THE BIBLE
AS RHETORIC

Good, but not useful for class
except · p 2. = use

6/24/90

Contemporary developments in literary studies and philosophy have focused attention on the literary and rhetorical dimensions of works whose primary concern is with issues of truth and falsity; at the same time biblical scholars have been attempting to find ways forward from the established history-based procedures of biblical criticism. These pioneering interdisciplinary papers explore the ways in which the persuasive strategies employed in the biblical texts relate (both positively and negatively) to their preoccupations with religious and historical truth. They clarify what is at issue in the apparently competing claims that the Bible should be read 'as literature' and 'as scripture'.

Uniquely, the volume brings together philosophers, literary critics, biblical scholars, theologians, and historians of ideas who combine the best biblical and historical scholarship with a range of contemporary approaches to the study of texts, from the deconstructive and the feminist through the Wittgensteinian to those of the heirs of the tradition of practical criticism. The volume is of importance both to those interested in the applications of contemporary literary theory and to all those concerned with the relation between religious and secular readings of the Bible.

Martin Warner teaches philosophy at the University of Warwick and was the founding Programme Director of its Centre for Research in Philosophy and Literature.

D0222792

WARWICK STUDIES IN PHILOSOPHY AND LITERATURE

General Editor: David Wood

In both philosophy and literature, much of the best original work being done today exploits the connections and tensions between these two disciplines. Modern literary theory increasingly looks to philosophy for its inspiration, as the influence of deconstructive and hermeneutic readings demonstrates.

The University of Warwick pioneered the study of the intertwinings of philosophy and literature, and its Centre for Research in Philosophy and Literature has won wide respect for its adventurous programme of research and conferences. The books published in this new series present the work of the Centre to a wider public, combining a sense of new direction with traditional standards of intellectual rigour.

Books in the series include:

EXCEEDINGLY NIETZSCHE
Edited by David Farrell Krell and
David Wood

NARRATIVE IN CULTURE
Edited by Cristopher Nash

POST-STRUCTURALIST CLASSICS
Edited by Andrew Benjamin

ABJECTION, MELANCHOLIA, AND LOVE:
The work of Julia Kristeva
Edited by John Fletcher and
Andrew Benjamin

THE PROVOCATION OF LEVINAS
Edited by Robert Bernasconi and
David Wood

WRITING THE FUTURE
Edited by David Wood

THE PROBLEMS OF MODERNITY
Edited by Andrew Benjamin

Forthcoming:

PHILOSOPHERS' POETS
Edited by David Wood

JUDGING LYOTARD
Edited by Andrew Benjamin and
David Wood

NARRATIVE AND INTERPRETATION:
The recent work of Paul Ricoeur
Edited by David Wood

THE BIBLE AS RHETORIC

STUDIES IN BIBLICAL PERSUASION AND CREDIBILITY

edited by

MARTIN WARNER

ROUTLEDGE

London and New York

First published 1990
by Routledge
11 New Fetter Lane, London EC4P 4EE

Simultaneously published in the USA and Canada
by Routledge
a division of Routledge, Chapman and Hall, Inc.
29 West 35th Street, New York, NY 10001

Disc conversion by Columns of Reading
Printed in Great Britain by
Richard Clay Ltd, Bungay, Suffolk

British Library Cataloguing in Publication Data
Warner, Martin
The Bible as rhetoric.
I. Title II. Series
220.6
ISBN 0-415-03617-8
ISBN 0-415-04409-X (pbk)

Library of Congress Cataloging in Publication Data
The Bible as rhetoric: studies in biblical persuasion and credibility
edited by Martin Warner.
p. cm. – (Warwick studies in philosophy and literature)
Bibliography: p.
Includes index.
1. Bible–Language, style. 2. Bible–Criticism, interpretation, etc.
3. Bible as literature. I. Warner, Martin. II. Series.
BS537.B52 1989
220.6′6–dc20
89-6248

CONTENTS

CONTENTS

NOTES ON THE
CONTRIBUTORS

CYRIL BARRETT, SJ is Reader in Philosophy at the University of Warwick. He edited Wittgenstein's *Lectures and Conversations on Aesthetics, Psychology and Religious Belief* (Blackwell, 1966) and is the author of *Wittgenstein on Ethics and Religious Belief* (Blackwell, 1989).

JOHN BARTON is University Lecturer in Theology (Old Testament) in the University of Oxford, where he is a Fellow and Chaplain of St Cross College. He is the author of *Amos' Oracles against the Nations* (CUP, 1980), *Reading the Old Testament: Method in Biblical Study* (DLT, 1984), *Oracles of God: Perceptions of Ancient Prophecy in Israel after the Exile* (DLT, 1986), and *People of the Book? The Authority of the Bible in Christianity* (SPCK, 1988).

DAVID CLINES is Professor of Biblical Studies at the University of Sheffield, joint editor of the *Journal for the Study of the Old Testament* and its monograph series, and a director and publisher of Sheffield Academic Press. Among his books are *I, He, We and They: A Literary Approach to Isaiah 53* (JSOT Press, 1976), *The Theme of the Pentateuch* (JSOT Press, 1978), *The Esther Scroll: The Story of the Story* (Sheffield JSOT Press, 1984), *Ezra, Nehemiah, Esther* (Marshall, Morgan and Scott, 1984), and *Job 1-20* (Word Books, 1989). He is currently editor and director of *The Dictionary of Classical Hebrew*, the first comprehensive dictionary of the ancient Hebrew language, to be published in parts by Sheffield Academic Press.

MICHAEL EDWARDS is Professor of English at the University of Warwick and former joint editor of *Prospice*. Among his books are *Towards a Christian Poetics* (Macmillan, 1984) and *Poetry and*

Possibility: A Study in the Power and Mystery of Words (Macmillan, 1988). He is also the author of several volumes of poetry and translations.

DAVID JASPER is Principal of St Chad's College, Durham, Director of the University of Durham's Centre for the Study of Literature and Theology, and editor of *Literature and Theology*. Among his books are *Coleridge as Poet and Religious Thinker* (Macmillan, 1985), *The New Testament and the Literary Imagination* (Macmillan, 1987) and *The Study of Literature and Religion: an Introduction* (Macmillan, 1989).

GEORGE KENNEDY is Paddison Professor of Classics at the University of North Carolina at Chapel Hill. He is the author of a number of studies in the history of rhetoric including *The Art of Persuasion in Greece* (Princeton University Press, 1963), *Classical Rhetoric and Its Christian and Secular Tradition from Ancient to Modern Times* (Croom Helm, 1980) and *New Testament Interpretation through Rhetorical Criticism* (University of North Carolina Press, 1984).

LYNN POLAND is Assistant Professor of Religion and Literature at the University of Chicago and the author of *Literary Criticism and Biblical Hermeneutics* (Scholars' Press, 1985).

MARGARITA STOCKER is Lecturer in English Literature at the University of Buckingham. She is the author of *Apocalyptic Marvell: The Second Coming in 17th Century Poetry* (Harvester, 1986) and *Paradise Lost: The Critics Debate* (Macmillan, 1988).

STEWART SUTHERLAND is Principal of King's College London, Vice-Chancellor elect of the University of London, and editor of *Religious Studies*; he was formerly Professor of the Philosophy and History of Religion at the University of London. He is the author of *Atheism and the Rejection of God: Contemporary Philosophy and The Brothers Karamazov* (Blackwell, 1977), *Faith and Ambiguity* (SCM, 1984) and *God, Jesus and Belief: The Legacy of Theism* (Blackwell, 1984).

ROGER TRIGG is Professor of Philosophy at the University of Warwick and Director of the University's Centre for Research in

Philosophy and Literature. Among his books are *Reason and Commitment* (CUP, 1973), *Reality at Risk: a Defence of Realism in Philosophy and the Sciences* (Harvester, 1980; 2nd edn 1989), *The Shaping of Man: Philosophical Aspects of Sociobiology* (Blackwell, 1982), *Understanding Social Science: A Philosophical Introduction to the Social Sciences* (Blackwell, 1985) and *Ideas of Human Nature: an Historical Introduction* (Blackwell, 1988).

MARTIN WARNER is Lecturer in Philosophy at the University of Warwick and was the founding Programme Director of the University's Centre for Research in Philosophy and Literature. He is the author of *Philosophical Finesse: Studies in the Art of Rational Persuasion* (OUP, 1989).

BIBLICAL TRANSLATIONS

While several of the contributors on occasion use their own translations of particular biblical phrases and sentences, most use for the body of their discussions the Revised Standard Version Bible (RSV), copyright 1946, 1952, 1971 by the Division of Christian Education of the National Council of the Churches of Christ in the USA, which is used by permission.

To this rule there are three exceptions. Professor Trigg makes use of the New English Bible (NEB) in his paper, while Professor Edwards and Dr Stocker use as the basis of their contributions the 'Authorized' Version (AV); extracts from the Authorized King James Version of the Bible, the rights of which are vested in the Crown in perpetuity within the United Kingdom, are reproduced by permission of Eyre & Spottiswoode Publishers, Her Majesty's Printers, London.

INTRODUCTION

MARTIN WARNER

RHETORICAL CRITICISM OF THE BIBLE

Rational argument is one of the most effective rhetorical modes we know. If such an assertion seems paradoxical, that is an index of the low esteem to which the study of rhetoric has fallen over the last two centuries; for the purposes of this volume rhetoric will be conceived, to quote John Stuart Mill, 'in the large sense in which that art was conceived by the ancients' (1843: 3). Aristotle defines rhetoric as 'the faculty of observing in any given case the available means of persuasion', and goes on:

> Of the modes of persuasion furnished by the spoken word there are three kinds. The first kind depends on the personal character of the speaker; the second on putting the audience into a certain frame of mind; the third on the proof, or apparent proof, provided by the words of the speech itself.
>
> (*Rhetoric* 1355b–1356a)

This account can be extended to cover both the spoken and the written word. In St Paul's notorious 'boasting' passage, where he appeals to his own manner of life as giving the Corinthian congregation reason to trust what he is now saying (II Cor. xi–xii), he is adopting the first mode – commonly known as that of *ēthos*. When Job seeks (unsuccessfully) to stir the emotions of his interlocutors – 'Have pity on, have pity on me, O you my friends, / for the hand of God has touched me!' (xix 21) – he is employing the second, that of *pathos*. And when Gamaliel counsels 'if this plan or this undertaking is of men, it will fail; but if it is of

1

God, you will not be able to overthrow them. You might even be found opposing God!' (Acts v 38–9) he does not invoke the fact that he is 'held in honour by all the people' (Acts v 34) (a consideration external to the speech which St Luke clearly intends us to see as contributing to its persuasive *ēthos*), but so far as his words themselves are concerned relies primarily upon force of argument – the third mode, *logos*. Aristotle is careful to include 'apparent proof' as well as 'proof' under the latter heading, but if it can be shown that what purports to be proof is only apparently such this radically reduces its persuasive power, and one powerful (but not infallible) way of warding off such loss of credibility is by presenting proofs which are genuine rather than apparent. Nevertheless, what Aristotle calls 'complete proof' is often difficult to come by; thus one may in good faith employ reasoning which is rationally powerful even though not fully conclusive in one's total persuasive strategy.

To examine a discourse from the point of view of rhetoric, therefore, is neither to impugn nor to endorse its message and procedures; it is to consider it in terms of its persuasive power. Nevertheless, such an approach may be less neutral in its results than is sometimes claimed; not only may the power of disingenuous techniques be fatally weakened by their unmasking, but even the tightest of arguments is unlikely to persuade us of an absurdity or obvious falsehood – a fact exploited by Zeno of Elea long ago (we shall never be persuaded that Achilles cannot overtake the tortoise) – thus considerations of persuasive power cannot ultimately be divorced from those of credibility.

If 'rhetoric' needs a word of explanation, so too does 'Bible'. The term is here taken to designate the Christian Bible, and the balance of the volume is tipped decisively towards consideration of the New Testament. There are of course relevant recent studies of the Hebrew Bible, such as that of Meir Sternberg, which provides the starting point for Lynn Poland's opening paper, but it is the Christian one – with its distinctive interpretation of the Hebrew as constituting an 'Old Testament' – which has been the more powerful influence on Western culture, and so it is with this that the following papers are concerned. In either case, to characterize such a heterogeneous collection of writings as a unity – the Bible – is already to presuppose an authority (or something comparable) by reference to which this (apparently non-literary) unity may be affirmed; the authority in each case designates the texts as 'scriptural', which specifies sets of distinctive relations to their standard readers and, as Stewart Sutherland argues below, their scriptural role is non-contingently related to the kinds of judgement to be made about them. To the extent that the differing Christian perceptions of the nature of Scripture (for most of which words are transcended by the Word) cannot be exactly mapped on to the (also varying) Hebrew perceptions, there are significant divergences in the frame of reference of rhetorical criticism depending on whether one is dealing with the Christian or Hebrew Bible; as Sutherland also argues, some of the apparently rhetorical ambiguities of our relation to the biblical texts are ultimately theological ones. Thus the easy solution of including papers from both frames of reference without significant comment would be disingenuous; on the other hand, in the present state of scholarship any serious attempt at integration or cross-comparison would be premature. (For a suggestive description of some of these issues from a different perspective, which seeks a quasi-literary unity for the Bible, see Josipovici 1988.)

For rhetorical criticism is a comparative newcomer to the field of biblical studies. It is traditional to divide the latter into textual (or 'lower') criticism, which is concerned with such issues as the comparison of manuscript sources and tracing the way that the texts have been transmitted to us, and 'higher' criticism which, narrowly conceived, is concerned to recover the biblical texts in their original forms and, more broadly, with the sources and literary methods of the relevant authors. One of the most influential procedures under this second head is that of 'form-criticism', which attempts to establish the origin and trace the history of particular passages by analysis of their structural forms. It was first developed to analyse the saga-like narratives of Genesis and gradually extended to the New Testament where its most influential use has been in exploring the supposed oral traditions lying behind the Synoptic Gospels. Its characteristic move is to break up texts into separate units, the forms of which are held to have been gradually fixed, and to explore the lived situation (*Sitz im Leben*) in which such units were created or preserved and transmitted.

Form-criticism has more recently been complemented by 'redaction criticism', which is concerned with the contribution made by the final editors or 'redactors' with particular attention to their theological concerns as revealed by the use of their sources. In principle, as George Kennedy points out, 'redaction criticism might be viewed as a special form of rhetorical criticism, which deals with texts where the hand of . . . an editor can be detected', but in practice attention is paid less to the editors' persuasive concerns than to their theological preoccupations and the circumstances of the communities within which they lived. Rhetorical criticism, to use Kennedy's formulation,

> takes the text as we have it, whether the work of a single author or the product of editing, and looks at it from the point of view of the author's or editor's intent, the unified results, and how it would be perceived by an audience of near contemporaries.
>
> (1984: 4)

('Intent' here, of course, should be construed in terms of 'the unified results' – the intention as manifest in the text – to the extent, that is, that the results can properly be characterized as 'unified'.)

There is certainly scope for exploration of the overlap between redaction criticism and rhetorical criticism, as Dr Jasper's contribution to this volume shows, but the former's focus on the way editors handle sources inevitably leads to what has been called a 'diachronic' preoccupation, with the way the materials have been reshaped through time; rhetorical criticism is free, also, to consider the texts 'synchronically', attempting to make sense of them as they stand – though the contrast is far from absolute. In this sense literary criticism of the Bible, as represented for example by Northrop Frye's *The Great Code* and by Robert Alter's and Frank Kermode's *The Literary Guide to the Bible*, is also 'synchronic'; but to the extent that its central preoccupations are with such issues as qualities of language, structure of plot and use of symbolism, with the author as poetic maker rather than as persuader, its focus is different from that of rhetorical criticism although, as we shall see, rhetorical criticism of the Bible cannot ignore the concerns of poetics. As Kennedy puts it, 'rhetorical criticism can help to fill a void which lies between form criticism on the one hand and literary criticism on the other' (1984: 3); it may also, as this volume shows, have a significant bearing on the scope and limits of these other forms of criticism.

It is with these considerations in mind that the contributors to this volume were invited to explore 'the ways in which the persuasive (and related literary) procedures of the biblical writers cut across or reinforce their concern with truth', and this brief bears some examination. First, the reference to 'biblical writers' was intended to capture both the variety of hands that contributed to the biblical corpus and the (no doubt problematic) integration of each of their works within a larger, scriptural, whole; the plural formulation is, of course, neutral with respect to any but the most extreme claims for the Holy Spirit as the author of Scripture – a doctrine of divine inspiration need not entail a theory of 'supernatural dictation' (Farrer 1948: lect. 3). Second, this formulation indicates that the texts in question may legitimately be construed in terms of intended communication between writer and reader or hearer, though whether the historically attested writers or merely the authors and editors which the texts seem to imply should have priority was left open – differing emphases with respect to this issue can be discerned in the papers which follow. Third, the invitation presupposes that at least some of these historical or implied writers were concerned both to persuade and with truth, though its parenthesis indicates that the notion of persuasion may be taken fairly broadly and that rhetoric may run into poetics; this, once again, is relatively uncontroversial though no doubt the notion of 'persuasion' is more appropriate to some biblical texts than to others. But, fourth, although relatively uncontroversial the reference to truth raises notorious problems which were gestured towards in the original invitation through the gloss that both religious and historical truth might be at issue, together with the relation between them; in some of the texts discussed – Job certainly and Judith probably – historical truth is not an important consideration, but for the prophets and most of the New Testament writers the matter is a good deal more complicated, as several of the papers in this volume demonstrate.

The term 'truth' is notoriously elusive. Part of the force of affirming that a claim is true is that in doing so one is underwriting the claim, but the same can be said of various other expressions such as 'well confirmed'. Further, the criteria relevant to establishing the truth of a claim vary radically with the type of claim in question: empirical, mathematical, moral and (probably) religious. The suspicion that there may be no more to truth than assertive force plus diverse criteria has led some to the relativist conclusion that the predicate 'true' makes sense only relative to some set of criteria which the claimant or the community of which the affirmer of the claim is a member treats as warranting assertibility (so what is true for one community or individual may not be so for another). Realist or absolute theories of truth, on the other hand, deny this conclusion, standardly maintaining that a claim is true if and only if it corresponds to the facts, independently of the beliefs and indeed criteria of individuals and communities; the problem is to characterize 'correspond' and 'fact' in a non-trivial and intelligible way, especially for those who seek to give an account of facts as items not essentially dependent on language or the mind. In this volume Roger Trigg presupposes his various discussions defending realism, while George Kennedy explores some of the ramifications of the relativist pole of the debate. But whatever one's position on this metaphysical issue, the relations between the different types of criteria used in judging truth-claims raise serious problems for biblical interpretation.

One familiar line of argument (the vocabulary deriving with doubtful propriety from Wittgenstein) maintains that the discourses concerning morality, mathematics, religion, history, natural science, and so on represent radically different and incommensurable 'language games', and that the attempt to use the criteria of one in judging the claims of another is illegitimate; religious truth and historical truth have nothing to do with each other, and the Jesus of history thus has no relevance to the Christ of faith. Part of the problem with this conclusion is that it appears to distort the claims of religions, such as the Christian, which claim that God is lord both of history and of creation, and to trivialize what to the religious mind are serious issues. Human suffering, whether on the large historical scale of the Lisbon earthquake and the Holocaust, or on the individual level of the type of suffering child instanced by Ivan Karamazov, is empirically constituted and takes place in human history; yet since before the time of Job it has been seen to constitute at best a trial to religious faith and at worst a bar to it by those of deep religious sensibility. Further, the historical event of the crucifixion of Jesus has been widely believed to have some bearing on the religious issue. Yet it seems certainly plausible to claim that the criteria for assessing religious truth are importantly different from those of the other discourses mentioned.

Analogous considerations could be adduced with respect to the interrelations of most if not all such language games. These 'games' take their intelligibility from and help to constitute varying 'forms of life', but most of us participate in many such 'forms' and it is only as a (somewhat misleading) metaphor that each of us may be said to lead more than one life. Further, the unity of our life has a bearing on the interrelations of the games we play in it. As Wittgenstein himself urged in his discussion of games, 'don't think, but look!' (1958: para. 66). All of which suggests that we are faced here with a subtle network of analogies, differences and interconnections which need to be unravelled. In its exploration of the ways in which the biblical texts seek to promote or deepen religious faith and insight rhetorical criticism can help to clarify these interrelations as they are found in some of religion's paradigmatic documents.

But whether truth is conceived relativistically or otherwise, and whether its criteria are understood to be incommensurable between language games or analogically comparable by reference to common human experience, there remains the problem, highlighted by Plato, that the aims of the persuader are not identical with those of the truth-seeker – a fact which has powerfully contributed to the low esteem in which rhetoric is commonly held today.

So far as the canonical Scriptures are concerned there is little reason to suppose the authors to be consciously disingenuous (though our lack of knowledge of the circumstances surrounding the editing of the Pentateuch on the one hand and of the pseudonymous Epistles on the other counsels caution here), but self-deception has many guises; it is perfectly possible for one's wish to persuade others of that of which one is personally convinced to allow one to stick somewhat loosely to the criteria generally regarded as having a bearing on assessing the truth of one's claims. In very different ways John Barton and George Kennedy explore this possibility with respect to the Prophets and St Paul respectively. On the other hand, one's vision may force a rethinking of the generally accepted criteria for establishing truth, and it is then wholly legitimate for one's persuasive strategy to involve commendation of these revisions and to allow one's case to stand or fall by reference to them. My own paper argues that the Fourth Gospel should be construed in these terms and that more attention than is customary should be paid to its own implicit canons of assessment. Rhetorical criticism of biblical texts should treat as live options not merely the possibility of their persuasive strategies undercutting those texts' avowed or implicit concern with truth, but also that of mutual reinforcement. Identification of persuasive strategies may undermine credibility, as in the case of the sort of rhetoric decried by Plato in his *Gorgias*, but it may do the reverse, as with the 'noble' rhetoric of his *Phaedrus*. Using the powerful tools of an influential trope-led version of rhetorical theory, David Jasper provides an instructive case study with his attempt later in this volume to assess which type of rhetoric is at play in St Mark's Gospel.

FROM RHETORIC TO POETICS

The terms in which the rhetorical criticism of the Bible has so far been presented might at first sight appear to involve something of an oversimplification, presupposing that the classic rhetorical categories are not themselves subject to disruption when applied to biblical texts – a presumption which is at least questionable. But over-sophistication can be misleading here; while it is certainly true that there are features of many of the biblical texts which either resist rhetorical analysis or else require the enrichment of its procedures and classifications, there are others where this does not appear to be the case, and the different features have a complex interdependence. To use the language of medieval exegesis, acknowledgment of the typological, moral and anagogical senses of Scripture need not involve the denial of the significance of that of the literal; to ignore those features of the biblical writings to which fairly simple categories are appropriate is itself to oversimplify.

At this preliminary level we might reasonably characterise one familiar, indeed traditional, way of reading the Bible as implying that the differing forms of truth presented in the texts mutually reinforce each other – at least to the eye of faith – in a relatively straightforward manner. Radically anomalous historical events (parting of the Red Sea, discovery of an empty tomb) are taken as persuasive signs whose truthful recounting helps lend credibility to certain religious claims. They do not stand on their own of course – the moral power of the teaching from Sinai or the Matthean mount play important roles, as do the narrative structures within which these events are set – and reciprocally the religious experience of readers will affect the degree to which the claims are seen as credible, together with the accounts of the signs which witness to them. Given this perspective, the rejection of the credibility of one type of constituent in this whole complex can be seen as disruptive of the whole. For example, a feminist rejection of the moral authority of the Ten Commandments or the Sermon on the Mount on the grounds that they are too imbued with patriarchal values, language and assumptions to be taken as moral touchstones ('You shall not covet your neighbour's wife' / 'Our Father who art in heaven') may be seen as putting a serious question mark against the validity of the whole Judaic or Christian vision. Similar considerations, notoriously, are frequently urged in the case of denial of the historicity of the allegedly foundational anomalous events; on one well-known variant of this approach, St Paul's 'if Christ has not been raised, then . . . your faith is in vain' (I Cor. xv 14) is taken as authoritative and Christ's 'raising' held to be incompatible with Jesus' body remaining in its tomb.

Concern that this set of issues should not be overlooked by rhetorical criticism lies at the heart of Roger Trigg's paper. He points out that emphasis on 'the way which the Gospel writers selected and constructed their material, and on the effects they wanted to produce' can direct attention away from 'questions about the possible truth of their accounts'. Such redirection can then form part of a strategy for driving a wedge between witness and reportage and hence between religious and historical truth which, on the traditional view, is illegitimate; he quotes Michael Dummett's claim that appeal to literary genres has degenerated into a procedure for enabling scholars to ascribe to the Gospels 'a sense consonant with the exegete's opinions without branding them deliberately deceptive'.

The Bishop of Durham's recent work is taken to exemplify this tendency. His strongly relativistic account of truth leads him to say of the writers of the Gospels that 'their world was not our world', so that it is inappropriate to apply our standards of historical truth to their texts. As presented by the Bishop the position invites at least two types of riposte, both represented in this volume. George Kennedy gently remarks that the claim for radical discontinuity between our cultural codes and those of the New Testament writers 'can pose a hermeneutic problem for orthodox Christians who wish to claim that the New Testament, as a text, is in some sense addressed to "us"'; more generally, if we inhabit different 'worlds' with respect to certain types of truth (such as the historical), why not with respect to others (such as the religious)? As Roger Trigg puts it, 'if the people of the New Testament were so utterly different from ourselves, . . . any religious message emanating from its pages would be pointless in our world, even if it could be made intelligible'. Since the Bishop maintains that 'the God in whom we believe is one and the same God' throughout historical change and that we 'have the opportunity to share' the faith of the Gospel writers (Jenkins 1987: 28 and 37), his position can only be stabilized by sustaining a strong doctrine of discontinuity between different types of truth together with the provision of reason to credit forms of continuity across time in the religious sphere which do not apply in the historical. This is, of course, hardly a matter of which the Bishop is unaware.

The second response is that of Trigg's denial of the relativistic premise: our distinctions between myth and claims to truth, and between poetry and history, are themselves ancient ones; they are embedded not only in Greek literature but also in the New Testament writings themselves; the thesis that there is a radical discontinuity between ancient and modern understandings of history and human nature which is a function of incommensurable conceptual schemes is to be rejected as embodying bad metaphysics; 'while we would be foolish not to recognize some differences between ourselves and our predecessors, the very recognition of difference only makes sense against the background of a fair degree of similarity'. Further, the attempt to keep the message of the Gospel narratives while denying their historical truth misinterprets the fundamental rhetorical strategy of their authors, which was to communicate what they saw as the truth – understood in such a way that historical and religious truth could be mutually reinforcing. The claim made by another contributor to this volume that the New Testament should be considered as 'mythical literature rather than as history', for it conforms 'to conventions and a culture which is not our own' and its writers would not have understood 'our modern distinction between fact and fiction' (Jasper 1987: 14, 13 and 15), is seen as vulnerable to the same critique.

The wider issue of relativism points beyond the confines of this volume to technical work in metaphysics, logic and epistemology, but Trigg's critique is salutary in its insistence on the relevance of these discussions to contemporary biblical criticism, as also on that of the scrupulous examination of a wider range of ancient texts than is always taken into account in generalizations about the biblical 'world'. The dispute also points, however, to matters fundamental to rhetorical criticism; Jasper's insistence on attention to the literary conventions embodied in the relevant texts goes together with a disinclination to separate what is said from the way it is said, content from form – a matter of some importance for his contribution to this volume.

Trigg proposes as one model for sifting truth from falsehood, which spans both the biblical and the contemporary world, that of cross-examination of multiple witnesses on an issue of fact in a court of law. Here the truth of what is said is ultimately independent of the way it is said even though words may be all we have to go on; St Peter's declaration in the first Christian sermon that 'we can all bear witness' to Jesus' resurrection (Acts ii 32) is construed on this model (though the fact that Trigg's title quotation is probably drawn from the pseudo-Petrine literature complicates the matter). But the words used to characterize the event to which witness is borne are 'the Jesus we speak of has been raised by God', and the 'speaking' in question has characterized Jesus as the Messiah of scriptural prophecy whose 'resurrection' was foretold. This characterization has closer analogies with the interpretative claims surrounding issues of law rather than those of fact in the law court, while the reference to being 'raised by God' seems to strain the model to breaking point; as Beckett sardonically remarks, 'God is a witness that cannot be sworn' (1963: 6). Given the assumption that religious and historical claims can interconnect, the legal model with its empirical teeth nevertheless still has some power. If the concept of being 'raised' has any objective empirical content then the denial of the instantiation of that content involves the denial both that God did any raising and that a prophecy of raising has been fulfilled. To reject the possibility that a claim may be empirically verified by sense experience is not to deny that it could be empirically falsified in this way. But clearly the main emphasis of the Petrine claim, as of most of the New Testament rhetoric, is on matters which transcend (even if they may to some degree depend on) the empirical, and here the assumption that

form and content can be neatly separated becomes radically
problematic. It is at this point that those elements of rhetorical
theory which are rooted in legal practice can become overly
limiting for rhetorical criticism of the Bible.

Traditionally it is poetics rather than rhetoric which concerns
itself with the creative powers of language. For Jasper, the New
Testament with 'its language of metaphor, symbol and myth has
produced imaginative fictions which demand an imaginative
response' (1987: 95); such demands can only be probed by close
attention to form and language of a type for which legal cross-
examination provides an exceedingly imperfect model – reminding
one of such questions as 'How many children had Lady Macbeth?'.
The divine reference points beyond the empirical, and here
qualities of insight, imagination and spiritual discernment are
required; the Kingdom of Heaven is to be spoken of in Synoptic
parables and Johannine images, and the texts which contain them
are themselves works which enact that same dynamic – pointing
beyond themselves yet also in some way emblematic of that of
which they speak, so that their own qualities are themselves
testimony, witnesses, to the significance of the claims they make.
On this account the Scriptures are best understood as sacramental
– 'outward and visible signs of an inward and spiritual grace' – and
any rhetorical analysis must take this into account, enriching the
standard rhetorical categories with ones developed by poetics. The
account is hardly a new one: St Augustine tells how at one stage he
attempted to approach the Scriptures wholly in terms of the secular
categories of classical rhetoric with the consequence that 'they
seemed to me unworthy of comparison with the grand style of
Cicero', but that eventually he was led to a less inadequate
understanding which pointed beyond stylistic concerns, relating
form to content: 'as for the absurdities which used to offend me in
Scripture, . . . I now looked for their meanings *ad sacramentorum*'
(*Confessions*, III, 5 and VI, 5). Thus it is appropriate that Lynn
Poland's approach to these contemporary problems through the
history of biblical exegesis should use St Augustine's work as a
touchstone.

One central problem is how rhetorical and poetic categories may
be integrated. Poland suggests that it has been made more difficult
by developments in poetics since the Romantic period which have
focused round the ideal of the 'union between form and content,

12

language and the world, and finally, between the eternal and the temporal', developments which have stressed formalist criteria and the Coleridgean idea of the 'symbol' – which participates in the reality it renders intelligible 'so that one directly apprehends the idea symbolized in the act of perceiving the symbol, in an "unmediated vision"'. Given such a context, the attempt to interrelate the communicative and expressive uses of language is radically problematic. Jasper's Coleridgean approach leads him to speak of the New Testament's 'language of metaphor, symbol and myth' in terms of 'imaginative fictions', which invites Trigg's riposte that the Gospels at least are presented as truth, not fiction. Poland's diagnosis would be that 'it is difficult for biblical scholars adapting the prevailing formalist literary critical tools to explore the Bible's peculiar relation to history or to examine the way its art is related to its truth claims'. Over against the standard preference for a 'poetics of the beautiful' which stresses the unifying symbol, she posits a 'rhetoric of sublimity' which exploits the discontinuities between text and truth – forms of incommensurability for which allegory is a more appropriate index than the Romantic symbol.

The traditional idea of the 'sublime' is of that which arouses amazement and awe, overwhelming the imagination through its resistance to the limits and categories within which we seek to contain it. On this account Scripture's religious power arises from its presentation of discontinuities between 'incommensurable orders', which to the young Augustine involved 'absurdities', and the manner in which the sublime endows truth with emotional power provides clues which suggest that 'a contemporary criticism is possible that is at once thoroughly historical and capable of addressing the Bible's rhetorical sublimity'. For Poland the diagnosis of those elements of the scriptural texts which fail to fit our own linguistic codes as the product of an alien culture – the Bishop of Durham's 'their world was not our world' – may be only partially correct; she points to the earlier tradition of reading the Bible as scripture as well as literature, where those elements which fit the standard rhetorical and poetic codes were represented as the Word becoming flesh and those which transgressed them reflected the text's divinity – 'the failure to signify becomes itself a sign, a sign of the presence of God's complete intention. Absence, in short, becomes a sign of presence, providing logical space for the operations of allegory with its 'disjunction of the faculties'. In positing originating communities for the Scriptures in which Augustine's 'absurdities' create no sense of shock one is attempting to domesticate the 'lawlessness' of divine speech in such a manner as to undercut its sublimity, and Augustine's sacramental understanding of them as linking two incommensurable orders collapses.

Augustine's own account is seen as exemplary but also problematic. It posits both the possibility of understanding 'the Christian economies of creation and redemption . . . in semiotic terms' and also that there is a 'discontinuity between language and the divine'. It is the interpreter's task to reconcile these two poles of Scriptural understanding.

> While Augustine already knows, through the rule of faith, the 'fullness of meaning' he seeks to recover through interpretation, the religious power of the texts does not lie in its truth so much as in the trials of its interpretation. Allegory combats the disdain and lassitude fostered by that which is too easily mastered.

But Poland points to a difficulty here; since he already knows the truths to be discovered, 'allegory threatens to become a rhetorical game of hide and seek; . . . it is a crisis "staged" to give the truth Augustine already believes affective power'. Nevertheless, although it would be idle to deny that allegorical criticism has often thus degenerated into the 'merely rhetorical', it is not clear that it need do so. Poland uses the *Confessions* for her main textual evidence, but any handling of that work needs to take account of its basic structural principles; its underlying model is that of the parable of the Prodigal Son, with Augustine himself cast in the role of the prodigal, and the concluding books are dominated by a consciousness of his own sinfulness and fallibility. Integral to their discussion of Scripture is his extended plea to those conservative exegetes, suspicious of his Platonizing tendencies, who seem cast in the role of the elder brother; it is as if the community is needed to validate the interpretation – and of course only a few years later Augustine reluctantly accepted the Church's condemnation of elements of Origen's teaching to which he had been strongly drawn and which plays a significant role in the Scriptural exegesis developed in the *Confessions* itself (see Warner 1984: 198–201). Poland, indeed, draws attention to the importance of the issue of the role of the community in establishing the sacredness of a text, but this goes further; the community has a say in the interpretation of that which it designates as 'sacred', and Augustine's belief that he 'already knows' the truths to be discovered may be false. Thus the labour of interpretation has a cognitive as well as merely 'affective' role; the 'fullness of meaning' one labours to recover may transform one's understanding of what one thinks one 'knows through the rule of faith'.

This issue relates to one raised by Stewart Sutherland in the paper that opens the New Testament section of this volume. To designate texts as 'scriptural' is to indicate a distinctive relation to the beliefs and practices of the community that accepts them as such; this relationship is symbiotic, the Scriptures both having a crucial role in the regulation and definition of faith and requiring to be read in a manner informed by some understanding of the nature of the faith; the community is in varying degrees both determined by the texts and determinative of them. There are indeed secular analogues here which also bear on historical, moral, and religious issues, and these help us to understand how texts can transform the understanding as well as elevate the feelings, but the claims to absoluteness and uniqueness implicit in a text being accepted as scriptural invite judgements which are ultimately theological, and these are every bit as problematic as Augustine suggests.

But if we are to make sense of a rhetoric which is transformative of the understanding through means which fall under the traditional poetic category of 'the sublime', some account must be given of what becomes of the traditional rhetorical claim to be concerned with truth, what we are doing in judging that the transformation in question is to be accepted as veridical or rejected as delusive, and here Cyril Barrett's concluding paper is relevant. His concern is with the most overtly 'poetic' parts of the Bible – presupposing, according to interpretative principles discussed above, that scriptural texts may be read as having religious significance – with an eye to the claim that the medium of the language itself enables them to communicate such significance. He compares these books and passages with visionary poetry and mystical writings; religious and related forms of ecstasy involve experience of or insight into the transcendental, and the attempt to treat the language associated with it as if it involved *reports* of experience runs against the boundaries of language. So understood it fails to signify, transgressing our linguistic codes in a manner analogous to that of the 'sublime' and 'lawless' divine speech which presents discontinuities between incommensurable orders discussed by Lynn Poland. But such writings are better understood as experience embedded in language – exemplifications of the 'ecstatic' or 'reflective aspect' of language which occupies a middle ground between its practical or propositional uses and empty bombinating, well described in the Sartrean phrase as setting 'a trap to catch a fleeing reality' (Sartre 1967: 6). On this account questions about truth and delusion can be reformulated in terms of the language's success in trapping 'reality'. It is argued that a characteristic feature of the language of distinctively religious ecstasy is the centrality of the symbol (as opposed to the metaphor or the analogy), and this provides criteria for distinguishing between valid and invalid ecstatic language and hence evaluating the biblical writings that employ it.

There is of course some tension between this claim and Lynn Poland's critique of the idea of the symbol, though caution is needed here. Poland's criticisms are directed specifically against the invocation of the Coleridgean symbol in this context, but the term can be understood in other ways and has an ancient theological lineage. The Augustinean 'rule of faith' which, as we have seen, can be seen as providing a (somewhat problematic) guide to religious knowledge is closely related to the Creed – traditionally known as *sumbolon*, a term which yokes together the notion of a mark of recognition with a sacramental sign. In analogous fashion the recognition of the Bible as scriptural acts as a distinguishing mark of the community which receives it sacramentally – as 'catching' aspects of the divinely revealed reality – and may therefore also be termed 'symbolic'. Nevertheless, Barrett's account of the symbol draws significantly on the Romantic tradition – though his claim that transcendental symbolism is 'largely negative' distances him from Coleridge – and this is symptomatic of a wider difference between the accounts given by Poland and by Barrett which itself reflects not only (as Poland puts it) 'a tension that has been present throughout the western tradition of biblical interpretation', but also (and relatedly) a long-standing and unresolved debate at the heart of Christian theology.

For Poland the problem with religious use of Romantic

symbolism is that it underplays 'the discontinuity between language and the divine'; for Barrett this discontinuity must not be conceived in such a way as to render it in principle impossible for us to be led 'from the sensory to the absolutely transcendental', a passage which requires 'some form of symbolism'. Poland's apparent exemption of the 'rule of faith' from the problems which attend religious language is deeply problematic, but without it her insistence on the 'discontinuity' and 'lawlessness' that subtend biblical sublimity leaves her with few resources to make sense of that distinction between valid and delusive interpretation which has always raised difficulties for allegorical interpretation of the Bible and was so important to St Augustine, whose *Confessions* are dominated by the question 'What, then, is my God?' (I 4). It remains to be seen whether 'some form', suitably finessed, of symbolism can provide what is missing without domesticating our sense of the *mysterium tremendum*.

THE HERMENEUTICS OF SUSPICION

Paul Ricoeur's distinction between theories and practices of interpretation, or 'hermeneutics', associated with suspicion and those associated with faith (1970: I, 2) usefully illuminates one way in which the remaining contributions to this volume bear on that ancient tension in biblical interpretation remarked by Lynn Poland. For Ricoeur the 'school of suspicion' seeks 'demystification', and its masters are Marx, Nietzsche and Freud; contemporary movements in literary criticism concerned with ideology, deconstruction and psychoanalysis would appear to be lineal descendants, while Nietzsche's sensitivity to the demystificatory potential of the tools of philological and historical scholarship enables other forms of contemporary criticism to be acknowledged as step-children. Members of the school seek forms of false consciousness or other types of incoherence inscribed within the texts they examine, and if Poland is right in seeing the scriptural 'rhetoric of sublimity' as operating in terms of discontinuities, incommensurabilities and failures of signification, the Bible is particularly apt for the application of the tools of suspicion. Indeed, the demonstration of such semiotic instability can be seen as an important element in the ascription of sublimity; without it there is danger of the 'blandness' and religious triviality which Poland sees as infecting much of the recent *Literary Guide to the Bible*.

Ascribing scriptural status to a text has normally been taken to indicate the possibility of the recuperation of religious insight beyond the level of Augustine's 'absurdities'. But there is a certain set of writings whose status for both Jews and Christians has long been ambiguous – those of the Apocrypha (found, with one exception, in the Septuagint but not included in the Hebrew Bible). Their marginal status has freed the imagination of readers to treat them as less 'tyrannical' (Auerbach 1953: 14) than fully canonical works and artists to play with them less respectfully. This provides Margarita Stocker with materials to explore in terms of feminist criticism (with psychoanalytic associations) the manner in which the apocryphal narrative of Judith has mythopoeic power, and thereby to mount a critique of such scriptural archetypes. The myth of Judith, she argues, represents a classic instance of the cultural construction of gender – more specifically of the heroine – but analysis of the text reveals a surplus of meaning which it fails to control despite explicit markers designed to do so. It is an unstable site of the three competing genres of epic, tragedy and romance contained within a myth of 'otherness' where woman's marginality makes for liminality – the sort of 'lawlessness' that in Poland's account should make for sublimity. But the ironic reversal of male tyranny by female weakness at the official narrative level has subversive undercurrents which undermine its authority and its procedures for the production and recuperation of meaning.

In discussing what he was accustomed to call 'the religious hypothesis' David Hume once distinguished between 'our inclination to find our own figures in the clouds' and our 'propensity . . . to believe in our senses and experience' (*Letters*, I, 155); only the latter provides ground for assent. It is a weakness of much feminist – and indeed psychoanalytic – criticism that it is often difficult to detect principled grounds for distinguishing propensities from inclinations in its ascription of sexual markers to texts. By appeal to the detail of what imaginative artists have made of the Judith narrative Stocker provides independent evidence that her analysis is more exegesis than eisegesis, and that a naive or surface reading can only be sustained by selective blindness.

For an example of a contribution to the Alter/Kermode *Literary Guide* which seriously addresses the Bible's rhetorical sublimity

Poland instances that on the Twelve Prophets, which is concerned to bring out 'discordant features that resist assimilation', and in this volume too the Old Testament prophets are seen as a suitable site for a variant of the hermeneutics of suspicion. John Barton argues that they characteristically presented the conduct of their contemporaries in such a way that it appeared to lead inevitably to divine judgement, when in fact they were justifying as best they could a premonition of approaching disaster. They were concerned to reason with their hearers, and their rhetoric skilfully assimilated the shortcomings of Israel and Judah to models which were generally held, in the ancient world, to cause divine displeasure. In the process they made the coming disasters comprehensible to their contemporaries. However, the appeal to reason is often rationalization and we should not be taken in by the force of their rhetoric. The fact that even modern readers are inclined to speak as if it really was obvious that God was bound to punish Israel is a tribute to their rhetorical skill.

As a counter to that unreflectively naive reading of the prophets which has such remarkably wide currency today, not least in liberation theology, Barton's analysis is salutary. But if one looks to the impact of the prophetic writings on subsequent generations, especially on those for whom they were scriptural, the possibility opens that it may represent only the first move in a (long overdue) dialectic. Certainly there was at best disproportion and at worst incommensurability between Israel's shortcomings and the models to which they were assimilated. But the effect of the assimilation was to lead the faithful to modify those models, to see what to the secular eye were relative trivialities as deserving of moral outrage. It is not for nothing that the prophets became known as 'the teachers of Israel'. They would hardly have gained a hearing if they had not used ethical models which resonated with the perceptions of their contemporaries, but the new teaching transformed the models. In this they may well have wrought better than they understood, but part of the significance of accepting a text as scriptural is that such an acknowledgement opens the possibility that it may in some way transcend conscious human artifice. To use categories already elaborated, Barton shows the untenability of the conventional reading of the prophets as exemplifying unmediated vision by demonstrating discontinuities between text and truth; but if these writings are to be read as possessing scriptural authority, exemplifying a noble – sacramentally transformative – rather than a false rhetoric, they must also be read as 'lawless' – with their discordant features being taken as indications of the divine speech's subversion of the standard rhetorical codes.

In a reading inspired by the deconstructive element within the school of suspicion, David Clines similarly seeks discordant features in the Wisdom literature. Distancing himself from the more radical strategies of deconstruction, he argues discriminatingly that the book of Job deconstructs itself in two respects. On the one hand, the stance taken by the central core of the book is that the doctrine of retribution is false, yet the epilogue affirms that Job prospers because of his piety, which is to say that it is true; on the other, the answers offered by the book to the problem of suffering are deconstructed by the insistence that Job's case is unique. Taken together, these discordances undermine the text's authority as 'trustworthy testimony', encouraging the post-modernist tendency to play uncommittedly with multiple perspectives. Here again the detection of dissonances helps bring into the foreground elements in a text which traditional modes of higher criticism mask; in this case the standard recourse to diachronic analyses of multiple authorship deflects attention from questions concerning the work's religious authority.

Nevertheless. if dissonance is an integral element in religious power, exploration of the religious dynamic of the work for those who have subdued themselves to it as authoritative may set these discrepancies in a different light. Generations of readers for whom the book is scriptural have identified themselves with the protagonist, and the feature that makes him unique, his blamelessness, has been taken as giving the comfort that it need not be the case that it is one's own sins that have led one into some analogue of Job's condition – more generally, that the 'doctrine of retribution' is false. There is, of course, no comfort here if the epilogue reinstates the doctrine, but it is at least arguable that the role of Job's final prosperity is a sign of God's justice and that to claim that this amounts to the same thing as affirming the doctrine of retribution is to presuppose the very interdependence between God's justice and the doctrine that the central core of the book is concerned to combat. In other words, the book may be read in terms of the rhetoric of sublimity, using divergences creatively instead of simply 'playing' with them in postmodernist fashion. There is room for debate as to whether the 'suspicious' or the 'faithful' reading is the better, but no reading can be seriously countenanced which does not at least take account of the dissonance.

The final exercise of suspicion here is that of George Kennedy. He focuses on some of those problems concerning truth and validity sketched above. To the extent that our linguistic codes constitute reality for us – and we have seen that this is a highly problematic issue – there is a certain circularity in attempting to validate our own code by an allegedly 'external' appeal to experience, whether of the individual or of the group which identifies itself by means of it. St Paul's statements about truth and his attitude to rhetoric are argued to exemplify this problem and to reveal some of the tensions involved between 'personal' and 'historical' validation; these tensions point to the challenge for modern Christianity 'to identify what in the "Great Code" of the Bible can be translated into modern codes and how'.

THE HERMENEUTICS OF FAITH

> The contrary of suspicion, I will say bluntly, is faith. What faith? No longer, to be sure, the first faith of the simple soul, but rather the second faith of one who has engaged in hermeneutics, faith that has undergone criticism, postcritical faith.
>
> (Paul Ricoeur 1970: 28)

Ricoeur is here drawing on his work in *The Symbolism of Evil* (see especially the 'Conclusion') where he distinguishes between a 'first' or 'primitive naïveté', which involves an 'immediacy of belief' to which an educated twentieth-century reader cannot with integrity return, and a 'second naïveté in and through criticism' which allows a 'second immediacy'. The former involves an 'ability to live the great symbolisms of the sacred in accordance with the original belief in them', and for those who aspire to such a condition the Bishop of Durham's 'their world was not our world' is salutary. Nietzsche maintained that 'what really triumphed over the Christian god [was] Christian morality itself, the concept of truthfulness that was understood ever more rigorously' (1974: V, 357). Whether it was indeed the Christian God that was overthrown or merely a deistic idol is open to dispute, but the claim that Christianity cannot renounce that concern with truth

21

which scholarship exemplifies without denying itself has considerable force. If there is indeed a way to a hermeneutics of faith it must lie through the hermeneutics of suspicion.

Such a thesis can itself claim some biblical warrant. Another of the contributors to this volume, Michael Edwards, drew attention in *Towards a Christian Poetics* to the possible application to language of the scriptural pattern of Eden, Fall and Transformation. The myth of Adam's Edenic naming of God's creatures gestures towards a wholeness of integration of language with reality that is broken with the Fall and exemplified at Babel. In a postlapsarian world any talk of God will inevitably involve fragmentary discontinuity, and 'the deistic model, in so far as it is constructed from a "religious" metaphysic ignorant or else negligent of the Fall, is fallacious and hallucinated' (231–2). However, 'Pentecost is the third term in the biblical dialectic of language, after the greatness of Adam's tongue and the wretchedness of the serpent's tongue, and of Babel' (12). Much modern literary theory is seen as 'genuine hygiene', undercutting logocentric deistic assumptions, but 'only a Christian, dialectical theory would seem capable of fully comprehending [the crisis of the sign] – of grasping both *grandeur* and *misère* and also the possibility that opens beyond them' (Edwards 1984: 221, 223). On this account, one might say, the hermeneutics of suspicion are concerned to diagnose the discourse of Babel and the hermeneutics of faith to explore that of Pentecost.

An outline of the dynamics of the latter discourse, at least so far as the central biblical writings are concerned and with the reservations mentioned above, is sketched by Lynn Poland; but we have seen that it can be a major issue whether a text is more properly to be diagnosed as exemplifying the discourse of Babel or of Pentecost. This issue is taken up by David Jasper with respect to St Mark's Gospel. He endorses the thesis which George Kennedy among others had previously argued that 'at the heart of religious rhetoric, quite distinctively, lies authoritative proclamation and not rational persuasion', arguing that in Mark language tends towards an absolute claim to truth without evidence and without recourse to logical argument; its rhetorical demands develop out of a newly established community (the Petrine church) wishing to assert its identity by an act of self-entextualising. He considers two models for interpreting this process. The first, deriving from the school of suspicion, is that of a group which derives its cohesion from the threat of alienation and whose defining text enacts a 'discourse of repression'; the second, which is adopted by St Paul in his letters to the Church at Corinth to help overcome its own crisis of self-identity, can be characterized in terms of the 'group-in-formation' of Sartre (1976) where the communal project can embrace the shock of radical discontinuity. The first model has remarkably plausible application to Mark, but a sufficiently careful reading – taking account of its radical irony – suggests that the latter is the less inadequate: that of a community realised as entextualised in the provision of the Gospel understood in terms of a radical newness which derives its absolute claims from that form of paradoxical transformation St Paul calls 'kenosis'.

The considerations Jasper adduces for preferring a Pentecostal model to one of Babel derive from his strategies of reading which have wide application and repay study. In particular the potential of Vico's structure of four 'master tropes' in rhetorical analysis is well displayed, though this fashionable version of rhetorical theory has a disconcerting tendency to perform the remarkable feat of simultaneously widening rhetoric's scope while narrowing its focus – thereby showing significant analogies with the Ramist attempt to streamline dialectic and rhetoric, from which it ultimately derives. Two specific reservations, however, are worth entering here. First, the reading is mainly developed in terms of the author and community implied by the text – sociological evidence concerning the existence of groups with these sorts of dynamic in first-century Rome is neither sought nor, probably, available; but the text's provenance in the Petrine church is assumed on evidence external to the text and the relation between these two types of evidence, internal and external, raises problems reminiscent of those raised by Roger Trigg and discussed in the second part of this Introduction. Second, although St Mark's Gospel certainly appears to fit Kennedy's specification of 'authoritative proclamation, not rational persuasion' (Kennedy 1984: 6), it remains to be shown that this characterization applies to 'religious rhetoric' as such, or even to all biblical rhetoric. Scriptural rhetoric may be more variegated than such doctrines allow, and there is room for debate concerning the legitimate boundaries of application of the term 'rational'.

Such considerations underlie my own analysis of the Fourth Gospel as developing according to a very different dynamic from that discerned by Jasper in Mark, but one that nevertheless also has affinities with Poland's 'sublimity'. I there argue that the text's avowedly rhetorical purpose is multilayered and that some of the disagreements between interpreters flow from a failure to take account of this. One crucial gradation, I suggest, is that of the symbolism on which Barrett insists, but at its deepest level it is to be understood in terms of Old Testament Wisdom models which it goes beyond in a strategy which seeks the transformation of the reader yet has powerful claims to rationality. Part of this strategy, I suggest, is such that several of the assumptions of the conventional higher criticism of the text appear radically problematic, and in particular it displays just the sort of historical vulnerability that according to Stewart Sutherland scriptural texts are supposed to avoid.

An obvious objection would be that one cannot be reading a text as Scripture if it is seen as vulnerable in such a way that discrepancies with other books in the same set of Scriptures discredit it. Part of the drive to cut the links between the Jesus of history and the Christ of faith, which on my reading runs counter to the strategy of the Fourth Gospel, has arisen from perceived discrepancies between the figure of Jesus as presented in the Fourth Gospel and that in the Synoptics. However, the presence of such allegedly anomalous and 'Johannine' elements in the Synoptic Gospels as Luke x 18 must put a question mark against any simple contrast here, while the nature and extent of such parallels and divergences is heavily trampled ground. This is not the place to go into the matter in detail, but it is worth pointing out that recent work in rhetorical criticism has some bearing on the issue. One contrast often alleged is that the Johannine Jesus openly declares his special status whereas that of the Synoptics is concerned to keep his Messianic claims secret. The problems with the notion of the 'Messianic Secret' are notorious, and Kennedy's *New Testament Interpretation through Rhetorical Criticism* throws useful light on the matter. He argues in chapter 2 that analysis of Jesus' rhetoric in all three Synoptic Gospels indicates common evidence of a change in his strategy from relative directness to indirection, apparently arising out of a crisis in his ministry; John tells of at least one such crisis after which Jesus 'no longer went about openly among the Jews' until he came up to Jerusalem for the last time on Palm Sunday (xi 47–54; see also vi 15 with its sequel at vi 60–6). If rhetorical criticism brings out features of the texts which indicate

24

that the Synoptics' sources are strongly coloured by memories of the later phases of the ministry, and if there is no good reason to doubt that the Fourth Evangelist relies on sources or memories for which earlier phases – including several visits to Jerusalem unrecorded by the Synoptics – were equally prominent, then perceived discrepancies may be read 'faithfully' instead of 'suspiciously'.

Perhaps the purest exemplification of the hermeneutics of faith is provided by the second of this volume's two essays on the Fourth Gospel, that of Michael Edwards. He points, indeed, to the elements of 'secrecy' in the teaching of the Johannine, as of the Synoptic, Jesus: 'They are not ready for him, or he is not ready for them, and they can only make themselves available to his teaching by a complete change of heart. . . . As a method of persuasion, this is precisely not what we are expecting'. It is the themes of transformation and of subversion of ordinary expectations that are seen as lying at the heart of this gospel. It reworks the Old Testament as a whole, from beginning to end, reconstructing it in its true meaning around the focal theme of Jesus as the Word which fulfils and absorbs the Scriptures and which confronts the fallen world as light in darkness. This conflict is not presented as a poetic vision to be contemplated but as an activity in which we are involved, for the Word is seen as the creative centre from which the world and language derive and in which they meet – a vision which renders coherent the otherwise unacceptable contemporary contention that any event is already textual, and undercuts the conventional distinction between fable and fact. The work seeks to persuade us, but not by inviting us into a dialogue or presenting itself for analysis; on the contrary, we are what is being analysed. Put differently, the Fourth Gospel moves without strain from the sphere of literature to that of religion, effecting a passage between Poland's incommensurable orders in the manner Edwards has termed 'Pentecostal' and which for St Augustine was sacramental.

Rhetorical criticism can thus incorporate and 'place' the hermeneutics both of suspicion and of faith, significantly contributing to discussions concerning which is appropriate where and in what respects. It helps give content to the aspiration expressed by Paul Ricoeur (1969: 349): 'Beyond the desert of criticism, we wish to be called again'.

PROLOGUE

Chapter One

THE BIBLE AND THE RHETORICAL SUBLIME

LYNN POLAND

I

I should like to begin by praising the announced purpose of the conference which provided the foundation for this volume: to explore 'the ways in which the persuasive (and related literary) procedures of the biblical writers cut across or reinforce their concern with truth'. This strikes me as a helpful way to describe the best work that has been done recently on the rhetorical and literary strategies evident in the biblical writings. It is helpful for several reasons, some of which are, I think, nicely formulated by Meir Sternberg, whose recent *The Poetics of Biblical Narrative: Ideological Literature and the Drama of Reading* is certainly one major example of the kind of project that seems to be described in this statement of purpose. Sternberg's description of the Bible as 'ideological literature' means to yoke together terms that many modern literary critics, under the dictum that art must be 'purposeless' and 'disinterested', have been schooled to dissociate. As Sternberg correctly notes, it is this dissociation of ideology from art that has made it difficult for biblical scholars adapting the prevailing formalist literary critical tools to explore the Bible's peculiar relation to history or to examine the way its art is related to its truth claims. By taking it as given that the Bible is above all 'interested', concerned with truth, Sternberg is free to ask how this function of biblical narrative works with or against its historio-graphic and aesthetic functions.[1] Sternberg, in other words, is free to take seriously the dilemmas of the literary craftsman faced with the task of producing a work under certain conditions – in this case, conditions mandated by the Bible's peculiar historiographic and ideological concerns. The editor's choice of the term 'rhetoric' also works to overcome the disjunction between artfulness and ideology because it situates discourse, understood as the artful representation of ideology, in relation to an audience. This Sternberg means to do as well, when he describes the functions of narrative as transactions between teller and reader.[2]

If Sternberg can be said to exemplify the kind of work prescribed for this volume, it could also be said that his work follows from and furthers the lines of inquiry represented by Erich Auerbach's *Mimesis*. Auerbach's essays certainly address the biblical writers' concern with truth – in his celebrated phrase, the Bible's claim to truth is 'tyrannical – it excludes all other claims' (1953: 14). By this he means that the biblical world not only claims to be historically true, but also claims to be the *only* world; it insists and promises that all of human history will be given a place within its frame. This claim to truth, as both doctrine and promise, is not separable from the stories, he argues, but is evident in their form. His essay therefore aims to describe the mechanics of biblical tyranny by defining biblical style, analysing what I should like to call the Bible's peculiar rhetoric of sublimity.

I do not know what the conference planners had in mind when they included in their statement the possibility that the rhetorical procedures of the biblical writers might 'cut across' as well as 'reinforce' their concern with truth. I shall therefore twist it for my own purposes (this is what Harold Bloom calls being a 'strong reader') and understand it as referring to a series of gaps, or discontinuities, that I would like to champion. For it seems to me that while Sternberg's, and the conference's, insistence on the ideological nature of the biblical writings works to overcome the modern critical prejudice against 'purposiveness', there is another critical dictum that also requires testing against the Bible, and that is the notion of the 'unity of form and content'. This phrase can mean a variety of things, and in its broadest sense, as I shall suggest shortly, it is an assumption about the nature of texts that is fundamental to western culture. Beginning with the Romantics, however, the 'unity of form and content' acquires a specificity that has continued to influence literary criticism into the present. One example of this specificity is the way, in the late eighteenth century, the term 'symbol' comes to supplant all other rhetorical terms for figural language, especially the term 'allegory'; in the process, symbol and allegory cease to be descriptive terms, and become normative judgements, with symbol, the privileged term, coming to stand for the 'poetic' in general (see de Man 1971: 188). The eclipse of allegory by symbol has a kind of counterpart in the eighteenth- and nineteenth-century critical distinction between the sublime and the beautiful: both the symbol and the beautiful posit a union between form and content, language and the world, and finally, between the eternal and the temporal, while allegory, and the sublime, insist upon their disjunction.

My reflections on these distinctions have been prompted by a certain irony in the reception of recent literary studies of biblical texts. For many, it seems, the literary critic's assumptions about unity – the unity of the Jewish or Christian canon, the acceptance of the received text as a unified whole, and the unity of form and content – were welcomed as a promising way to rescue the Bible from the fragmenting procedures of historical criticism and thereby as a way to save the Bible for religion. Instead, these literary studies have sometimes been accused of doing precisely the opposite. I think here, for example, of the biblical scholar James Kugel's polemical reproach in *Prooftexts*, that literary methods ignore the Bible's religious character (Kugel 1981b: 217–36; see also the reply by Adele Berlin (1982) and Kugel's (1982) response). He writes:

> This literary reading, which has been around since antiquity is not now a mere 'also' that has come to heighten our appreciation of the Sacred Writ, it is not simply 'another dimension' of a great book, but rather the modern rival of an older reading, 'The Bible as Scripture'. Our new reading is the creation of a modern tradition of exegesis that brackets what used to be the most fundamental aspect of the Bible, the tradition of its divine character (and the reading(s) that that implied). . . . Even today, the Bible presents itself to us as something unique, Scripture, and if we are interested in reading it, that interest is, directly or *par personne interposée*, religious.
>
> (Kugel 1982: 329; 1981b: 234)

The literary critic George Steiner offers a related complaint in his review of the new *Literary Guide to the Bible* edited by Robert Alter and Frank Kermode. 'Of this tome', he writes, '. . . a terrible blandness is born. . . . We hear of "omelettes", of "pressure cookers", not of the terror, the *mysterium tremendum*, that inhabits man's endeavour to speak to and speak of God' (Steiner 1988: 97). It is important not to mistake Kugel's and Steiner's criticisms for what they are not. Neither are merely complaining about the imposition on biblical texts of literary competencies foreign to it, although this is, of course, a significant concern. If this were all that was at issue here, however, it would be possible, at least in principle, to remedy – and I think the work of Auerbach, Alter, and Sternberg, to continue my examples, have in their different ways at least attempted to do so. What Kugel and Steiner are suggesting is that literary analysis domesticates the religious power, or what I should like to call the 'sublimity', of the biblical texts. What is not clear in either of their essays, however, is just where this religious power – the *mysterium tremendum* – is located. To speak of the text as sacred scripture is to isolate it as unique and to invest it with authority of a special kind. Is its sacrality wholly the work of the community that reads it as such, then, or is there something about the text itself that invites or makes necessary this investment? Neither Kugel nor Steiner address this point directly. Steiner seems to hold that the Bible's 'concern with truth' is implicated in its form, and he therefore implies that there is something in the biblical texts themselves which the essays in the Alter/Kermode volume fail to see. He writes, for example, that 'the voice and that which it speaks can never be considered as separate'. Similarly, he praises Karl Barth, Rudolf Bultmann, and the 'masters of rabbinic exegesis', remarking that 'for such writers there are no divorcements between the literary understanding of the word and the fathomless question of the Logos – of that whose formulation is indeed of this world . . . but whose source and level of meaning, of demand upon us, are *other*' (1988: 97). Yet this observation seems to push us toward the other pole, toward the notion that the 'sublimity' of the texts lies wholly in the reader's investment in them. Neither the rabbis nor Bultmann, that is, could be said to find the 'question of the Logos' as 'incarnate' in the biblical writings in the way that form is continuous with content for romantic and modern literary critics. Bultmann, after all, found the 'true scandal' of the Word in 'event' rather than text – the event of the bare kerygma proclaimed, a kerygma that must be separated from the 'false scandal' represented by the specific cultural forms in which it was expressed. And for the rabbis Steiner praises, as, in a different way for Christian allegorists, it is the disjunctions, the disunities, in the text that signal that 'source and level of meaning' Steiner speaks of as 'other'. When Steiner then concludes by praising these exegetes as readers 'whose intensity is fully consonant with the words before them', we are left without knowing the source of this 'intensity of the words'.

I do not promise that I can, finally, offer any more of a solution than Steiner or Kugel, but I do think that the question of the source and nature of the Bible's 'sublimity', its capacity to provoke in at least some readers a sense of what Rudolf Otto spoke of as the 'holy', deserves to be raised again and again. What I wish to offer here is one way of reflecting on the problem. I have attempted to ask the question in the context of the history of biblical interpretation, and to isolate one strand of that tradition. I have tried to focus on the questions of the relation between form and content, and of text and truth, by exploring the contrast between allegory and symbol, or, put differently, between a 'rhetoric of sublimity' and a 'poetics of the beautiful'. The latter has dominated modern criticism since the Romantics, although its hegemony has been challenged in various ways by many recent developments in criticism that implicitly or explicitly seek to rediscover the allegorical, to re-insert the 'gaps' collapsed by the Romantic notion of the symbol.[3] While George Steiner does not say so (and, indeed, probably would not do so), his discomfort with the Alter/Kermode volume may have to do with the editors' dismissal of just these modes of contemporary criticism.[4]

II

The difficulty I have been pointing to in Steiner and Kugel's laments reflects a tension that has been present throughout the western tradition of biblical interpretation. It is a tension between two understandings of the relationship between God and language, the one positing that relation as continuous, the other as discontinuous. Let me speak briefly about each.

In *Beginnings*, the critic Edward Said distinguishes the notion of beginning from that of origin.[5] An origin, he argues, founds a set of relationships linked together by a familial analogy: 'father and son, the image, the process of genesis, a story' (Said 1985: 66). The series is dynastic, biological, bound to sources and origins, and mimetic. A beginning, in contrast, is specifically verbal – its logic is not found in biological succession, but, like the Oedipal complex, in departures and divergences from it. For words stand at the beginning, indeed are the beginning, of a series of displacements; to use words is to substitute them for something else – call it reality, nature, historical truth, or a kernel of actuality. To begin, in and with language, then, is to replace the familial/biological series with an intentional verbal structure: 'the brother, discontinuous concepts, paragenesis, construction' (65–6).

Said's contrast between image and language, mimesis and displacement, unproblematic, continuous familial reproduction and problematic, Oedipal substitution, however interesting, ignores the fundamental way these two strands have been linked in Western culture. In the beginning, God created by word: this posits a unique, unrepeatable origin and a foundational unity of word, intention and referent – an original plenitude in which meaning is complete and self-sufficient. From this verbal origin proceeds a continuous chain of signification – God, word, language, revelation, text, writing and reading, form an implicated series. In turn, the implications of this for Western notions of texts and textuality have been significant and persistent. The notion of God as Author authorizes human authorship, just as it provides the theological basis for the notion of a unified self. God did not have to create: human creation is therefore understood as the freely intended, that is, 'original', as opposed to determined, project of an individual agent, and as a unique, once for all, activity. Furthermore, the text, like the unity of thought, action, and word in God's creation, is therefore conceived as the realization, or actualization, of the author's intention. Criticism of various kinds – textual criticism, modes of historical criticism, formalist and hermeneutic modes of literary criticism – all share in this powerful theological impetus to understand a text as the act of one person at one time: such an understanding actually demands these kinds of criticism, in order to repair the wrecks of history (see, for example, McGann 1983). Interpretation is understood to be the work of recovering an original plenitude of meaning. Western culture, then, also privileges order, unity, and structure as normative categories. God's existence can be proved by arguments from the design of his creation, just as literary critics of the Bible now employ a version of the argument from design to posit a unified 'intention' in the biblical writings.[6]

This first side of the tension is perhaps most vividly – and influentially – articulated by St Augustine, for whom the Christian economies of creation and redemption are understood in semiotic terms. In Book 13 of his *Confessions*, Augustine pictures the firmament dividing the 'heaven of heavens' from the terrestrial sky as the unfolded scroll of scripture, stretched out like a skin. Above this firmament are the angels who have no need of reading to understand God's word, for they can read God's face: they read without syllables spoken in time, and their reading is perpetual, for what they read, God's will, never passes away; it is a book never closed (Augustine 1963: XIII, 15). Unlike the angels, human beings must read, and seek to recover, God's pre-existent and eternal will – his full intention present from the beginning – the way they read a sentence: because they must read in time, the syllables emerge and pass away, and complete meaning will be accessible only at the end of time. Salvation, like language, is a kind of tautology, ending where it began.[7] Augustine's image of scripture as a scroll that will one day be folded up both posits history, the temporal order, and subsumes it: he seems to imagine readers moving through time under the scroll, reading scripture part by part, while at the same time he envisages the scroll as written into the order of creation itself, 'from the beginning'. The mediating 'scroll' is both firmament and scripture, both nature and language, the verbal manifestation of God's intention in the two texts of creation and scripture. Language here is not displacement, as Said would have it; it does not substitute, as he puts it, one method for another. Rather, the 'natural' biological order is actualized as semiotic.

This confounding of scripture with nature becomes especially clear as Augustine continues his interpretation of the Genesis account. He is puzzled by the fact that the command to 'be fruitful and multiply' is extended to Adam and Eve, and to the creatures of sea and air, the fish and fowls, but not to the herbs, trees, beasts and serpents, which also bring forth 'according to their kind'. Because God does not speak without purpose, Augustine reasons, this must be understood allegorically: 'for I know that what is understood by the mind in a single way can be represented corporeally in a number of ways, and also that what is understood by the mind in a number of ways may have only one corporeal expression' (Augustine 1963: XIII, 24; his exegesis of this extends through chapters 20-4). Augustine finds the warrant for his allegorical reading of scripture, and the answer to his puzzlement, at the same time: the creeping creatures of the deep (as sea, and as depths of the flesh) are corporeal signifiers; they are the sacraments, which manifest God's intention in physical ways for those estranged by the deep from eternity, and they are corporeally pronounced signs, the 'material' aspect of language. The birds, born in the sea (and flesh) fly free of the sea, over the dry land, as thoughts are released from the material body of words to increase and multiply as things intellectually conceived. 'Be fruitful and multiply', then, refers not to biological generation, but rather to the generation of language as multiple signs and multiple meanings. Furthermore, the capacity to allegorize is what distinguishes human beings from the mere biological generativity of other creatures. What prevents this human activity of increasing and multiplying thoughts and words from becoming an endless and therefore meaningless chain of allegorization, is that the birds nevertheless fly 'under the firmament'. The possibilities and the limits of their semiotic flight are inscribed in the linguistic structure of creation. While signs continually point beyond themselves, all signs are ordered to and by God: creation is the sanctioning allegory of allegory.

While Said's contrast between beginning and origin remains problematic, his understanding of language as an Oedipal divergence from the unity of Father and Son, God and Word, is nevertheless helpful as a way of describing the second side of the tension I have mentioned, that of the discontinuity between language and the divine. The inadequacies of human language for speaking of or to the divine – Augustine is clearly an example here as well – is as persistent a theme in the history of Christian thought as the notion of original plenitude.[8] James Kugel also helps to elaborate this. In *The Idea of Biblical Poetry*, he notes that throughout the Christian and Jewish traditions, the question of biblical style has traditionally been approached through a distinction between divine and human speech. 'What was recognizably rhetorical or poetic', ('recognizable', that is, according to the secular norms for rhetoric with which the interpreter was familiar) was attributed to the notion that the Divine Word was accommodated to human capacities, or to the fact that human beings were the vehicle for God's word. What seemed 'awkward, unrhetorical, and even incomprehensible' in scripture, on the other hand, was explained by the text's divinity. Scripture is a 'lawless' text, as Kugel puts it, and it is precisely its stylistic breaking of the rules that signals its divinity (Kugel 1981a: 205–6). In contrast to the continuities between God's will and words, and between divine and human authorship, here we find that the divine is that which escapes writing. As Kugel also observes, until the modern period, we find biblical interpreters adopting two, rather contradictory, procedures at once. On the one hand, interpreters worked to identify the metres, tropes and figures of 'pagan' literature in the biblical writings, while on the other they attributed the Bible's departures from these rules to its special divine eloquence. Thus Augustine the rhetorician documented the figures of classical rhetoric in biblical texts. On the other hand, when the Augustine nurtured on the Hellenistic classics found the style of scripture in comparison rude and vulgar, Augustine the allegorical interpreter found in this same roughness the evidence of its spiritual eloquence. For Augustine, as for others, it is the gaps and difficulties in the text that point to divine intention without semiotically representing it. Human language is here discontinuous with divine rhetoric, even as, in its failure, it provides it a place.

For Augustine, the two poles in the tension I have outlined are in principle reconcilable – indeed, we could say that it is the task of interpretation to reconcile them. Where the surface rhetoric of the text breaks down, where it fails to signify, the interpreter assumes that God manifests himself here in a different kind of language, a language of things, like the allegorized aquatic creatures in the Genesis account. In this process the failure to signify becomes itself a sign, a sign of the presence of God's complete intention. Absence, in short, becomes a sign of presence.[9] This interpretative act thus requires a leap, or in Augustine's terms, a 'passage', between incommensurable orders: from human rhetoric to God's, and from temporality to eternal significance.

There are several things here that deserve closer attention, since they are related to our, and Steiner's, question about the locus of the religious power of Scripture. For Augustine, allegorical interpretation is not simply a cognitive exercise, but an emotional one. Allegory, as he puts it, kindles ardour, arouses the affections, and strengthens the soul; it provides truth with affective power. Indeed, Augustine's central justification for allegory is precisely its capacity to combat Steiner's 'terrible banality': a truth laid bare, he says, falls into disrepute; revelation without mystery loses its worth. While Augustine already knows, through the rule of faith, the 'fullness of meaning' he seeks to recover through interpretation, the religious power of the texts does not lie in its truth so much as in the trials of interpretation. Allegory combats the disdain and lassitude fostered by that which is too easily mastered. As he writes in *Epistle* 137, 'Lest what is easily understood should beget satiety in the reader, the same truth in another place more obscurely expressed becomes again desired, is somehow invested with a new attractiveness, and is thus received with more pleasure into the heart' (Augustine 1973–4: I, 480; *Epistle* 137, IV, 18). Stated this bluntly, Augustine's way of reconciling the tension through allegory seems 'merely' rhetorical, without theological necessity. Because he already knows the truths to be discovered, that is, allegory threatens to become a rhetorical game of hide and seek, for the purpose of producing pleasure. I think that it is finally correct to say that Augustine's reconciliation of the tension is 'merely rhetorical', but in a more subtle way than this statement suggests.

First, it needs to be said that the affective power of allegory is, for Augustine, considerable, and that it includes a sense of terror, of the '*mysterium tremendum*', as well as pleasure. As Augustine undertakes his exegesis of Genesis in the last books of *Confessions*, for example, he continually re-begins his quest for origins with a prayer that the ardour kindled by his interpretative activity be directed to the right object and that it be subject to God's control. As he petitions in Book XI, 2, 'From all rashness and all lying circumcise my lips both within and without. . . . Let your scriptures be my chaste delight'. And in Book XIII, 15: 'we know of no other books so destructive of pride, so destructive of the enemy and the defender who resist reconciliation with you. . . [I know of no] writings so apt to persuade me to bow my neck to your yoke and take service with you for nothing'. Augustine's concern here with circumcision (as symbolic castration), with submission to the Father, and with chaste delights, betrays his anxiety that the nature of his interpretative ardour will not serve to uncover the fullness of God's intention hidden in the text, but will instead be lost in an endless movement from sign to sign without closure, or the fear that what he will 'discover' behind the veil will not be God's visage, but the projections of his own temporal desire.

What we learn from Augustine, I suggest, is that the '*mysterium tremendum*' of scripture is located in the labour of interpretation to reconcile the two poles of our tension, to match fulfilment with 'gap'. But we also learn that the specifically religious power, the terror of interpretation, lies in experiencing the possibility that these tensions are not reconcilable. Augustine's belief that God's intention is inscribed in the grammar of creation is an article of faith. Textual obscurity creates a crisis for faith; confronted with the failures of human rhetoric, Augustine experiences affectively the question of what, if anything, lies behind the letter. The pleasures of discovery depend upon this prior negative moment of interpretation. The veil, or the gap, in the text functions to introduce doubt. I speak of this process as 'rhetorical', because there is something gratuitous about the hide and seek of allegory. It is a crisis 'staged' to give the truth Augustine already believes affective power.

This structure of estrangement motivating reconciliation, this means of enhancing the affective power of religious belief, is reproduced and displaced in the eighteenth- (and nineteenth-) century taste for the 'sublime', which influenced Bishop Löwth's *Lectures on the Sacred Poetry of the Hebrews*. Throughout the medieval period and the Renaissance, we find Augustine's understanding of allegory linked to rhetoric by the notion of the grand, or sublime, style, the *oratio gravis*. Medieval theorists tended to translate *gravitas* as *difficultas*, however: the grand style is therefore characterized by *difficulta ornata*, difficult ornament. The sublime style, whether of the Bible, or later, of secular poetry, was thus the allegorical or enigmatic style – the 'lawlessness' of which Kugel spoke. The eighteenth-century sublime may be understood as an intensification, and translation, of the notion of 'lawlessness' as textual 'difficulty', into qualities of the landscape, painting, architecture, and literature that convey wildness, power, or infinity, and produce in the beholder mixed feelings of terror and delight. Analyses of the sublime were numerous, and theorists were far from unanimous in their articulation of this critical idea. Nevertheless, the experiences they describe can be seen to share the structure I have suggested is evident in Augustine's allegory: sublimity concerns transport to a transcendent ideal (and by the eighteenth century this could refer to the Christian God, or, say, Kant's notion of the 'transcendental' or 'supersensible' Ideas) by means of 'enthusiasm' or 'vehement passion'. By 'kindling ardour' for this ideal, to use Augustine's description, the beholder is moved to rise above the limits of the merely human to discover a superior nature or destiny. This kindling of passion, as I have suggested, has its locus in an encounter with some experience of 'difficulty'; one must first experience the limits of one's capacities, must first feel frozen in terror or astonishment, before the positive moment and movement of transport can occur. David Hume makes this plain when he writes:

> 'Tis a quality very observable in human nature, that any opposition which does not entirely discourage and intimidate us, has rather a contrary effect, and inspires us with more than ordinary grandeur and magnanimity. In collecting our force to overcome the opposition, we invigorate the soul, and give it an elevation with which otherwise it would never have been acquainted.
>
> (Hume 1878: II, 480)

This encounter can arise from the apprehension of one's powerlessness before the forces of nature, or from a sense of one's intellectual limitations – one's incapacity to master, to comprehend, what appears vast, difficult, obscure, or infinite.

We also find here that there is something gratuitous about the moment of sublime crisis, just as I suggested there seems to be in the hiding and seeking of allegory. We see this most clearly when the sublimity in question involves a confrontation with natural force, since for the soul to experience the 'transport' of sublimity, it must not be in actual physical danger – as Hume noted, the opposition cannot 'entirely' overwhelm us. The 'terror' one feels is thus already the work of the imagination, which – as Kant describes it – 'pictures to itself' an attempt to resist, and feels terror as it sees that such resistance would inevitably fail (Kant 1951: 110–11). (Since it is not so much 'nature', as the idea, or imagination, of nature, that is involved here, the transition from a sublimity of nature to a rhetorical, or literary sublime, is therefore an easy one to make.) The gratuity of the crisis is evident when we recognize, further, that, as in allegory, the 'transport' that occurs here involves an unmediated leap between two incommensurable orders, a shift in which failure or absence of meaning or mastery, again comes to signify the presence of the transcendent. The soul is elevated in a vertical relation to the transcendent, by the breakdown of its horizontal relation to nature or to cultural artifact. And in these modern versions of the sublime, too, it must be said that the nature of the 'transcendent' is, as it was for Augustine, known in advance. The transcendence that is experienced as 'emerging from' the experience of terror is clearly not derived from what occasions it – it must have already been assumed. If in the sublime moment, for example, one stands before infinite spaces, or confronts a text that exceeds comprehension, and experiences not just confusion or terror but transport to a higher order, what this experience means depends upon what one assumes, *a priori*, to be the nature of the transcendent: whether some version of God, or Kant's 'supersensible destiny'.[10] Thus, as I have suggested regarding Augustine, there is a sense in which the sublime crisis is 'staged' so that the existence and nature of the transcendent order which one already knows can be affectively confirmed. The sublime, too, is a way of endowing truth with emotional power.

Most importantly for our purposes, what the sublime and allegory have in common as a way of 'reconciling' the two poles of our tension – the inadequacies of human rhetoric with a posited original fullness of meaning – is that both depend upon a felt sense, however momentary, that these orders are indeed incommensurable. The sense of the text's religious power arises both from the 'terrified' perception of their incommensurability, and then from the feelings of assurance and joy when the 'passage' has been made.

III

In his lament in *Prooftexts*, James Kugel locates the loss of the Bible's 'sublimity' (although this is not his term) in the Renaissance. While biblical interpreters have always read the Bible according to the norms of secular texts – finding in them the tropes of classical rhetoric, for example – with the Renaissance, to read the Bible in a literary way means to read it as one text among others – to read it, as he put it, as literature, as opposed to, scripture. This continues his argument in *The Idea of Biblical Poetry* that with the Renaissance the simultaneous, if contradictory, reading of scripture as both human rhetoric and as 'lawless', divine speech, is replaced by a third option: the 'lawlessness' of the biblical text is attributed to the foreignness of the conventions governing the world of the Bible's composition. The texts become, from a stylistic standpoint, human creations that differ from our own compositions chiefly because they were written in another land centuries ago (Kugel 1981a: 206). Kugel's argument here is misleading, in so far as it suggests that both historical and literary criticism necessarily entail the eclipse of biblical sublimity. While criticism that explains away the 'lawlessness' of biblical rhetoric, or collapses the tension between 'gap' and 'fulfillment', will have this effect, it seems to me that a sense of the 'terrors of interpretation' can be preserved without foregoing modern criticism altogether. I would suggest that the danger lies not in Renaissance humanism, as Kugel has it, but instead in the emergence of the specifically Romantic notion of the poetic symbol, and in the identification of the Bible as the *locus classicus* for 'the poetic' so defined. Coleridge can serve as paradigm for this turn. The biblical narratives are, he writes:

> the living *educts* of the imagination; of that reconciling and mediatory power, which incorporating the Reason in images of Sense, and organizing (as it were) the flux of the Senses, by the permanence and self-circling energies of the Reason, gives birth to a system of symbols, harmonious in themselves, and consubstantial with the Truths, of which they are the *conductors*. . . . Hence . . . The Sacred Book is worthily entitled *the* WORD OF GOD.
>
> (Coleridge 1972: 29)

This passage is confusing, but its language of reconciliation and mediation, of symbols consubstantial with truths, should suggest how this Romantic aesthetic refuses to countenance the incommensurability of the two poles with which we began. It collapses the distinction between experience and the representation of experience in language, between what Auerbach spoke of as the tension between 'sensory appearance' and 'meaning', and between divine and human speech. Coleridge's version of the nineteenth-century valorization of symbol over allegory may help to clarify this, as it makes clear the relationship between the symbol and an aesthetics of beauty, as distinct from allegory and an aesthetics of the sublime. The symbol, for Coleridge, is akin to the 'beautiful' of idealist philosophies, for it is characterized 'by the translucence of the Eternal through and in the Temporal' (1972: 30). Like Kant's definition of the beautiful as entailing a harmony between the understanding and the object perceived (in contrast to the sublime, which entails a disharmony of the faculties), the Coleridgean symbol 'partakes' of the reality which it renders intelligible, so that one directly apprehends the idea symbolized in the act of perceiving the symbol, in an 'unmediated vision'. Allegory, in contrast, he writes, 'cannot be other than spoken consciously', because the reader is independently conscious of the system of ideas to which the allegorical text refers (Coleridge 1936: 30). Allegory entails, then, a 'disjunction of the faculties', the imagination engaged by the concrete textual surface, the reason by the ideas to which they refer.

It is this disjunction of the faculties, I have argued, that exhibits the sense of incommensurability between the divine plenitude of meaning and the human order. Both allegory and the sublime, I have suggested, repeat this tension in the forms of text or nature and so produce in the reader or beholder that dual sense of terror and delight Otto called the experience of the holy. Coleridge, in contrast, experiences from the 'poetic', as we have seen, a 'reconciling and mediating power': poetry 'reconciles opposite or discordant qualities' into a new, health-giving harmony. (See, for example, *Biographia Literaria*, chap. XIV, reprinted in Adams 1971: 471.) From the perspective of the creative process, the poetic 'genius' is endowed with the capacities posited of the divine creator: the relation between intention and its manifestation in signs is thought to be – to recall Said's catalogue – seamless, unproblematic, familial and biological: the poem's unity is 'organic', plant-like, its intention and transcendent referent 'incarnate' in its form. The plenitude and self-sufficiency of meaning posited for the symbol leaves no room for real history or real time, then; the symbol can posit the possibility of the coincidence of image and idea because they are understood as part and whole of the same order (like the relation between God and his Word); their relation is therefore one of simultaneity, spatial rather than temporal, a relation in which the intervention of time is merely a matter of contingency. For allegory, in contrast, time is constitutive because the incommensurability of the two orders is its starting point. As Paul de Man puts it, 'renouncing the nostalgia and the desire to coincide, [allegory] establishes its language in the void of this temporal difference' (de Man 1971: 207).

When the Bible, or any other literary work, is read in accordance with this poetics of the beautiful, then, we see the assumptions about unity I characterized at the beginning of my essay take such precedence that they tend to cancel out, to forget, the problematics represented by the second side of the tension. We find a criticism that, in the words of the flamboyant early twentieth-century critic T.E. Hulme, 'cannot look at a chasm or a gap without shuddering' (Hulme 1924: 4). We find criticism that seeks to establish the coherence, autonomy and organic unity of the biblical text and tries to find a way to preserve the notion of a single 'intention' informing it, whether in the single author, the redactor, or the process of canon formation. This is a criticism that finds it difficult to reckon . with pluralism of any kind, whether of authors, redactors, ideologies, or traces of the temporal evolution of the texts. One thinks here of the Hans Frei of *The Eclipse of Biblical Narrative*, for whom the history of biblical interpretation does not seem to include allegorical interpretation, and for whom the 'realistic' 'history-like' biblical narrative forms an organic unity that orients rather than disorients its readers. Like the Romantic symbol, Frei's narrative, in his words, 'does not illustrate a meaning that already exists independent of it' (an allusion to allegory) but instead 'constitutes' its meaning: the meaning is located somehow 'in' the text itself. Meir Sternberg, despite his interest in 'gaps' and 'tensions', finally shares these biases as well: he finds a single poetics of biblical narrative, a single 'ideology' informing the poetics, and ultimately a single reader, a reader located nowhere in particular, the reader he becomes as he voices the questions and hypotheses this 'reader' is expected to construct. Sternberg's difficulty in dealing with history is also, perhaps, evidence of the Romanticism still guiding his work. As Terry Eagleton and others have pointed out, the elevation of the 'poetic imagination' over the mundanely 'prosaic' can be seen as an attempt to deal with the fragmentation, alienation, and secularization that emerged with the industrial middle class, the symbol's autonomy and remoteness a solution to the artist's loss of a social function, and an antidote to the social and cultural conflicts in the actual world (Eagleton 1983: 17–53). To see the Bible as belonging to a higher, more 'poetic' order than prose can also be understood in these terms, as a response and antidote not only to the cultural conditions Eagleton describes, but also to the raging sectarianism in biblical interpretation and the search for political consensus.[11]

Finally, this is a criticism that is, inevitably, unrhetorical, in the sense that language is understood as proceeding from, produced by, and manifesting the 'spirit' of an author or 'age'. There is no room here for the possibility that rhetorical figures may, on the contrary, generate the 'spirit'. Auerbach's essay on Homeric and biblical narrative, for example, takes as its point of departure certain stylistic details: in contrast to the complete 'externalization' of all elements and interconnections in Homeric epic, he argues, biblical narrative is reticent, paratactic, multilayered and therefore 'fraught with background' (Auerbach 1953: 12). But style, for Auerbach, is mimetic; it is an index of a culture's mode of comprehending and representing things. Thus his central notion of 'figura' is for him a theological principle and a way of seeing before it is a rhetorical form: style and language are essentially innocent. One could argue to the contrary, however, that ways of seeing and theological principles are instead (at least in part) derived from linguistic categories – that, in fact, the 'figura' is the rhetorical structure of the literary history Auerbach produces in *Mimesis*.[12]

I think that a contemporary criticism is possible that is at once thoroughly historical and capable of addressing the Bible's rhetorical sublimity. I think here, to give a single example, of the essay on the Twelve Prophets in the Alter/Kermode *Guide* by Herbert Marks. Marks focuses on the persistence in the texts (because or in spite of its redactions) of discordant features that resist assimilation – in particular on the way the received text juxtaposes antithetical traditions – oracles of judgement, oracles of salvation – with only abrupt transitions and unmotivated reversals. Marks is not so much interested in discovering the 'causes' for this discord, nor in assigning their presence to the intention of a redactor, as he is in the text's 'aesthetic impact', and its religious effect. In Marks's reading of the book, we find again and again the structure of the sublime, estrangement juxtaposed with reconcilia-tion, with nothing mediating between them but the reader's experience of terror and hope. The book of the Twelve Prophets, to recall de Man's words about allegory, renounces the nostalgia and the desire to coincide, establishing its language in the void of this difference.

To conclude, it should be clear that the structure and experience of sublimity I have sketched here is not confined to the Jewish or Christian Scriptures. As my discussion of the eighteenth- and nineteenth-century sublime was meant to suggest, the experience of the terrors of interpretation extends beyond biblical interpretation. I do mean to suggest two things, however. First, we need not think of allegorical interpretation as something left behind, outgrown and replaced by the 'better', Romantic understanding of the poetic imagination. Similarly, the modern critical turn in biblical interpretation represented by the 'higher criticism' need not be understood to be as absolute a critical watershed as our common accounts of this history often maintain. From this perspective, allegory as a mode of interpretation can be understood as a persisting tradition in the West, momentarily eclipsed by the Romantic disparagement of it.

Second, by using the term 'rhetoric' of the sublime I have meant to insist upon the importance of the language of the biblical texts. It is language in its 'lawlessness', in its failures to signify, that provides the occasion and the motivation to pass, experientially, through terror to assurance. I have thus offered this 'tradition' of interpretation as a counterweight against two ways of reconciling the tension with which I began. On the one hand, it corrects those who would so stress the unity of form and content that the disjunctures between divine and human rhetoric are forgotten. On the other, it balances a position often manifest in protestant neo-orthodox theologies – in Bultmann, and, more recently in the work of Paul Ricoeur on biblical interpretation. Ricoeur writes:

> Maybe in the case of Christianity there is no sacred text, because it is not the text which is sacred, but the One about which it is spoken. . . . The critical act is not forbidden by the nature of the text, because it is not a sacred text in the sense in which the Qur'an is sacred.
>
> (Ricoeur 1979: 271)

While Ricoeur is undoubtedly correct to contrast Christian scripture with the Qur'an, the effect of his emphasis on the 'One about which it is spoken', like Bultmann's stress on Word-Event, is to dislocate the religious power of scripture, to remove it altogether from the text to something outside of it.

The question I have pursued here is, in some sense, the question of the 'genesis of secrecy'. As Frank Kermode observes, 'We are programmed to prefer fulfillment to disappointment, the closed to the open. . . . We are all fulfillment men, *pleromatists'* (Kermode 1979: 64 and 72). We in the West are 'programmed', that is, by assumptions about unity of intention and its manifestation in language that unfold from our notion of origin, from God's creation by his Word. Nevertheless, as Kermode also notes, it is our perception of the 'radiant obscurity' of texts that terrifies and consoles us. It is this that makes us not simply fallible but, as he puts it, 'blessedly fallible'.

NOTES

1 I am not convinced that Sternberg himself has done justice to the question of history, but in principle his framework allows for it.

2 Here, too, despite this description and his own use of the term 'rhetoric', Sternberg unfortunately does not finally mean a historically situated audience or reader: the 'transaction' occurs between an implied author and a hypothetical, ideal, if fallible, reader.

3 See, for example, Paul de Man, *Blindness and Insight*, Walter Benjamin's reinterpretation of the allegorical and emblematic style of the baroque in *Trauerspiel*, *The Origins of German Tragic Drama*, and J. Hillis Miller, 'The Two Allegories' (1981: 355–70).

4 In their 'General Introduction' to the volume, the editors dismiss: 'critical approaches mainly interested in the origins of a text in ideology or social structure', 'Marxist criticism', 'psychoanalytic criticism', 'critics who use the text as a springboard for cultural or metaphysical ruminations', 'Deconstructionist', 'feminist critics' (Alter and Kermode 1987: 5–6).

5 I am grateful to my colleague, Professor Anthony C. Yu, for recalling Said's work in this context.

6 This was suggested by Anthony C. Yu, by way of contrasting Asian with Western attitudes toward order.

7 As John Freccero nicely puts it: 'Like language itself, the redemptive process is tautology, ending where it began.' (1975: 35)

8 Augustine often uses language to illustrate the problem of temporality as he does, for example, in his analysis of time in Book XI of his *Confessions*.

9 Cf. Thomas Weiskel's analysis of the sublime in similar terms in *The Romantic Sublime*.

10 On this point see Weiskel, *The Romantic Sublime*.

11 On this point see Stephen Prickett, *Words and The Word*, 1986: 39.

12 Timothy Bahti develops this point in 'Vico, Auerbach, and Literary History', 239–55, and 'Auerbach's *Mimesis*: Figural Structure and Historical Narrative', in Jay and Miller 1985: 124–45.

Part One

OLD TESTAMENT
AND APOCRYPHA

Chapter Two

HISTORY AND RHETORIC IN THE PROPHETS

JOHN BARTON

The books of the classical prophets of the Old Testament contain two themes which are so interwoven that they strike the modern reader as indivisible parts of a single whole. Oracles denouncing the sin and apostasy of Israel and Judah alternate, in such books as Isaiah, Jeremiah, Amos, and Hosea, with predictions of national calamity – usually at the hands of foreign powers, though sometimes apparently by means of natural disasters. The predicted calamity is said by the prophets to be the direct result of the sins they denounce, and this leads in some places to a third theme, the urgent call to repent before it is too late.

This whole package of ideas deeply influenced the later generations who wrote the history of Israel, first in the books from Joshua to Kings (the so-called 'Deuteronomistic History', or Former Prophets, as the Hebrew Bible perhaps significantly calls them), and then, during the Persian period, in the books of Chronicles. In all these works there is a strong tendency to present the history in such a way that the prophetic message is shown to be exemplified in the events that befell. The nation sinned, both corporately in turning aside to worship other gods and individually in crimes against the person; consequently God punished them, by sending in foreign armies to invade, destroy and deport. Only when the people repented did divine judgement abate, though (at least in the more optimistic version of the history in Chronicles) *whenever* repentance was forthcoming, God relented. The moral for the reader of these histories is scarcely concealed: in every generation, sin leads to national disaster, but repentance to new life and salvation. Indeed, sometimes prophets are planted at salient points in the historical account to make just this point in so many words. Thus the history of Israel becomes an extended illustration of the justice and mercy of God, an acted parable of the prophetic message. As Josephus was later perceptively to put it:

> The main lesson to be learnt from this history by any who care to peruse it is that men who conform to the will of God, and do not venture to transgress laws that have been excellently laid down, prosper in all things beyond belief, and for their reward are offered by God felicity; whereas, in proportion as they depart from the strict observance of these laws, things otherwise practicable become impracticable, and whatever good thing they strive to do ends in irretrievable disasters.
>
> (*Antiquities* 1:14)

But the seamless unity of the prophetic message as it formed the Jewish consciousness in later generations may not necessarily imply that the prophets themselves came to it in a single moment of illumination. In this paper I shall be arguing that there is a great deal more artifice in the message of the prophets than appears at first sight. So far from hanging together naturally, the different parts of their reading of the historical experience of Israel form a considerable rhetorical *tour de force*. The genius of the classical prophets was to take the highly recalcitrant facts of history, whose religious and moral implications were in fact extremely ambiguous, and to give an account of these facts which would convince people not only that the hand of God could be seen in them, but that the operations of the divine hand were entirely comprehensible in human moral categories – indeed, that given the right ethical framework one could see that history could not but have unfolded in the way that it did. Prophetic rhetoric is designed, that is to say, to make the contingencies of human history look like divine necessities. Another way of putting this would be to say that the chief concern of the prophets is theodicy, the justification of God's ways with his world. In the interests of a coherent theodicy, great rhetorical skill needed to be employed. Even if we can hardly avoid questioning the prophets' theology, we are bound to admire their literary talent.

A traditional Anglo-Saxon way of interpreting the prophets minimizes the degree of artifice in their message, and enables us to go on believing that they were essentially right when they spoke of inevitable judgement on a sinful nation. This line of interpretation is most attractively summed up by E.W. Heaton in his little classic *The Old Testament Prophets*, where he talks of Amos and his successors as 'morally sensitive laymen' (Heaton 1977: 36). What this means is that the classical prophets did not receive their message of coming judgement as a revelation, but arrived at it as the conclusion to a moral analysis of the contemporary social and political scene. Far from being visionaries filled with a non-rational foreboding, they were clear-sighted commentators on the society of their day. Their conviction that disaster was coming was a moral conviction: a God such as they believed the God of Israel to be *could not but* destroy a nation such as Israel had become. Filled with this sense of moral outrage, the prophets then surveyed the international scene, and identified more or less plausible candidates for the role of the 'staff in Yahweh's hand' (cf. Isaiah x 5). Sometimes, in fact, they were carefully reticent about the identity of this divine agent: Amos said simply 'An adversary shall surround the land' (iii 11), and Jeremiah spoke merely of a 'foe from the north' – playing very safe, for (unless the Egyptians were to invade) any foe was likely to approach Jerusalem from the north. The very vagueness of such threats helps, on this view, to confirm the impression that the prophets began from moral sensitivity and concluded that judgement was coming – unless the people repented.

I shall return briefly at the end to the suggestion that the prophets should be seen as 'laymen', because I think it highly illuminating in other ways. But its association with this rather rationalizing explanation of their oracles of judgement seems to me less well grounded. The mainstream of German Old Testament scholarship has been right, I believe, to argue that the prophets' moral analysis does not, as this would imply, invariably have the priority in their thinking. The main difficulty in seeing the ostensible argument from sin to inevitable judgement as also, historically, the way in which prophetic thinking actually worked is that it does not do justice to the political realities of the prophets' times. Amos, the first of the classical prophets, has been rather a misleading example here. When he prophesied, perhaps in the 760s, well before the expansion of Assyrian power that began with the accession of Tiglath-Pileser III in 745, it was indeed unlikely that many people could have foreseen the eventual extinction of the northern kingdom of Israel. Israel was apparently enjoying an Indian summer of prosperity. But all the later prophets lived in times when the threat to national security was palpable, and Jeremiah and Ezekiel of course actually lived through national disaster and went on prophesying after it. The certainty such prophets had that Israel's existence was threatened was certainly unwelcome: they were regarded as lowering morale, perhaps even as agents of the Assyrians or the Babylonians paid to lower morale. But it can hardly have been incomprehensible, or have struck their contemporaries as a totally implausible product of the prophetic obsession with national sin. On the contrary, it was the prophets who said 'Peace, peace' who were peddling an implausible message, as Jeremiah was quick to point out. The plausibility of the classical-prophetic proclamation of judgement in political terms was very high, however much in the popular mind wishful thinking prevailed over it.

This being so, it seems unlikely that the prophets for the most part arrived at their expectation of disaster only because of their unique sensitivity to the moral condition of the nation. The counsellors of Hezekiah or Zedekiah had already arrived at the same conclusion by a simple consideration of diplomatic dispatches and news from border towns: that was why they paid so much attention to improving the national defences. The originality of the prophets lay not in what they had to say about the future as such, but in the fact that they gave a particular theological interpretation of it not as the result of *Realpolitik* but as the working out of the will of Yahweh, offended by national sin; and corresponding to this, in their insistence that national repentance, not military measures, was the only possible means to avert the disaster that threatened.

This strongly suggests that moral sensitivity came in to provide explanations of a foreboding of the future that had originally been derived from a quite different source: *political* sensitivity. As a matter of fact, even Amos may not really be an exception to this. If the 'adversary' he so vaguely describes was indeed the Assyrian empire, then we should have to ascribe a more-than-human prescience to him or, if we wanted to avoid this, fall back on the position that he was indeed 'morally certain' of Israel's downfall. But a good case can be made for seeing the 'adversary' in question as the Aramaean kingdom of Damascus, with which Israel was actually at war in Amos's day. To think that the temporarily successful anti-Aramaean campaigns were about to go into reverse may have required more political astuteness than most of Amos's contemporaries possessed; but it is not an idea of a different order from the forebodings of doom in later prophets. We do not have to rationalize all such prophetic forebodings as political insight, or exclude the possibility that their antennae were more sensitive than those of their colleagues in the royal court, but there is still no need to rationalize them in the other way, by deriving these political predictions from their moral insight. It is the predictions about the future that are primary, not the moral analysis.

A great deal more could be said about the question of which came first, moral analysis or prediction of doom; but let us at least for the sake of argument accept that a case can be made for regarding the moral analysis as secondary, and ask where this leads. It seems to me that, as I have already suggested, the moral condemnation in the prophets functions essentially as part of a theodicy. The prophets' object is to demonstrate not only that disaster is coming, which many suspected, but that it is coming for a good and adequate reason, and that it vindicates (rather than impugning) the justice of Yahweh, Israel's God. This is indeed something of a *tour de force*, for there is no reason to suppose that a neutral observer would have seen anything in either the religious practices or the social relationships of Israelites in the period of the great prophets greatly different from what had been current in earlier times or what was to be common later on. The distinctively new feature from the eighth to the sixth centuries was the international situation. This made the two small kingdoms of Israel and Judah pawns in the ambitions of various superpowers, and the historian is bound to say that they would have been that whatever their internal moral or religious character had been. The prophets' task was to make these perfectly contingent political circumstances look like the most obvious and inevitable outcome of national sin: to create, in fact, exactly the impression which has been accepted for the truth by the English-speaking tradition of talking of the prophets as morally sensitive critics who felt that the sins of Israel cried out to heaven for vengeance. At the simplest level, the prophets do this by liberal use of words such as 'because' (*ki*) and 'therefore' (*laken*) to link denunciations of sin with predictions of disaster. But they are far from content merely to use such logical connectives to suggest causal connections that were in fact not at all evident. They manifest extreme ingenuity and resourcefulness in the way they present history as determined by moral forces.

An important point to note here is that the prophetic concern to show that historical events reflect divine decisions, not merely human intentions, is not in itself any kind of *novum* in the ancient Near Eastern context. Everyone in the ancient world, so far as we can tell, believed that the rise and fall of nations was determined by the gods. While this in no way inhibited political leaders from acting in the light of normal political and military calculations, it meant that the eventual outcome of such decisions for good or ill was commonly given a theological interpretation. One of the achievements of Bertil Albrektson's *History and the Gods* was to remind Old Testament scholars that there was a widespread theology of history in the ancient world. According to this theology, military defeat, invasion, and national disaster were the working out through human instruments of the will of offended gods. The prophets of Israel refined this common theology in various ways, but they certainly did not invent it. When they announce the coming downfall of *foreign* nations as a divine judgement on them, they are often saying nothing that would have been strange either to their Israelite contemporaries or, in principle, to the nations concerned. People in the ancient world regularly predicted and gloated over the collapse of their enemies and neighbours, and as regularly attributed this collapse to divine displeasure.

In the ancient Near East there were two kinds of offences against the gods in particular which were widely believed to call down their wrath and to lead to the fall of kingdoms. These provided the raw material for prophetic rhetoric to get to work on, though (as we shall see) in a very subtle and ingenious way. The first is what we generally call *hybris*: arrogating to oneself the privileges and status of the gods. Of course kings in the ancient Near East were never noted for their humility, and one may ask whether the idea of pride as a sin was conceivable at all to some of the Assyrian rulers. But there is a difference between what is regarded as a sin in moral codes of a sapiential or legal kind, or in conventions for royal proclamations and propaganda, on the one hand, and the sins for which people cast around once a disaster has already struck and requires theological justification. Barnabas Lindars made this distinction very helpfully in a little article on 'Ezekiel and Individual Responsibility':

Thought about the divine retribution proceeds from a point quite different from that of criminal responsibility. The laws concerning crime start with the fact that a crime has been committed and impose the appropriate remedy. But ideas of divine retribution start with the recognition of a state of affairs which appears to be brought about by God, e.g. prosperity or adversity, and seek to account for it by tracing it back to God's favour or displeasure.

(Lindars 1965: 456)

Furthermore, people will frequently castigate as sins in fallen enemies qualities they regard as admirable in themselves – I do not think one needs much proof that this is a constant feature of human nature. *Post eventum* explanations for national decline, and predictions of the decline of foreign powers, operated both in Israel and among its neighbours with a concept for which *hybris* is a perfectly serviceable shorthand term. It is the commonest reason adduced for the downfall of foreign nations in prophetic oracles against the nations in the Old Testament, and widespread also outside Israel.

A second major model for interpreting disaster thinks in terms of divine anger at offences against humanity. As a number of studies of international conventions about war, diplomacy, and international relations have shown, apparently modern ideas such as 'atrocity' or 'outrage' were current, *mutatis mutandis*, in many ancient cultures. Wars waged without regard to such conventions risked the anger of the gods. Again, we must distinguish between propagandist glorifications of atrocities, such as we find in Assyrian annals, and rationalizations of decisions to go to war against enemies or explanations of defeats that have already occurred. Of course all nations practised atrocities, and justified them. But when defeat struck, people might look around to find atrocities – oath-breaking, massacres of innocent populations, infringements of diplomatic immunity, and so on – which could account for the divine anger that had caused the defeat. When cursing their enemies or praying for their downfall, they would point to similar crimes and call on the gods to avenge them. There is often in this a sense that such outrages are offences against a kind of order of nature.

Now the skill of the prophets lies in deploying the almost instinctive feeling that such offences as these form a sufficient ground for divine retribution in order to show that the state of the nation in their own day was inviting the wrath of Yahweh. When the prophets looked around at society in the times of the Assyrian and Babylonian threats, they did not in fact see much that appeared obviously to smack of either *hybris* or transgression of natural law. Israel and Judah were not expanding an aggressive empire, but fighting for their lives; and often they were relying not on their own military might but on the help (fruitless as it proved) of such allies as the Egyptians. Nor were Israelites and Judaeans committing war-crimes or otherwise offending against common humanity. Indeed, in the time of Amos or Isaiah there seems little that can even be called crime for the prophets to batten on: outwardly society is quite calm and prosperous. (Hosea and Jeremiah do admittedly reflect a more disordered society.) Yet the prophets contrive to dress up the sins they can detect in language which assimilates them to these dominant models. Thus they make them seem to lead inevitably, even obviously, to the disaster which they are sure (on quite other grounds) will fall on the nation. Four examples of the technique may be considered.

1. We begin with the second kind of sin, offences against natural order. As a number of commentators have suggested, both Amos and Isaiah show considerable familiarity with this way of thinking. Isaiah's ultimate condemnation of Judah's rulers takes the form 'You turn things upside down!' (xix 16), while Amos describes the perversion of justice he claims to see around him as being like an attempt to plough the sea with oxen: an absurd contravention of the order of nature (vi 12). The technique most commonly used to make this point is in fact, as in this example, the rhetorical question expecting the answer 'no': 'Can horses run upon rocks? Will you plough the sea with oxen? yet you have turned judgement into poison, and the fruit of righteousness into wormwood'.

All the prophets deploy this form, whose natural home is generally thought to be in the Wisdom literature, in order to convey a sense not just of moral condemnation but of uncomprehending moral outrage. What the nation is doing cries out to heaven; no rational person can begin to understand how such things are even thinkable. The verse from Isaiah just referred to continues, 'Shall the potter be regarded as the clay, that the thing made should say of its maker, "He did not make me"?' This sounds as though it ought to be a condemnation of overt blasphemy; but in fact it is part of an attack on those who 'hide deep from the LORD their counsel, and whose deeds are in the dark'. Probably, therefore, it is no more than part of the prophet's opposition to the secret diplomatic negotiations in which Hezekiah's counsellors were engaged, in their desperate attempt to save the nation from the Assyrians. But Isaiah presents it as an attempt to hide from Yahweh – something which, as the Psalms or the book of Job testify, is a vain hope; and this makes it possible for him to speak of it as though it were a most impious reversal of the natural order in which the Creator has pre-eminence over his creatures.

The best examples of the technique come, however, from Jeremiah, who conveys throughout his oracles a sense of half-choked fury at the absurdities of his contemporaries' conduct. The tendency in his day to worship gods other than Yahweh, which we now know was not widely felt to be wrong in pre-exilic Judah, *he* presents as a ludicrous breach of every natural sense of loyalty, even as an offence against common sense: 'Can a maiden forget her ornaments, or a bride her attire? Yet my people have forgotten me days without number' (ii 32); 'Has a nation changed its gods, even though they are no gods? But my people have changed their glory for that which does not profit' (ii 11). On a number of occasions Jeremiah contrasts the regularities and predictabilities of the natural world with the irregularity and unnaturalness of the conduct of Israel. 'Hear this, O foolish and senseless people, who have eyes, but see not, who have ears, but hear not. Do you not fear me? says the LORD; do you not tremble before me? I placed the sand as the bound for the sea, a perpetual barrier which it cannot pass; though the waves toss, they cannot prevail, though they roar, they cannot pass over it. But this people has a stubborn and rebellious heart; they have turned aside and gone away' (v 20–3); 'Even the stork in the heavens knows her times; and the turtledove, swallow, and crane keep the time of their coming; but my people know not the ordinance of the LORD' (viii 7); 'Does the snow of Lebanon leave the crags of Sirion? Do the mountain waters run dry, the cold flowing streams? But my people have forgotten me, they burn incense to false gods' (xviii 14). Compare Isaiah: 'The ox knows its owner, and the ass its master's crib; but Israel does not know, my people does not consider' (i 3).

This is a technique pioneered in the old Egyptian wisdom schools, in which the pupil's stupidity and recalcitrance is compared unfavourably with the orderliness and obedience of dumb animals and inanimate objects. Compare, for example, this passage from an Egyptian scribe's rebuke to his pupil:

> You do not hearken when I speak. Your heart is heavier than a great monument of a hundred cubits in height and ten in thickness, which is finished and ready to be loaded. . . . The cow will be fetched this year and will plough by the return of the year; it begins to listen to the herdsman; it can all but speak. Horses brought from the field have already forgotten their mothers; they are yoked and go up and down on every manner of errand for his Majesty. They become like those that bore them, and they stand in the stable, whilst they do absolutely everything for fear of a beating. But even if I beat you with every kind of stick you do not listen.
>
> (Caminos 1954: 377; cf. Blackman and Peet 1925)

The effect of this way of thinking, when applied to the sins of Israel, is to remove any suspicion of arbitrariness in the punishment which Yahweh is about to exact, by showing that the people, contrary to popular belief, have sinned in ways that cry out to heaven.

2. In Amos we find the commonplace belief that the gods vindicate breaches of natural morality used rhetorically in order to justify the coming fall of Israel. This can be seen in the way the opening oracles of the book are arranged. As I have argued elsewhere (Barton 1980), the oracles against the nations at the beginning of Amos all deal explicitly with war-crimes committed by Israel's neighbours. Here the prophet can count on it that his audience will, like him, expect divine judgement to fall on those who commit such offences. This cleverly prepares the way for the oracle against Israel itself in ii 6–16. Here the sins singled out for mention fall far short of what most people in the ancient Near East would have regarded as atrocities. Many of them are highly 'respectable' sins, such as breaches of trading standards, which were certainly forbidden in Israelite law but no doubt widely connived at in practice. But by juxtaposing these things with the atrocities in i 3 – ii 3,

60

the prophet contrives to make the reader feel that they lead just as obviously to divine judgement. Here the rhetorical trick lies at the level of structure. The patterning of the oracle against Israel on the same model as those against foreign nations constrains the readers (or hearers) to overlook the very different nature of the offences being highlighted, and so to suppress the feeling they would otherwise have that the kinds of sin condemned in the two units do not really play in the same league.

3. A further technique for creating an impression that the predicted judgement is only what the nation should have expected, and that its sins can hardly fail to be avenged by God, may be found in the 'poetic justice' pattern of many prophetic oracles. The prophets like to show that divine punishment takes the form of tit for tat. In Isaiah Judah has sinned, in the prophet's view, by disregarding the proper ordering of society, with upstarts trying to direct the affairs of state. Shebna, the king's chief secretary, was a 'new man' with no family background in Jerusalem (xxii 16); and according to iii 12 'children and women' are being allowed to rule in the capital, which Isaiah – a much more reactionary figure than the modern picture of an Old Testament prophet might suggest – deeply disapproves of. Now of course the overthrow of the country by military invasion would be bound to cause anarchy, with the natural rulers removed and their place taken by Assyrian puppets. Accordingly Isaiah links the punishment with the crime: voluntary anarchy will be punished by compulsory anarchy: 'I will make boys their princes, and babes shall rule over them . . . the people will oppress one another, every man his fellow, and every man his neighbour . . . woe to them, for they have brought evil upon themselves' (iii 1–9). Just so those whose ambition is to 'dwell alone in the midst of the land' by enclosing the fields of peasants will find their houses left desolate and without inhabitants altogether (v 9); those whose appetite for food and drink makes them drunkenly disregard the works of the LORD will die of thirst and hunger, and will become food for Sheol: 'therefore *Sheol* has enlarged its appetite, and opened *its* mouth beyond measure' (v 14). Little of this, I think, should be seen as the prophet's attempts to devise punishments suitable for the crime; rather, it is a matter of presenting the crime in such a way that it becomes manifest that it merits the coming punishment (cf. Barton 1979).

4. If we now turn to the other traditional theme which accounts for national disaster, we shall find the same kind of material. Pride or *hybris* is certainly the commonest explanation of the downfall of foreign kingdoms. But given the weak and dispirited condition of Israel and Judah in much of the period when the classical prophets were active, it is in some ways rather surprising to find it as an accusation against them. Particularly in Isaiah, however, it is one of the major categories for interpreting the disaster foretold by the prophet. 'Jerusalem has stumbled and Judah has fallen, because their speech and their deeds are against the LORD, defying his glorious presence' (iii 8); they are 'wise in their own eyes, and shrewd in their own sight' (v 21), 'heroes at drinking wine and valiant men in mixing strong drink' (v 22). The inhabitants of the northern kingdom 'speak in pride and arrogance of heart' (ix 9). Given Isaiah's highly hierarchical vision of the ideal human society, it is not too difficult for him to assimilate sin to pride, suggesting that rulers and those in positions of trust are lording it over their subjects and therefore that they have incurred the kind of judgement that was generally believed to fall on foreign rulers whose pride led them to despise the people of Yahweh – as in the case of the Assyrians, condemned for arrogance in chapter x.

Even the worship of other gods is assimilated, perhaps oddly from our point of view, to pride. To the modern reader, the proliferation of gods that seems to have occurred in eighth- and seventh-century Judah looks like an acknowledgement of human weakness and a desire, in a crisis, to appropriate the power of as many divine forces as possible. But Isaiah consistently presents 'idolatry' as an expression of human *arrogance*. He stands at the beginning of the tradition that comes to be typical of Judaism, presenting 'idols' as 'the work of human hands' rather than as alternative sources of divine power, or rivals for Yahweh. In chapter ii he sets out the three charges 'their land is full of silver and gold', 'their land is full of horses', and 'their land is full of idols' as parallel accusations, all three alike symptoms of human self-aggrandizement and signs of a failure in humility towards the true God. In the same way, in all the prophets sacrificial worship (even of Yahweh himself) is regarded as a form of self-assertion, rather than of self-abasement before the divine.

All such attempts to be 'like God' come under the judgement of the 'day of Yahweh' described by Isaiah:

The LORD of hosts has a day against all that is proud and lofty, against all that is lifted up and high; against all the cedars of Lebanon, lofty and lifted up; and against all the oaks of Bashan; against all the high mountains, and against all the lofty hills; against every high tower and against every fortified wall; against all the ships of Tarshish, and against all the beautiful craft. And the haughtiness of man shall be humbled, and the pride of men shall be brought low; and the LORD alone will be exalted in that day.

(ii 12–17)

Here, as with the appeal to natural orders in the world, patterning human sins after analogies from nature is designed to bring out their sinfulness – though (in this somewhat cutting across the prophets' other arguments from nature) it seems to be implied that the natural order, too, is out of joint and is afflicted by the same insubordination as the people of Judah. Consistency on this sort of point is not the prophets' main concern. What they are concerned to do is to paint contemporary society in colours that will make its imminent collapse seem reasonable and even inevitable. The analogy of a tree which grows too high and so is felled by the wind suggests itself to them, because overweening pride was a classic example of the sin that causes the fall of nations.

To sum up. Prophetic rhetoric skilfully assimilated the short-comings of Israel and Judah to models which were generally held, in the ancient world, to cause divine displeasure. In the process the prophets sought to make (and succeeded in making) the coming disasters comprehensible to their contemporaries, who learned to see in them not the hand of a capricious tyrant, but the chastening of a good and consistent Creator. The constant appeals to the order of nature in particular show how much the prophets saw their task as being to reason with their contemporaries; and if a prophet in the ancient world was essentially someone who reported non-rational experiences and premonitions and appealed simply to his divine authorization, not to the reason of his hearers, then the classical prophets were very far from being 'prophets' in this technical sense, and we might well follow Heaton and call them 'laymen'. But as we have seen, the appeal to reason may sometimes fairly be called a rationalization, and we should not be taken in too much by the force of their rhetoric. It was not really obvious that God was bound to punish Israel. The fact that even modern readers of the Bible are inclined to speak as if it was is a tribute to the rhetorical skill of the classical prophets.

NOTE

The ideas in this paper were outlined in my 'Begründungsversuche der prophetischen Unheilsankündigung im Alten Testament' (Barton 1987).

Chapter Three

DECONSTRUCTING THE BOOK OF JOB

DAVID CLINES

At least since the time of Gregory the Great's 35 books of *Moralia in Job*, the book of Job has been regarded as a vast quarry for moral truths and wise sayings about the human condition. In particular it has been thought to offer the answer to the knottiest questions about the meaning of life, the problem of suffering, and the moral order of the universe. In the bibliography of my forthcoming commentary on chapters i–xx of Job (Clines 1989) I have listed more than 1,000 books and articles that profess to state the unequivocal answers of Job to such questions. It is high time, then, to wonder whether the book of Job also, like many other works of literature, if not indeed all, is woven from a seamless cloth, or is not perhaps open to a deconstruction.

In this paper I shall be arguing that the book does indeed deconstruct itself in several fundamental areas. I shall try to distinguish these deconstructions from simple incoherence, and suggest that its rhetoric innoculates it against its deconstructability.

As a point of departure I take the well-known formulation by Jonathan Culler of the strategy of deconstruction: 'To deconstruct a discourse is to show how it undermines the philosophy it asserts, or the hierarchical oppositions on which it relies' (1983: 86). Not every deconstructionist would be happy with such a transparent account of what in most hands is a very much more esoteric and mystifying procedure. Nor does this formulation lend itself to that aspect of deconstructionism that is a strategy in philosophy. But for deconstruction as a procedure with texts this is a statement which both seems understandable and sounds promising.

Some distinctions need to be made. To deconstruct a discourse is not simply to show its incoherence – which some writers have indeed attempted to do for the book of Job. For if a discourse should undermine the philosophy it asserts in the same manner and with the same degree of explicitness that it asserted it, we should be merely confused or else amused at its incompetence as a discourse, and pronounce it simply incoherent. For a discourse to need deconstructing or to be susceptible of deconstruction the undermining has to be latent, as indeed the metaphor of undermining already tells us. In deconstructing, we are distinguishing between the surface and the hidden in the text, between shallow and deep readings. We are allowing that it is possible to read the text without seeing that it undermines itself, and we are claiming that the deconstructive reading is more sophisticated and at the same time more true to the text itself. It would therefore not be possible to challenge a particular deconstruction of a text by producing a non-deconstructionist reading; a deconstruction could only be called into question by arguing that those elements in the text that the critic thinks undermine it do not actually do so, and that the discourse is perfectly coherent throughout all the levels on which it can be read.

I

The first arena in which we may see the book of Job deconstructing itself (or, we might prefer to say, in which it is open to deconstruction by the reader) is the issue of moral retribution, the doctrine that one is rewarded or punished in strict conformity with the moral quality of one's deeds. This is a view widely supported in the Hebrew Bible, above all by the book of Proverbs, but no less by the theology of the book of Deuteronomy or of the prophets. Pride goes before destruction and a haughty spirit before a fall (Prov. xvi 18). In the path of righteousness is life, but the way of error leads to death (xii 28). If Israel obeys the voice of Yahweh, its God will set it high above all the nations of the earth (Deut. xxviii 1). And if it is not careful to do all the words of the law, then Yahweh will bring upon it extraordinary afflictions, afflictions severe and lasting, and sicknesses grievous and lasting (xxviii 58–9).

If we ask, What is the stance of the book on this central dogma of old Israelite religion?, which is to say in Culler's words, What is the philosophy this book asserts?, we are at first disposed to say the following. The plot of the book of Job affirms that in the case of Job the traditional dogma is false, for he is a righteous man who, to the surprise both of himself and his readers, suffers the fate of the wicked. On this reading, which is an ordinary reader's view as well as the scholarly consensus, the issue of the book is whether the conventional nexus between piety and prosperity, sin and suffering holds, and whether it is possible to make the usual inferences backwards, from prosperity back to piety and from suffering back to sin.

Given that this is the general impression we have of the book as a whole, we are bound to have some difficulty with its opening chapter, where it is the opposite that seems to be affirmed. For there the impression is definitely given, though it is not said in so many words, that the story of Job illustrates not the falsity but the *truth* of the traditional dogma.

We first encounter what we suspect is the old dogma enshrined in the opening verses of the prologue:

> There was a man in the land of Uz . . . blameless and upright, fearing God and turning away from evil, *And* there were born to him seven sons and three daughters, *and* his possession was seven thousand sheep and three thousand camels . . .
>
> (i 1–3).

The simple '*and*', technically the *waw*-consecutive indicating a subsequent action to that of the previous verb, is admittedly all we have to go on. Nothing here says explicitly that we are dealing with *cause and effect*, nothing prevents us from insisting that here there is a mere temporal progression or even perhaps the laxness of a naive story that orders contemporaneous facts into a temporal sequence to give the impression of narrative, the only real temporality being in the movement of the narrator's eye, first resting on this item, then on that. Nevertheless, most readers find here more than mere temporal succession; they notice at the very least a sense of the fitness of things, an inner bond between the piety of the man and his prosperity, between rather his superlative piety and his superlative prosperity, a fitness not only in kind but in degree, a fitness that is nothing else, when expressed theologically, than the dogma of retribution.

So is this book *for* the principle of retribution or *against* it?

Suppose that we leave the question open for the moment and read further down the chapter. Before very long we come to realise that in the interchange between God and the Satan the old traditional causal nexus between piety and prosperity is being taken for granted – in heaven no less than on earth. Says God: 'Have you considered my servant Job, that there is none like him on the earth, a blameless and upright man, fearing God and turning away from evil?' (i 8). And the Satan replies: 'Does Job fear God for nothing, gratuitously?' (i 9). According to the Satan, God must be thinking that Job *does* fear him gratuitously, that the piety of Job is the origin of his prosperity. The Satan's own suspicion is that it is Job's prosperity that is the origin of his piety, that it is only in order to become prosperous or remain prosperous that Job is so exceptionally pious. When the point is put to him, God has to admit that he does not know the difference; he had been assuming all along, as do most humans, that the principle of retribution runs from the deed to the result. God has to allow an experiment to be carried out on Job to discover whether the dogma is true. Now if the narrator has God believing in the doctrine of retribution, may we not suppose that the narrator was willing us also in these opening sentences to accept it, naïvely, yes, and unquestioningly, the way such dogmas are generally accepted?

This philosophy is not, of course, sustained throughout the prologue. For once the suffering of Job is determined upon it suddenly becomes the case that piety does not necessarily lead to prosperity and that what leads to suffering is not necessarily sin. In this second philosophy it is the righteous man who suffers. In the first philosophy only the wicked suffer.

Does then the first philosophy deconstruct the second, or, does the second deconstruct the former? Can we speak of either of them undermining the other?

No, not undermine. Just confront. There are conflicting philosophies here, indeed, but the warfare between them is all above board. For against the view that piety leads to prosperity the narrative affirms both the blamelessness of Job and the reality of his divinely imposed suffering. And against the correlative view that sin leads to suffering the narrative affirms that, on the contrary, in Job's case it is piety that leads to suffering, indeed that exceptional piety leads to exceptional suffering. What happens in the narrative of the prologue is that the philosophy that is at first affirmed is then negated by the philosophy inherent in the events of the narrative as it is deployed. The first philosophy stands to the second as exposition stands to complication in a narrative; no narrative can get moving unless it begins to contradict the *status quo ante*, no philosophy is worth affirming unless in contradiction to that already affirmed or implied. That is all as it should be, and no more than we should expect of any narrative. There is no deconstructing going on here.

Where then stands the philosophy asserted by the poem of iii 1 – xlii 6, the core of the book as a whole? On the side of the first or the second philosophy? This seems open to no doubt. It is the same side as the second philosophy of the prologue; all it does is to expound it at length, dramatically and unarguably. What the poem does, philosophically speaking, is to prove over and over again that the doctrine of retribution is wrong. Every time Job's friends fail to carry us with them in their denunciations of Job, and every time Job excites our admiration for his injured innocence, the poem convinces us again that the doctrine of retribution is naïve, dangerous, inhuman and, above all, false. If ever for a minute in the course of the dialogue we are tempted to believe that Job after all must deserve something of what he suffers, or if for a moment we find it hard to believe that anyone can possibly be so blameless as Job is making himself out to be, the affirmations of both the narrator and God in the prologue stride forward in our memory: there is none like him on earth.

Not that we are ever permitted to forget that the standpoint of the poem is, Athanasius-like, in opposition to the world that surrounds it. For the friends of Job, each in his individual way, begin all their thinking from the conviction that the traditional dogma is true, and Job himself makes no secret of the fact that he too, until these recent calamities, has always thought that way. He is the first to acknowledge that his sufferings are, *prima facie* at least, witnesses against him (xvi 8); he has always thought suffering was ammunition *against* humans, not testimony *for* them. It is this very break with convention, this brave shouldering of an unpopular commitment, that makes the philosophy of the book of Job so universally recognized and treasured.

So far there has been the confrontation of philosophies, and the massive assertion of the second, that the doctrine of retribution is false. A surprise, however, is stored up for the last eleven verses of the book (xlii 7–17), which deconstruct the second philosophy in the direction of the first. Which is to say – since the second philosophy is affirmed by the great bulk of the book – the epilogue deconstructs the book as a whole.

The epilogue has often made readers uncomfortable. I suspect that the discomfort is the psychological registering of the deconstruction that is in progress, though until recently we did not have this name for the process, and so did not perhaps properly appreciate its character.

The discomfort is expressed sometimes in aesthetic terms, as if it were a lapse in literary taste to have the tortured Job first brought to a new religious and intellectual perception of the world that enables him to accept his suffering and bow before the author of it in reverence if not penitence, and then to recount how on top of that he gets double his money back, for all the world like a contestant on some game show.[1]

At other times the discomfort takes the form of a historical judgement that the epilogue is to be assigned a secondary status in the history of the book's composition.[2] If we can affirm that it does not come from the hand of the master poet and thinker the lack of fit between the poem and the epilogue can be lived with. There is here indeed a curious but commonly entertained assumption that to understand the origin of a discrepancy is somehow to *deal with* the discrepancy, to bring about a new state of affairs in which it is as if the discrepancy did not exist. It is, indeed, something of an oddity with this move in the case of the epilogue to Job that by most accounts the epilogue is not a chronologically secondary accretion to the poem, but the earlier folktale frame into which the poem has been slotted; so what is literarily secondary is not the work of some late redactor (archetypically of limited intelligence) but pre-existent narrative stuff which the poet of Job simply did not excise. The discomfort is multiplied.

Yet another form the discomfort takes is a moral decision that the epilogue is not really very important. The story of Job, it is said, would be essentially the same without the epilogue. All that needs to be achieved by Job and for Job has taken place by xlii 6, and the epilogue adds nothing to the poem religiously or philosophically. Job's restoration comes as a bonus to him and to those readers who require a happy ending, but it is really neither here nor there from the point of view of the meaning of the book.

Amid all this discomfort, it is even more disconcerting that what one hardly ever sees argued is the view that in fact the epilogue undermines the rest of the book of Job. This is worse than uncomfortable, and that is perhaps why it is not argued. For who wants to argue that a world-class work of literature is so much at odds with itself as that, so determined not to speak with a single voice; or, even worse, that a work of great theological penetration ends up by giving assent to the very dogma it set out to annihilate?

For that is the position of the epilogue. It tells us, and not at all implicitly, that the most righteous man on earth is the most wealthy. If in Chapter i he was the greatest of all the easterners, in Chapter xlii he is simply a hundred per cent greater than that. And if there was any doubt in Chapter i whether his piety was the cause of his prosperity and whether perhaps it was not the other way about, by Chapter xlii no one, not even in heaven, is left in any doubt that it is the piety of Job, somewhat eccentrically expressed, to be sure, that has led to his ultimate superlative prosperity. What the book has been doing its best to demolish, the doctrine of retribution, is on its last page triumphantly affirmed.

Why not call this an incoherence? Should it be dignified with so glamorous a title as a deconstruction? In the switch from the first philosophy to the second in the prologue to the book we could see the familiar enough process of setting up a straw man that the rest of the book will demolish. But we are so unused to, or so uncomfortable with, the last page of a book pulling the rug from under all that has been going on throughout the book that we do our best to maintain that that is not what is happening at all. The very fact that the ending of the book of Job is not normally regarded as logically incoherent with what precedes it is an evidence that the contradiction is an *undermining*.

Should we not, however, before we throw up our hands in aporia and cry deconstruction, seek a reconciliation of the two philosophies? Could we perhaps argue that the central part of the book of Job only sets out to show that the doctrine of retribution is not *inevitably* true, that there can be notorious cases of its inapplicability? That the ending of the book wants to assert that, despite the failure of the dogma to explain all human fortunes, in the end and in the main it is perfectly true after all? That even, perhaps, the case of Job is a special case, indeed an extraordinary case, maybe an utterly unique case? Is not the story itself at pains to point out that this man Job is a man unlike other humans, that this man's fate is wholly to be explained by an unparalleled set of circumstances in heaven? So does that not mean that whatever may be true for Job is as like as not to be untrue for every other human? That the book of Job is not about Everyman, but entirely about the lone and remarkable individual Job?

If that is so, and that is where taking the ending 'seriously' (as they say) leads us to, then the poem has no philosophy to set forth, being about nothing at all except the unfortunate man Job. That is indeed a short way with dissenting philosophies: showing that one of them is not a philosophy at all, and that there is therefore no dissension.

No, perhaps that is too extreme. Rather than assert that the book of Job in its central section is only about the individual Job, let us argue that it propounds the view that quite often the righteous suffer the fate that typically belongs to the wicked. Whether in the case of others it is heaven that is to blame or not hardly affects the position. It is the *fact* of the suffering of the righteous that constitutes the philosophical position of the poem. Can we reconcile the epilogue of the book with that philosophy? Could the epilogue be saying that if the righteous suffer, that is only a temporary setback? That the doctrine of retribution is to be applied to the broad sweep of things, and not to the trifling ups and downs of human fortunes? That, in such a case, what all the interlocutors should have been stressing was that Job, being by all accounts a perfectly innocent man who by cruel misfortune had been brought to calamity, could confidently expect that the dogma of retribution would come into its own in the long run and his end would be sure to be at least as good as his beginning? If that is so, then the book of Job is not about Job himself particularly, but about Job as a representative of a humanity that suffers what it does not deserve but is on the way to a happy dénouement. But if that is the philosophy of the book, how shall we accommodate the fact that Job is introduced to us at its beginning as an utterly exceptional human being and his suffering is attributed to a unique event in the heavenly realm?

These two quests for a reconciliation of the philosophies fail. If we attempt to house the anti-retributionist philosophy within the dogma of retribution, as a kind of modification or tempering of it, we denature the drama of the book. But equally if we assert the retributionist philosophy of the epilogue over against the anti-retributionist stance of the poem, we rub the poem out of the book. That the poem should supervene upon the naïvety of the prologue in its opening makes sense; but that the epilogue should undermine the grand poem and return us to the first naïvety is disorientating, to the point of being deconstructive. What are we to make of a narrative that purports to conclude with a happy ever after but only returns us to the point where it all started, with what assurance that the same calamities cannot befall the doubly innocent Job? Is it so certain that lightning never strikes twice in the same place?

For a text to deconstruct itself means that there is no firm ground in it for the reader to take a stand on. Each time we begin to state the view the book takes of this fundamental question in theology and ethics – retribution – we find ourselves headed towards an aporia that is not merely a morass of indeterminacy in which it is difficult to discern what it is the book asserts but a truly deconstructive state of affairs where each of the philosophies it actually does assert is undermined by the other. Where that leaves us as readers is a point I want to return to at the end of this paper.

II

The second arena in which the book of Job is deconstructible is its handling of the question of suffering. If we take as our starting point our general impression of the book (and why not? for that only means the preunderstanding we bring to it), we shall probably agree that a prime concern of the book is the problem of suffering.

What *is* the problem of suffering, in fact? Most of the textbooks on ethics and the commentaries on Job accept the commonsensical view that the problem of suffering is its *cause*, which is to say, Why suffering?, Why this particular suffering? And the book itself encourages us to regard that as its concern too; for it begins its narrative precisely with an account of how the suffering of the hero is decided upon in heaven – which is to say, with a narrative of a causal chain. Job himself of course has no idea of why he is suffering, but the book insists upon the readers knowing, and knowing in advance, and knowing all there is to be known about the matter. There is no question of any deferment of disclosure of real purposes or causes to the end of the story. Everything is up front; this is no story beguiling us with half-truths and false clues.

But the moment we ask, And what exactly *was* the reason for Job's suffering?, we run into a problem. The story bears retelling, if only for the soupçon of hermeneutic suspicion that can be introduced into the telling. What happens in heaven is that a question is raised that has apparently never before been asked, in general or in particular. The particular question is, Does Job fear God for nothing? The more general question is, Do humans fear God gratuitously? Job fears God, no doubt, but is it gratuitous, or is it for the sake of the reward? Heaven has been up till now as accepting as earth of the doctrine of retribution: the pious become the prosperous. But now the question is raised: Assuming there is a causal connection between the two, in which direction does it operate? Could prosperity be, not the result of piety, but its *cause*?

The difficulty is that neither God nor the Satan know which comes first, the chicken or the egg (or, as they say in Italian, as if to underline the problem, *l'uovo o la gallina*), the piety or the prosperity. This is no doubt because when the principle of retribution is functioning properly the pious are the same as the prosperous, and so you can never separate out cause and effect. We readers who have persevered to Chapter xlii of course know by now what we think of the principle of retribution, but the God of Chapter i has never engaged in deconstructions, dwelling as he does in an informal and somewhat rustic court, where there are none of the typical oriental courtesies but plenty of blunt speech, and no divine omniscience but only a willingness to find out, whether by report or experiment.

Experiment. That is the word. Job's suffering will be (not a wager, for the Satan has nothing to win, or lose, by the outcome, but) an experiment in causality. To prove whether the piety hangs on the prosperity, remove the prosperity and see if the piety falls. The experiment has to be done, not only for the sake of the truth, but even more for the sake of God's well-being. How could God ever look himself in the face if it were to turn out that none of his creatures, not even the most godfearing man of all, loves him for his own sake but only for what they can get out of him?

Which means to say that the reason for Job's suffering lies not in Job, not in the way the world works, nor in the principle of retribution, nor in any dogma, but deep in God and his need to know the truth about humankind and thus about himself (creators, like trees, are known by their fruit). Job suffers to prove God's integrity and to lay to rest the doubt the Satan has raised that perhaps no one in the wide world really reverences God for his own sake but that everyone is simply trying to *use* him.

Now the reason for Job's suffering is presumably not the reason for anyone else's. Once God has been convinced that gratuitous piety is possible, he does not need to experiment again to find that out. If none of the piety of this superabundantly pious man hangs upon his prosperity, the lesser piety of lesser mortals may also be equally clear of self-interest. Job has answered the question of the causal connection between piety and prosperity paradigmatically and definitively.

Which means: The reason for Job's suffering is never the reason for anyone else's. What the narrative gives with one hand it takes away with the other. For a moment we thought, when we were told the reason for Job's suffering, that we had penetrated to the book's explanation for human suffering in general. But that cannot be, for Job's case is unique. For a moment we were encouraged to believe that there is no mystery at all about suffering, that all is plain as day: Job suffers for a reason that can be simply told and which he could have understood as well as we can. But the instant we recognize that this reason is unique to Job, at that moment we are in the dark again about the meaning of human suffering generally.

So to the problem of suffering inasmuch as the problem is its *cause*, the book says, No problem. Here is the cause. But the moment we see it we realize that this answer is no good to us, for we wanted to know the reason for human suffering in general, and the book's answer has nothing to do with that.

How is it then that we thought in the first place that the book was about the origins of suffering? Is it because it *purports* to be telling us in its opening scenes about origins, causes? Not really, because it was claiming nothing, nothing more grand than to be a tale about an antique patriarchal figure from the days when wealth was measured in camels. But it succeeded in misleading most of the people most of the time. Can that be because it was really a deconstructive narrative, reaping where it did not sow, and more especially, sowing where it did not reap, sowing in our heads grand ideas of universal truths and never reaping but letting them run rank? Or is it deconstructive in the other direction, innocently maintaining it had no designs on the universe but all the time winning its way into world literature on the strength of its evident global human sympathies?

That deconstructive discomfort makes us wonder whether we should be trying another tack over this question of the problem of suffering. What will happen if we suggest that the real problem of suffering, for the book as much as for ourselves, is not the problem, Why suffering?, but the problem, What must I do now that I am suffering? or, How am I to suffer? That is, the existential question rather than the more intellectual question of origins.

On that route we encounter in the book first, not a deconstruction exactly but certainly a conflict. For the prologue makes plain that the response of a truly pious man to unexplained suffering is to bless the God who has given and who has taken away. The pious Job sees God in the predations of Sabeans and Chaldeans as much as in the fire from heaven and the whirlwind, and he accepts without demur that God has the same right to hand out 'evil' as he has to deliver 'good'. But the moment we turn the page into the poem in Chapter iii (by a happy accident, I have to do literally that in my edition of the Revised Standard Version) we strike against another image of Job, whose response to 'evil' is to abuse the author of it and demand he give an account of himself. It is an enormous shock to the system when we find God in Chapter xlii approving of this rebellious and irreverent Job, and declaring that this Job has spoken of him 'what is right', unlike the friends who have spoken only orthodox theology in careful circumspection of God.

So although the book proffers two answers to the question, What kind of sufferer is approved of by God? or, What should I do when I am suffering?, it leaves us in little doubt about which is its preferred answer. It is not even a matter of its recommending pious acceptance so long as that is possible and the stiff upper lip does not quiver, with approval being given to hysterical and venomous outbursts once they can be no longer restrained. On the contrary, it appears to be the outbursts that are being recommended. But that conflict of ideologies or behaviours is not one that leads in itself to a deconstruction, since the book resolves it, at least ostensibly, no matter how shocking the resolution may be.

Where deconstructive thoughts gain a toehold is over the issue (again) of whether the book speaks for humanity at large, or only of the isolated man Job. There seems little doubt over what was the right thing for Job to do, but does the book mean us to follow Job's example? We cannot help remembering that Job is the most pious man on earth, testified to by both the narrator and God (the former the more omniscient, but the latter presumably the more authoritative) as a blameless man. From the perspective of the narrative, he has a perfect right to protest against the treatment he is receiving, for he knows, and we all know, that he does not deserve it. But what of the rest of us? Does the book mean to suggest that protesting against one's suffering is a form of asserting one's innocence? Is it an indirect warning that no good will come of behaving like Job unless one is in Job's moral position to begin with? If that is so, we no longer know whether the book offers an encouragement or a warning. Is it saying, Behave like Job, or Don't dare behave like Job? What we are told about Job deconstructs the example he affords. Job becomes an example for no one, for is it not the case that 'there is none like him on earth'?

Thus, over the question of the meaning of the book in relation to the problem of suffering, we find ourselves forced into accepting by the logic of the narrative that Job's case can have no relevance to humanity at large, while every instinct we have about literature and life compels us in the opposite direction. It looks as though this book of Job is another self-deconstructing artifact.

III

When a text has been deconstructed, what happens next? This is a question not often raised by professional deconstructionists, but it is a pressing question for many other readers.

One thing that happens is that the text goes on being read by readers who have never heard of deconstruction. Which is to say that it goes on, to a greater or lesser extent, having the meanings it always has. Saussure's treatise has not ceased to be the foundation of modern linguistics just because Derrida has deconstructed it. A deconstruction does not mean that a text cancels itself out and becomes a mere cipher. Simple conflicts and incoherences may do that, but a deconstructed text loses little of its power in the deconstruction, though it may lose all of its authority as a trustworthy testimony to the way things really are in the external world.

What sustains a book's life beyond its deconstruction is its rhetoric, that is, its power to persuade beyond the bounds of pure reason, its ability to provoke its readers into willing its success even beyond its deserts. The book of Job had already enjoyed a notable victory of rhetoric over logic long before the word 'deconstruction' was ever breathed. For it had been persuading generations of readers to take sides with its hero Job in his ignorant reproaches against heaven even while they have had perfect knowledge of what was hidden from Job. They know that in heaven it is entirely accepted, even by the Satan, that Job is the most righteous of men, and they recognize that if Job knew that his tirades would be sapped of their energy. He would still have something against heaven, for it would still be unreasonable of God to make an innocent man suffer in order to establish some theological point to the satisfaction of heavenly disputants; but Job would not be able to protest that his innocence was going unrecognized, and he would not be able to call God to account for branding him an evildoer. So he would not be able to speak many of his most moving speeches, for example:

> Let me have silence, and I will speak,
>   and let come on me what may.
> I will take my flesh in my teeth,
>   and put my life in my hand.
> Behold, he will slay me; I have no hope;
>   yet I will defend my ways to his face. . . .
> Only grant two things to me,
>   then I will not hide myself from thy face:
> withdraw thy hand far from me,
>   and let not dread of thee terrify me.
> Then call, and I will answer;
>   or let me speak, and do thou reply to me.
> How many are my iniquities and my sins?
>   Make me know my transgression and my sin.
> Why dost thou hide thy face,
>   and count me thy enemy?
> Wilt thou frighten a driven leaf
>   and pursue dry chaff?

(xiii 13–15, 20–5)

But we readers happily endure the contradictions of our position, privy to knowledge that undercuts Job's position, and siding with Job nevertheless. Rhetoric triumphs over mere fact, and we would not have it otherwise. We are willing, as we listen to Job, to entertain the possibility that the prologue to the book does not exist and that there is no such perfectly simple explanation of Job's suffering as the prologue suggests. We recognize in the unenlightened Job the human condition, embattled against an unjust fate, and we will him to succeed in his struggle even at the moment when we know it is ill-conceived and unnecessary. Our assent to the logic of the story, in which Job cravenly withdraws his charge against God the moment God chooses to communicate with the man, is wholly sincere, but we do not regret for an instant that Job has been kept in the dark so long; we were overjoyed that a man had the opportunity, so properly seized and so long sustained, to approach his God 'like a prince' and 'give him an account of all [his] steps' (xxxi 37). It did not matter in the least that it was all, in a manner of speaking, a huge mistake.

In just the same way, no deconstruction can rob readers of what they have savoured in the book of Job. Even when it has been deconstructed, the book can still go on exciting or entrancing us, enraging us against heaven or compelling our admiration for the divine, even assuring us that these are the truths about God and the universe. But when we believe its hero, we will believe him because we want to, because it suits our sense of the fitness of things, and not because he has divulged a truth about a transcendental signified that is one and incontrovertible.

The problem with the dogma of retribution, or any other dogma, is not that it is wrong, but that it is a dogma. And you cannot cure the problem of a dogma with another dogma. Whenever you have a case of dogma eat dogma, you always have one dogma surviving and snapping at your heels. The heart craves dogma, even a dogma dying a death of a thousand qualifications. But the deconstructive strategy eliminates dogma as dogma, and in recognizing that multiple philosophies are being affirmed in the deconstructible text loosens our attachment to any one of them *as dogma*. It does not however follow that it weakens their persuasive force, their seductiveness. It may even be, sometimes, that when a fearsome dogma has been overpowered and shorn of its authority, we take to it more kindly and are attracted by its defencelessness, begin to find it charming, and even fall to wondering whether there was not perhaps some virtue in it that made it into a dogma in the first place.

NOTES

1 R.A. Watson commented (though he went on to reject this line of thought): 'Did Job need these multitudes of camels and sheep to supplement his new faith and his reconciliation to the Almighty will? Is there not something incongruous in the large reward of temporal good, and even something unnecessary in the renewed honour among men?' (1892: 409).
2 'As an essential part of the old Folk-tale, [the Epilogue] could not be discarded. To have made the hero die in leprosy would have been too audacious a contradiction of what may have been a well-authenticated tradition' (Strahan 1913: 350). Similarly Pope 1973: lxxxi.

Chapter Four

BIBLICAL STORY AND THE HEROINE

MARGARITA STOCKER

All myths are necessarily narratives first, although powerful myths also tend to centre on a narrative moment of dense symbolic value. Those are the moments which appeal to pictorial non-narrative art, and in which the need for complex visual interest can bring out the polysemous potential of that moment. I make this contrast between the still-frame of pictorial representation and the dynamic successiveness of narrative in order to suggest the formal process by which meaning is produced. Narratives are constructed not only by what they say, what they represent, but also by their significant silences; and by what they explicitly deny. The archetypal narrative myth on which I want to focus here is refracted in various ways in subsequent literature and art, as such myths tend to be, and these refractions require scrutiny here, as themselves consequences and interpretations of the original myth.

Of that original story its wide dissemination, and relative authority, have resulted from its inclusion in what has been itself the archetypal 'Book' of Western culture, the Bible. Needless to say, all texts in English have inscribed a culture determined in some part by the biblical collection of narratives and saws. It is 'The Book' with the most insistent claims to authority and (in some sense, immediate or derived) authenticity. Those claims have been complicated by the history of institutionalized religion, with which this text exists in a sometimes awkward dialectic. The simplest example of this external interference with the text is the very existence of a body within it distinguished as the Old Testament 'Apocrypha': books of uncertain status, even though, like the Vulgate before them, the translators of the Authorized Version of 1611 nevertheless felt compelled to translate them.

Although some early issues of the Authorized Version included the Apocrypha, before long it was omitted. In the previous century, the Geneva Bible (1560) had prefaced the Apocrypha with a careful explanation of its status: these texts were not to be read in churches, nor did they possess doctrinal authority, but 'were received to be read for the advancement and furtherance of the knowledge of the historie, and for the instruction of godlie manners', and as a witness to God's providence. Already the status of these texts has a problematic ambivalence: the texts possess knowledge but not authority; they are to be read privately, but not recited in the public religious house; they have not canonical, 'underwritten' authority but yet attest to something, as witness; they witness to God's providence, 'prove' it in the relation of actions, yet they are also tropological and exemplary, for the private practice of 'godlie manners'. They are passive as witnesses, active as exempla. They are of history, yet for the private reading subject. (That distinction, private from public, subsists even when we remember the communal reading of the Bible in Protestant households; the household is in the domain of the private.) These are authoritative non-authoritative texts, whose signification alters in accordance with the context of signification. One might say that their ambivalence, and their openness, were *instituted* by a rubric like the Geneva's. There is, paradoxically, a formal warrant for us as readers to make of these texts what we will.

Similarly, the kind of text which we are to expect is also left unfixed. In the Renaissance the term 'history' was still ambiguous, denoting either a chronicle of actual occurrences or a fictive story. Either is a narrative (and sometimes both are myths, of course), although only one makes claims to factual truth. The fictive can also claim a truth – psychological, cultural, social, or metaphysical – but not the mundane accuracy of the actual. From the position of modern anti-essentialism, neither genre could correspond to anything 'actual', since both represent no more and no less than textuality. In a sense, then, the Renaissance ambiguity of 'history' inscribes that slippage between 'history' and 'story' – the unlocatability of fact, the instability of meaning. What that slippage implies, above all, is the absence of 'authority'.

The most recent, most strenuous critique of authority has been feminist. In that critique, gender difference has been portrayed as primary, more decisive even than racial difference, in the construction of our cultural and social systems. Of those systems the central text has been identified as the Bible, as the prescriptive Book of Judaeo-Christian patriarchy (see Rogers 1966; Daly 1985). In a familiar process, when seventeenth-century writers examined the nature and scope of the patriarchy within which they lived, they went to the Bible for the *fons et origo* of woman's status (Woodbridge 1984: 28–9 *et passim*; Ezell 1987: esp. 55–60). What she was, was defined by what Eve had been; and by what she had done, by the Genesis narrative. It was a myth of Woman as Other. Woman supplies the difference whereby the male subject defines an identity for himself. As Other, she is without identity, yet constitutes that which gives him his.

> Once the subject seeks to assert himself, the Other, who limits and denies him, is none the less a necessity to him: he attains himself only through that reality which he is not, which is something other than himself. . . .
> Woman thus seems to be the inessential who never goes back to being the essential, to be the absolute Other, without reciprocity. This conviction is dear to the male, and every creation myth has expressed it . . . in her mate was her origin and purpose; she was his complement in the order of the inessential.
>
> (de Beauvoir 1972: 172–3)

So Woman is herself a myth, that of Otherness: whether natural or supernatural. 'Because of woman's marginal position in the world, men will turn to her when they strive through culture to go beyond the boundaries of their universe and gain access to something other than what they have known' (ibid.: 163; cf. 174–5). Marginality makes for liminality. That women have been excluded from the male world of public action, from history, makes for their mythic constitution. As man is Self, woman Other, so history is masculine, and femininity is myth. That is not to say that myth is feminine, that Woman has power over it; the reverse is true, because Woman is constructed by male mythologies. Gender is culturally constructed rather than biologically determined, so that women learn what to be by means of the cultural determinants replayed in story, myth and history. They learn that they are Other. In a series of binary oppositions reflected throughout our literature, male is to female as art is to nature, intellect to instinct, reason to passion, action to passivity, authority to the ruled, public to private, order to disorder, possessor to possessed. Yet, as Other, she is necessarily mystery. And mystery is what myth is designed to deal with, in every sense of 'deal with': to inscribe, control, and proscribe. (The political determinants of that process I shall describe more fully elsewhere.)

The myths contained within the Apocrypha are, by dint of that label, themselves marginal by comparison to other biblical texts. Their claims to authority are provisional. And here is one of the few biblical books named for a woman: Judith. I wish to examine not only the book of Judith, but also the myth of Judith in representation, as a site of the cultural construction of gender. Amongst other things, this myth highlights something about narratives of femininity which, like gender difference itself, cuts through historical changes to the replaying myth beneath them.

Although the Apocryphal books were excluded from the canon on linguistic grounds, the nature of that decision is not of interest here; I am concerned not with such causation, but with effects. The book of Judith has multiplied itself in literary and artistic representations more variously than the Testamental books either of Ruth or of Esther. Its influence has been exerted not despite, but because of, its marginality. The provisional authority of the book of Judith has rendered it susceptible to exploration, liberating subsequent interpretations. This myth is, too, of a type distinct from those of Ruth and Esther. At the simplest level of synopsis, Ruth succeeds in getting married. By contrast, Esther's marriage is the plot-event necessary to something more important, saving the Hebrews; Judith does that, too, but she does not marry. To focus on marriage as present or absent in these stories is not as arbitrary as it may seem. In gender-construction, mating and reproduction are what women's activity should wholly consist in. Ruth's devotion to Naomi is the powerful moment in her myth; however brave in intention, its activity becomes a rite of passage – a passage to rights – leading to marriage. While at one level the myth may represent ethnic taboo and practice, as story it is domestic. Similarly, Esther's ability to save her countrymen is wholly dependent on her marriage to Ahasuerus, who possesses might and power; salvation is achieved by influence upon him. Meanwhile, the prophetess Deborah has a henchman, an army and Jael to do her work for her: Jael is no sooner introduced to perform an assassination, than she is dismissed from the narrative. Only Judith fully performs an action, at once by direct agency and with public consequence. Her story signifies an action in history, devised and performed by a woman despite women's marginality in history. Whether the history here is accurate is not relevant (it is, as Renaissance authors well knew, inconsistent with the factual history which can be recuperated from elsewhere in the Bible). This is a myth which shows a woman intervening in history.

The narrative of the book of Judith begins in the reign of Nebuchadnezzar the Assyrian emperor (an 'unhistorical' setting). He goes to war with Arphaxad, king of the Medes, and is victorious despite the refusal of the Israelites and others to help him. In due course, having nothing better to do, and being like most tyrants anxious to assert his omnipotence, Nebuchadnezzar declares a punitive war upon those who had ignored his summons for aid, and orders his chief commander, Holofernes, to lay waste 'the west country'. Holofernes is to make good 'the afflicting of the whole earth out of [Nebuchadnezzar's] own mouth' (ii 2). He proceeds to do precisely this, for seven chapters. His intention is 'to destroy all the gods of the land, that all nations should worship Nabuchodonosor only. . . as god' (iii 8). As he turns his attention to the town of Bethulia, key to the subjection of the Israelites, Achior the Ammonite warns him that their God has never failed to protect them except when they wandered after idols. Since at present they were not a-wandering (typical of the Israelites' perversity, experienced Bible-readers might say), he counsels Holofernes not to risk defeat by harassing them. Achior suffers the usual fate of truth-tellers, which is to offend: the Assyrians reply that they're damned if they'll show fear of this insignificant nation (v 23, vi 4). Achior is abandoned before Bethulia, Holofernes promising that he will suffer massacre with the Israelites. The Bethulians bring Achior into their city and he tells their elders of Holofernes' resolution. The Israelites pray for rescue, but the Assyrians besiege Bethulia and cut off its water supply. Ground down by the effects of famine and thirst, the people demand that their elders surrender the city. Temporizing, Ozias the elder concedes that if the situation has not changed within five days, they will surrender. Only now, at the beginning of the eighth chapter, does Judith enter the story. She reproaches the elders for tempting God by setting him a time-limit. They should trust in him. They cannot allow themselves to become the means by which Israel is laid waste and the temple at Jerusalem profaned. The Lord is trying them. Ozias pays tribute to her wisdom in this reproach. Then Judith announces that she will do something which will go down in history: 'But inquire not of mine act: for I will not declare it unto you, till the things be finished that I do' (viii 34).

With their assent, Judith leaves to pray. Having attired herself in her finest garments, she makes her way to the Assyrian camp, declaring that she has fled from a doomed city. She says something along the lines of 'take me to your leader'; Holofernes is suitably impressed with her, accepting her claim that she is a prophetess, and that she will receive a revelation from her god of the means whereby Bethulia may be taken. She says that her god is displeased, for in the extremity of famine the Bethulians have consumed unclean things. In the following days, Judith establishes a routine whereby she leaves the camp to purify herself and to pray, returning to eat only the kosher food which her maid has brought with her. Nothing changes until the fourth day – the eleventh hour, so to speak – when Holofernes, intending to seduce her, sends his servant Bagoas to invite Judith to a private feast. Judith complies, though she still eats only the food she has brought with her. When the other guests have left in anticipation that Holofernes will want to be private with Judith, and he has fallen onto his bed in a drunken stupor, Judith takes up his sword and decapitates him. Placing the head in her bag, she returns with her maid to Bethulia – unchallenged by the Assyrians, who think that she is following her usual routine. She shows the Bethulians Holofernes' head, stating that he was slain by her as the instrument of God. At her behest, Achior is summoned, and swoons at the sight of the head. Recovering, he does obeisance to Judith, and her relation of events convinces him that he should convert to Judaism. She instructs the Bethulians to display the head on the city walls, and to raise the alarm in the Assyrian camp by obvious preparations for an attack: predicting that, when they discover Holofernes' corpse, the Assyrians will scatter, and the Israelites may slay them at will. And so it turns out. The high priest, Joachim, comes from Jerusalem to salute Judith as a national heroine, and she leads the women of Israel in thanksgiving.

She returns to Bethulia, frees her maid, and lives in celibate retirement. 'And there was none that made the children of Israel any more afraid in the days of Judith, nor a long time after her death' (xvi 25).

I shall not linger on the manifest improbabilities of this narrative, except to note that the elders' respectful response to Judith's reproach, and their willingness to remain ignorant of her purposes, are not the least of these. Ozias's attestation of her wisdom and her renown, at this point, is obviously present to explain this strange obeisance of patriarchs to a mere widow. Her beauty, status, and riches, emphasized at her entry into the narrative, underprop her ability to speak forthrightly in her society. Most important in this respect, though, is the precise nature of her renown: 'there was none that gave her an ill word, for she feared God greatly' (viii 8). She is irreproachable: faithful worshipper, inconsolable and celibate widow. The key to this irreproachability, its invulnerability so to speak, is the correspondence between loyalty to God the Father and loyalty to the husband, even beyond his death. When Judith reproaches the elders they cannot (in tropological terms cannot) reproach her for impudence, because her absolute commitment to God and husband – the two lords of her life – stands in contrast to the failure of faith which they have publicly admitted. Therefore their ready acquiescence to put faith in her mysterious purpose represents, in the tropological pattern, a submission to faith in God's mysterious purpose. To refuse this acquiescence would be to make the same mistake twice: once again to question God, in the person of Judith. That is, the elders' submission is not to Judith herself, but to the providential mystery which she embodies at this point in the narrative. The mystery of the woman figures, momentarily, the mystery of supernatural governance. The elders resubmit themselves to the patriarchy of God. That his ways are at once omnipotent and unknowable, Judith has just reminded them: 'And now who are ye that have tempted God this day, and stand instead of God among the children of men? And now [you] try the Lord Almighty, but ye shall never know any thing' (viii 12–13). This is nothing if not forthright.

In the course of the eighth chapter, then, Judith makes her first appearance and, having rebuked the elders, declares her purpose. This is the turning-point in narrative structure, halfway through the sixteen chapters of the book. Not the slaying of Holofernes, but its motivation, turns the narrative. For the structure is, so to speak, broken-backed. The first seven chapters are all leisurely epic sweep: empire, pomp, war, and devastation. The eighth chapter inaugurates a swiftly conducted, intimate drama in which armies hang fire until their fate is already sealed. Instead of battle, there is a single killing. Murder under the name of assassination, that is: nationally, publicly pronounced just, in the same way that soldiers are murderers by licence. Judith and the elders reiterate that licensing several times. Even Judith's name signifies her national responsibility, for she is Jewry in the sense that nations are rendered female by time-honoured symbolic logic (see Warner 1987: esp. 160-6). In the final chapter her song of thanksgiving elides Israel and her Judith into the same 'she'. Not a private woman, Judith is national identity in symbolic form. She sings of the Assyrian's boast 'that he would burn up my borders. . . and make mine infants as a prey, and my virgins as a spoil. But the Almighty Lord hath disappointed them by the hand of a woman' (xvi 5–6). In the gap between those two successive sentences, 'Assur' has reverted to 'them', whereas Israel has reverted to Judith the woman. It is to the Assyrians' shame that she reverts to individual woman, conqueror of their vast number; and to the honour of Israel, for she is a mere woman and weakest of instruments. (That fact is reiterated too.) Nevertheless, the symbolic logic of the passage links the sentences at a level which is meant to override their broken syntax. Israel's virgins have not been made a spoil. The invariable connection between defeat and the rape of the conquered nation's women has both its barbarous factual existence and its semiotics. Invasion, conquest, rape and pollution are all aspects of the same phenomenon. Holofernes is frustrated in his purpose to sleep with Judith; the virgins of Israel remain unviolated; the Temple at Jerusalem remains unpolluted. The symbolic logic of Judith's thanksgiving is that the national Judith is *virgo intacta*.

That is why, in this representation of a national myth of resistance, Judith the character is defined as chaste. In order to be socially prominent yet still a private individual, she must be rich. To be a free agent, she must not be under a private male authority, whether of father or husband, yet in patriarchy she must carry some reflected male authority; so she must be married, but a widow. Awkwardly, this means that she cannot be a virgin, but she can be the next best thing, celibate. And as a widow, she is still in some sense 'possessed' and controlled, from the grave by her husband, to whose memory she is devoted. The first thing that we are told about Judith is who her father was (viii 1) – conventional enough in the Bible. In the next verse we are told that she is the widow of Manasses, and then we are told of her eremitic and self-abnegating devotion to mourning him ever since. No sooner are we told of her great beauty than we are assured that her reputation was spotless, for she was god-fearing (viii 7–8). Loving God and her husband, Judith's sexuality is voided. Indeed, God's sanction for her actions is guaranteed finally by her chastity. At the end of her story, we are told that she returns to her solitude, refusing all offers of marriage, and remains 'honourable' till her death (xvi 21). Hence the final verse, which assures us that Israel remained inviolate too: Judith has lived out the price of the nation's honour. As she tells the elders, surrender would be shameful, 'servitude' and 'dishonour' (viii 23). The Authorized Version's translators lived in the period when honour for a woman was chastity, for a man courage and dignity. Here the word carries both connotations for the Jewish nation. Yet these are in fundamental conflict, for the plot requires Judith to conquer by means of sexuality; to achieve masculine honour through feminine sexuality, while guaranteeing national honour through chastity.

As a result, the whole question of Judith's sexuality is overdetermined. During her sojourn in the camp, her daily purificatory ritual is recounted with the pointing, 'So she came in clean, and remained in the tent' (xii 9). The point is, she came *out* of the tent clean too, despite Holofernes' intentions. Her access to the fountain for her daily ritual (xii 7) is in imagistic contrast to Bethulia's drought; water, the symbol of spiritual infusion, sanctifies her as godly, which is to say, chaste. On her return to Bethulia, Judith announces her exploit, with an insurance clause that 'As the Lord liveth, who hath kept me in my way that I went, my countenance hath deceived him to his destruction, and yet hath he not committed sin with me, to defile and shame me' (xiii 16). Rather, her womanliness is to be *his* shame, that 'the Lord hath smitten him by the hand of a woman' (xiii 15). In her prayer before leaving Bethulia, Judith had requested this of the Lord: that the weakness of a woman would mock the Assyrians' might, thus rendering proof of God's omnipotence through the humblest and feeblest of instruments (ix 10). Judith's femininity, the 'lack' or absence which is Woman as Other, reflects back God's presence and power. In contrast, sexual activity would intervene in that reflection, by rendering a form of power to the human male, Holofernes. He and God are rivals here. At another level of that duplication, Holofernes is an avatar of his master Nebuchadnezzar, 'next unto him' as we are told (ii 4), and Nebuchadnezzar sets himself up as a false god rivalling Jehovah. His tyranny, cruelty, and pomp are rendered in Holofernes, as his instrument. Both he and Judith are instruments of their gods. Yet in his case, sexuality is not problematic; it matches perfectly its correspondent in the signifying system here, which is lust for power and power as lust. In Holofernes and his hubristic master, desire signifies a lack which is metaphysically significant. Whereas in Judith, lack of desire signifies no absence; it signifies the presence of God in her.

Another system of correspondences duplicates these. Tyranny is servitude, to the lust for power: so the Assyrians form a chain of subordinations. Nebuchadnezzar is served by Holofernes, who is served by Bagoas and the Assyrian host, which exacts surrender and tribute from client nations. Because of this psychology of servitude, Holofernes' assassination effectually defeats his whole reliant host, almost literally at one stroke. On the other hand, the Israelite configuration breaks the chain of subordination. The elders submit to Judith's wisdom, Judith liberates Israel from the foreigner, Judith gives her maidservant manumission. The maid is to Judith as Bagoas is to Holofernes: on entry into the narrative, each is described as having 'the government' of all that belongs to mistress or master (viii 10, xii 11). Bagoas conveys his master's invitation to Judith. Replicating his mentality, 'he thought that he had slept with Judith' (xiv 14) – the ambiguous pronouns are very much to the point – and this misapprehension allows her time to escape. Bad servants and bad masters deserve each other, the irony suggests, for by evil thought their intended evil is obviated.

It does not pay, the text implies, to think ill of Judith – whether you are Holofernes, Bagoas, or the reader. So what does the maidservant reflect of her mistress? Why, of course, that she is indeed a 'maid'. The maidservant is present in the narrative as a duenna and a witness. Her mere presence ratifies Judith's story. Equally, at the end she can go free, reflecting Judith's godly capacity to emancipate their nation; but also, emphasizing by contrast Judith's imprisonment in asexuality. As duplication of Judith, the maidservant serves the illusion of Judith's free agency by being freed from involuntary constraint: Judith's constraint is rendered as not imposed, but voluntary, because she is mistress of her duplicate's fate. As duplicate, the maid hives off Judith's freedom of action, while as witness she has attested to Judith's sexual restraint. As bondservant, though, she at once reflected Judith's status as a mistress and, by duplication, her status as servant of patriarchy. It is the patriarchs – Joachim and Ozias – who repeatedly confirm Judith's right to act, her status as handmaiden of the Lord (viii 29, 31; xiii 18–20; xv 8–10). By their statements they ratify the patriarchal control which Judith's initiative and action might threaten. For what they, and Nebuchadnezzar, and God all share is patriarchal power. If Nebuchadnezzar's tyranny is a false counterpart of divine omnipotence, the difference depends upon a likeness which causes slippage. If Judith's courage is feminine mockery of male might, it must be controlled, must not overflow from its reflection of another patriarchal power, which is God's.

The story's polysemousness – politics, religion, sexual politics – is at once necessary to it, and explodes its coherence. Its strategies for the production of meaning produce uncontrollable signification; correspondence slides into ambiguity, replication turns upon itself. Where does right end and oppression begin? When is murder sanctified assassination? When is sexual guile chastity? Where does correspondence end and ironic reversal begin? These questions emerge from the surplus of meaning in the narrative of the book of Judith: a surplus which the text fails to control, despite explicit markers like the elders' blessings of the heroine. As the Other, she evinces the dialectic of difference: that, 'once the subject seeks to assert himself, the Other, who limits and denies him, is none the less a necessity to him: he attains himself only through that reality which he is not, which is something other than himself' (de Beauvoir 1972: 171). The process of individuation by difference contains its own negation, in that identity depends on an otherness not itself, self depending on not-self. As a power-relation, difference must involve a continuing dialectic if it is not to collapse:

each separate conscious being aspires to set himself up alone as sovereign subject. Each tries to fulfil himself by reducing the other to slavery. But the slave, though he works and fears, senses himself somehow as essential [to the master's self-definition]; and, by a dialectical inversion, it is the master who seems to be inessential.

(de Beauvoir 1972: 171–2)

In the book of Judith is refracted the myth of Otherness, the master-slave construction of essentialism. It is a narrative of resistance to tyranny, as constructed in political, religious and gender relations. All three act polysemously upon its 'moment of mythic power', the assassination of Holofernes. In that moment the apparent master – in power, in might, in gender – is revealed as a slave. The humble are exalted, as the Geneva Bible in particular insists. Yet also, the Other swallows the subject – almost literally. Holofernes' head goes into Judith's foodbag. This moment of discovery replicates the narrative's moment of reversal, the decapitation itself. For at this point we begin to see the significance of the story's insistence upon taboos relating to food. In severing Holofernes' head Judith has broken a taboo which her conscience about kosher food is designed to reassert in advance, so to speak. To murder Holofernes she takes him in sleep, as a siren would; she grabs his hair to hold the head for her stroke, like Delilah about to cut off Samson's source of strength. Judith lops off his head, as Salome takes the Baptist's. Symbolically and traditionally, the head is the seat of selfhood, rationality and control – the 'king' of the body. Of course, Judith is the obverse image of those biblical villainesses, the female as castrator. The hair and the head are displaced signifiers of phallic power, a power she appropriates the moment she uses Holofernes' own sword to kill him.

The narrative moments which separate the head on and the head off – the severance in the text – are vital to inflexions of the Judith myth. Those inflexions are clear from the selectiveness of its pictorial representations. Botticelli's Judith, all pellucid beauty and mobile drapery, unconscious of the sword in her hand, is returning to Bethulia with a similarly youthful maid in attendance, the head tucked away neatly in a basket on her head. In Ruskin's opinion, this was one of the few portraits of Judith which eschewed prurience (Ruskin 1906: 335–7). As in Ghirlandaio's similar composition, this picture of Judith after the event is triumphalist without being intimidating. By the early seventeenth century, the followers of Caravaggio are more concerned with the story's sensationalist possibilities. Depicting the very moment of decapitation, the chiaroscuro rendering of Caravaggio is one of the most disturbing.[1] The painting divides into two distinct halves. To the left, a bleeding Holofernes writhes under the stroke; to the right, a youthful Judith in virginal white is attended by a yellowed ageing crone of indeterminate sex, who holds a napkin at the ready. Whereas the crone is aghast yet not afraid, Judith's expression conveys at once fastidiousness and a concentration on the task in hand. As a whole, the picture is a beautiful brutality, titillating yet powerful. While imitating the master's brilliant chiaroscuro, the less outrageous renderings of the Caravaggisti usually focus on the aftermath. A standard pose is Judith holding the head up to the viewer by the hair, as in Fede Galizia's portrait. (This pose is characteristic also of the boy David with the head of Goliath, like Delilah another favourite subject.) Alternatively, another standard representation shows Judith and the maid after the murder, either holding or stowing the head. Antiveduto Grammatica gives us the heroic version, Judith as an armoured Minerva, in conspiratorial intimacy with her maid. Orazio Gentileschi's version, a most popular and most copied picture, shows the two figures turning from each other to stare out of the frame in differing directions. A Judith painted by his daughter, Artemisia, stares out to the left, her admonitory raised hand throwing half of her face into deep shadow against the candlelight. Developing the hint in Orazio's double-headed composition, this shows the face of Judith half-dark, half-light, half-sinister, half-illumined, a figure of radical ambiguity. Her powerful build, contrasted by the maid's kneeling posture, suggests fearsomeness rather than girlish attractiveness. In another picture by Artemisia, Caravaggio's bold treatment of the decapitation itself is imitated in a composition more kinetic and therefore more evidently brutal. The maid forces Holofernes' body down while another hefty Judith saws determinedly at his neck. As it is the most violent of representations, so also Artemisia's picture is rare in giving the maid so active a role as accomplice to murder. (It has been said that Artemisia's fascination with the subject was attributable not only to her desire to exploit the market successfully mined by her father's picture, but also to a feminist conviction not unrelated to her own traumatic experience of rape (Greer 1981:

189–207); but intentionalism is unnecessary to the viewer's recognition of an evident violence.)

In each of these representations erotic elements depend upon the violence. In the Artimisian decapitation Holofernes' head and body are foreshortened towards the viewer, his thigh-like arms feminized as if for rape. (Alternatively, an implicit image of childbirth is suggested by the midwifely co-operation of the two women; see Pointon 1981.) Here as in other versions, emphasis upon Holofernes' mouth, dilated by pain, provides an appropriate orality which can be (as in the Caravaggio) duplicated by the severed neck. This effect is even more evident in the Botticelli diptych, where the lopped and bleeding neck is remarkably vaginal: a sensationalism contrasting with the diptych's demure Judith, for in this wing all the figures are male and military. It is as if the diptych divides the ambiguous Judith into sainted woman and, sundered from her, a brutal military assassination. In contrast to these, Veronese's Judith shows a simply decorative titillation, in which the maid becomes a blackamoor to contrast the whiteness of her mistress's skin, echoed by her pearls; Holofernes' dark head is casually balanced in Judith's hands like a fashion accessory. Such inflexions suppress meaning, so that the sword is literally neither here nor there in this picture. Yet in all of these pictures the very fact of the subject seems to import a distinctive horrification of the composition. This even though the fifteenth-century Judiths of Botticelli and Ghirlandaio, for instance, were more subtle in their suppressions. In both the sword is more exotic than menacing, simply by means of authenticity – just as the Authorized Version specifies a 'fauchion', it is for them a scimitar rather than the slim razor-sharp blade of the Caravaggio. Heroic inflexions are banished to the background: in Botticelli the distant armed camp, in Ghirlandaio wall-decorations depicting the maelstrom of battle. Perhaps, though, the very calmness of the female figures carries its own disconcerting implication. (One may compare the impudently calm and steadfast gaze of Sebastiano's Salome.) Even the Orazio Gentileschi is only prepared to be half-disturbing: two heads turned from one another, while another, male head sits in a container between them. Neither woman looks in the least heroic. Again, the horror seeps in, for only the sword, seeming like an awkward afterthought in Judith's overloaded hands, gives icono-graphic proof that this is Judith rather than Salome. For Judith with a sword is Judith: Judith with a severed head but no sword slides into Salome. She is the ambiguous Other, assimilating a Salome – whose own function is directly sensual and evil – to a more menacing, because sanctified, destroyer.

Judith, who mythologizes the Other, cannot be pinned down, her meaning cannot be stabilized. In the Renaissance controversy over woman's nature, pro- and anti-female writers select one from Judith's two faces. She is always there in the list of heroic women, biblical and classical (as, for instance, in Le Moyne 1652 and Shirley 1686): she is woman as resistance. Equally, as a typing for Elizabeth I (see, for example, Nichols 1823: II, [the Norwich pageant] 145–7), she is woman as power. Female power cashes out in the way we might expect, as the Judith myth itself signifies: Elizabeth is an honorary man because she is a Virgin Queen. In a characteristic celebration of heroic 'Viragoes' like Thomas Heywood's, Judith and Boadicea both provide prolegomena to the final, subsuming example, an Elizabeth who is the national heroine surpassing all others. The Heywood hagiography naturally recounts Elizabeth's speech at Tilbury, in which she lays claim to kingship and to the 'heart and stomach' of a man (Heywood 1640: 185, 211; on Judith 20–42). In her embodiment as the classical Astraea,[2] who is another sword-woman because she allegorizes justice, Elizabeth is power and just power because she is a virgin, and the virgin Astraea is a goddess. Chastity is the site of signification for justice, power, national integrity and sanctification (see Stocker 1986: 168–73; and 1987: 159–79). Alternatively, in Joseph Swetnam's philippic, *The Arraignment of Lewd. . . women*, Judith is ranged with Delilah and other traitorous sirens. With righteous anger, Esther Sowernam's riposte, *Esther Hath Hang'd Haman*, accuses Swetnam of folly and blasphemy in this compounding of the virtuous Judith with biblical villainesses (Swetnam 1615: 23–4; Sowernam 1617: 241–2). Yet *The Arraignment*'s strategy is easily achieved. If the Other is a mystery, undifferentiated within Otherness, then the various configurations of mythic woman must slide into each other, reveal themselves as their apparent opposites.

The ambiguity of the Other necessarily destabilizes the subject. In the book of Judith, the male point-of-view which constructs myth shows its instability in generic terms. We move from empire and war to private seclusion and the war in the bedroom; from the epic of hubris to the melodrama of resistance. That generic switch formalizes the narrative irony, the reversal of male tyranny by female weakness. The story's exemplary and tropological force depends upon that reversal, but also founders on it. Judith's exertion of female and private resistance in the bedroom has to be recuperated for epic by her reabsorption, at the end, into Israel singing of victory. (Not surprisingly, it is that recuperative moment which was selected for inclusion in the Roman Catholic Breviary.) Epic is a masculine genre, public, warlike and historical. Epic is the opposite of the romance's feminine 'invagination' of narrative.[3] Where epic culminates in triumphalism, romance depends upon deferral of climax, upon replications of incident and characters. In one sense, the Book of Judith does have a climax, which substitutes death for consummation. (Equally, in the Renaissance love-lyric eros and thanatos meet, in the customary description of orgasm as a 'death'.) In another sense, death denies consummation and is itself absence. As the one entirely explicit absence in existence, death reveals deferral as a kind of death. It is the lack which impels desire, as textual deferral is the pleasure of desire in anticipation, endlessly offering itself because it is never fulfilled. Death is the Other by which desire is constituted. So Judith, object of desire, is necessarily death. It is not accidental that the Decadent artists of the nineteenth century should have favoured Judith/Salome in their representations of morbid eroticism.

The Apocryphal narrative watches with the voyeur's eye as she decks herself to allure (x 3–4), a voyeurism which the Bishop's Bible translation tries to counter by insisting that she remained pure in heart even as God mystically magnified her power of attraction for all men.[4] She is the innocent object of desire. Yet, in the construction of the Other, the power of the object of desire is a threat which must be turned back upon the object. The guilt of desire is repudiated by the subject and displaced onto the Other. In the narrative's attempt to block this repudiation of Judith, the effects of her castrating are placed and displaced by replication. The shock of the reversal is at once ironized and proleptically diluted by Holofernes' duplicate, who is introduced as 'Bagoas the eunuch' (xii 11). The sexual invitation to Judith is voiced by one already emasculated. Another correspondence, overdetermining the sign, is placed after the reversal, when Achior is motivated by Holofernes' decapitated head to convert, to be circumcised (xiv 10). That symbolic castration in the rite recuperates emasculation for the positive order of patriarchal signification: it is a submission to God and his elders, in which Judith is returned to instrumentality within the divine governance. Any subsequent representation of the myth omits at its peril Achior, Bagoas and the maidservant. That is one of the reasons why visual representations include the maid in their portrayal of the decapitation and its aftermath. A Decadent painting like Gustav Klimt's omits the maid for the same reason. It also omits the sword, which is why Klimt's second picture of Judith, lacking the title in the frame of the first, has usually been known as a Salome. Yet, as in the narrative so in the pictures, the maid and the sword are ambivalent. She fetishizes Judith, old age texturing youthful beauty. The sword says that this is not the evil Salome, yet as phallic symbol it signifies that this death is castration. The maidservant's fear and inactivity sensationalize Judith's activity, and emphasize its appropriation of male power by showing it to be deviant. In a similar fashion, the narrative's drive to overdetermine by correspondence and contrast reveals the endless replication of meaning, beyond its control. For Judith's myth produces a story which is, in effect, peculiarly intractable to control.

Even the Authorized Version, which is in many ways the most successful in its unsuccessful strategies, cannot evade those immanent problems which modern versions of the story simplify by selection. One such modern preoccupation is represented in, for instance, the nineteenth-century play by Hebbel, where a misogynistic thesis about Judith's supposed 'penis-envy' is all too clear.[5] To discover the Apocrypha's more complex representation, and its consequent ability to valorize the castrator's action, we need to examine this issue from another perspective. Because of the Apocrypha's concern for sanctification, its Judith cannot be so readily reduced to the negative image. Even a Freudian reading of this text, then, does not necessarily recapitulate Freudian misogyny.

The castration complex, in Freud's analysis, is the critical process for the formation of sexual identity. It summarizes 'within its instance the totality of loss', including the fear of death (Mitchell 1975: 76). The reversal in the book of Judith activates that totality. In the psyche, fear internalizes the castrating agent as authority, conscience. In having desired his own death and punishment, Holofernes renders the tropological signification of the complex. Holofernes claims that the Israelites have brought massacre upon themselves; ironic reversal reveals instead his own death-wish, which is closely related to the castration complex. Equally, in sexual identity, 'the encounter with the castration complex produces, for men, three choices: fetishism, acknowledged or denied homosexuality, or – "manhood", which is itself only a makeshift resolution of the other possibilities' (Mitchell 1975: 76). Fetishism is a sign of fear of the mother as an apparently castrated being, as 'lack': the fetish supplies woman with a phallic substitute, displaced to another part of the body. The Medusa's head, like Judith and Salome a favourite subject of the Caravaggisti, is an instance. Usually, David with the head of Goliath exemplifies 'might humbled by the weak' in a manner which is much less complex than that of Judith's myth. Yet for Caravaggio's homosexual audience, David with the severed head has implications similar to those of Judith. And in representations of Judith, the severed head is fetishized by the morbid eroticists. In a similar way, Salome in Oscar Wilde's Decadent play suggests a transvestite expressing a male desire for Jokanaan.[6]

The translation of desire into words reveals the cultural constructions of gender relations. Instructing Bagoas to deliver his invitation to Judith, Holofernes explains his desire: 'For, lo, it will be a shame for our person, if we shall let such a woman go, not having had her company;' – a word with sexual connotations in the Renaissance – 'for if we draw her not unto us, she will laugh us to scorn' (xii 12). If Holofernes does not seduce Judith, he will lose face, both before his army and (from his master-slave viewpoint) before Judith herself. Simultaneously, Holofernes attributes to Judith the male construction of feminine admiration for mastery, and rationalizes his own desire, in a manner which suggests that he is a champion of Assyrian honour rather than a captive of her allure. The *machismo* here explicitly involves sexual with power relations. That classic translation of the desiring male gaze into power-play has already been anticipated, and generalized, in the narrative. As Judith prepared to leave Bethulia for the Assyrian camp, the Israelites 'saw her. . . they wondered at her beauty very greatly, and said unto her. . . the God of our fathers, give thee favour, and accomplish thine enterprizes to the glory of the children of Israel. . . . Then they worshipped God' (x 7–8). The power of Judith's beauty is instrumental for God and to the glory of the nation: a power which is being exercised *through* her. A few verses later, the Assyrians

> wondered at her beauty, and admired the children of Israel because of her, and every one said to his neighbour, Who would despise this people, that have among them such women? surely it is not good that one man of them be left, who being let go might deceive the whole earth.
>
> (x 19)

Admiration immediately flips over into antagonism, the will to destroy. Before, the Assyrians had insisted that the Israelites were too weak to be spared. Now they are too much of a threat to be spared, for Judith's beauty represents their dangerous power to seduce. Apparently, then, the Assyrians do need reassurance that the Israelites will be vanquished, and that this 'national beauty' will be possessed by Holofernes. Desire and conquest, admiration and destruction, are necessarily correspondents in the lust for power.

Similarly, Chaucer uses allusion to Judith's assassination in *The Man of Law's Tale*, to explicate the divine inspiration which gives Constance strength to kill a rapist who enforces power as lust. Cultural construction works differently in *The Tale of Melibee*, where Patience cites Judith as an exemplary figure for women's 'good counsel' (Chaucer 1957: 72, 11, 911–45; 1, 1098). For the elders this is Judith's attribute. She has two forms of power within masculine culture: the artifice of allurement, for which she decks herself, and the art of words. 'There is not such a woman from one end of the earth to the other, both for beauty of face, and wisdom of words' (xi 21). On three occasions she beguiles Holofernes by the use of ambiguity. 'God hath sent me to work things with thee' (xi 16); she will do something great for her lord, she says (xii 4), and he understands her to mean himself/Nebuchadnezzar. When Bagoas delivers his invitation, Judith says that she cannot gainsay her lord (xii 14), which Bagoas/Holofernes takes to mean sexual submission. On these occasions Judith lies by telling the truth. Although she does mean to state her servitude to a master, he is God, not Holofernes. By ambiguity she avoids the perils hazarded by that other truth-teller, Achior, while serving her own (which is to say, her real Lord's) purpose. Ambiguity is a weapon like the sword, an appropriation of the man-made language just as Judith appropriates the phallic symbol. For if she deceives Holofernes, so 'he [had] waited a time to deceive her, from the day that he had seen her' (xii 16). His purposes, seduction or if necessary rape, are appropriated and inverted by Judith's self-presentation as sexual object and her role as castrator. Sexual mastery becomes the mistress.

In history, de Beauvoir insists, women have been able to act only by instrumentality or indirection – as Judith does. Her prayer evokes both:

> Smite by the deceit of my lips the servant with the prince, and the prince with the servant: break down their stateliness by the hand of a woman . . . hear thou my prayer: And make my speech and deceit to be their wound and stripe.
>
> (ix 10–13)

Through the language of prayer Judith invokes her Lord's power, so that her eloquence may be transformed into a language with power to destroy. Her words must become the Assyrians' 'wound', a punishment to fit their crime. For her prayer has already described their pollution of Israel: a national rape, which in the time of Simeon 'opened the wombe of the maide, and defiled her' (ix 2, in the Geneva's graphic translation). The image of this womb slips into that of the rapist's punishment, for Judith has two sets of lips. Her sexual allure and her verbal artifice are signifiers of the same feminine power. The ambiguity of her speeches is, in fact, covert resistance. Feminine power is indirect, mediated, the sliding effect of the ambiguity in Otherness.

On the other hand, the story of Holofernes can be, and sometimes was, extrapolated out of this two-faced narrative of epic and Freudian 'family romance'. When extrapolated, Holofernes' story becomes an exemplum of 'tragedy' in the medieval sense of the genre, as a fall from high to low estate. As such, the 'tragoedia' of 'Olofernes' forms a part of Chaucer's *Monk's Tale*, where Judith is not even mentioned. The Monk, indeed, shows a remarkable capacity for rendering his tales anticlimactic. His tediously didactic retailing here manages, by major omission, to rob the narrative of its perplexities. At the same time, this procedure is a failure of storytelling which accounts for the reader's fatigue long before the Monk is impatiently interrupted by the Knight.

In effect, then, the book of Judith is a site of three competing genres. Within the myth of Otherness are played out the epic of masculine aggression; the tragedy of a masculine fall from power, a loss of potency; and the romance of feminine power. In this book genre, like discourse, is unstable. The severance in the narrative of Otherness is that reversal which is implicit in the feminine. Remembering the broken back of this narrative, we can re-examine the much-criticized structure of Shakespeare's *The Winter's Tale*. Between the opening and the closing movements of the play stands a gap of sixteen years, signified by a speech from Time personified. That gap separates Court from Country, but it also divides the masculine tragedy activated by Leontes' jealousy from the feminine romance which restores him and his Court. While Hermione's existence remains hidden and subversively 'unauthorized', Paulina becomes her mouthpiece and Leontes's conscience. The statue of a 'dead' Hermione embodies and memorializes her absence but, in an ironic and liberating reversal, is in fact Hermione herself. Her son was a scapegoat of Leontes's madness, but her daughter is a regenerative presence. Productions which double the parts of Perdita and Hermione recognize the replication here, although Paulina is also a corresponding figure. When the mystery of Perdita's identity is revealed, when the lost is found and recognized, when the mother throws off the disguise of inanition – in short, when the women's intended and inadvertent deceptions come to fruition – the mystifications of romance work out the mysterious ways of providence. In this text, only secrecy, indirection and irony can effect the feminine restitution of life, liberty and the pursuit of happiness.

Equally, in the Apocryphal myth of Otherness, Judith's song, celebrating Israel's emancipation and triumph, reverses its signification of the essential, into the feminine carnivalesque:

And they put a garland of olive upon her and her maid that was with her, and she went before all the people in the dance, leading all the women: and all the men of Israel followed in their armour with garlands, and with songs in their mouths.

(xv 13)

101

Of course, in this text that cannot be the last word. The book of Judith ends, necessarily, with two words: 'her death'.

NOTES

1 For studies of the Caravaggisti see Friedlaender (1974) and Spear (1975).
2 Yates (1977: 29–88). For Elizabeth's representations generally, see Strong (1977); and in literature, Tennenhouse (1986).
3 The generic difference between epic and romance is given its most amusingly explicit statement in Lodge (1985: 322–3).
4 *Bishops' Bible* (1568): 'The Lorde gaue her also a speciall beautie and fairnesse: for all this decking of her selfe was not done for any voluptuousnesse, but of a ryght discretion and vertue, therefore did the Lorde encrease her beautie, so that she was exceeding amiable and welfauoured in all mens eyes' (x 4).
5 See Jacobus (1987: 110–36), for 'The Phallic Woman' and Hebbel; for Freud on Hebbel, see Freud (1957: 207–8).
6 For a 'transvestite' reading of Wilde's *Salome* see Millett (1977: 152–6).

Part Two

NEW TESTAMENT

Chapter Five

HISTORY, TRUTH, AND NARRATIVE

STEWART SUTHERLAND

INTRODUCTION

There are two central questions which constitute the background of
this paper. The first is: what is the nature of the text or texts which
we are considering? What *sorts* of text are they? The second, which
is closely related to this is: what is the appropriate relation between
the text and the reader? Whether there is an appropriate answer to
the latter question is itself a problematic matter.

These two are clearly interconnected not least in that some
philosophers and critics might argue that there are no legitimate *a
priori* answers to these questions. Equally, however, if there are
legitimate answers, whether *a priori* or *a posteriori*, then the answer
to the former will set limits to the possible answers to the latter and
perhaps have an even closer influence than that.

The choice of text to be considered has been set by the terms of
this volume. But within that 'text', which is in fact a library of
texts, I shall be addressing my remarks to the first four books of
what Christians call the New Testament – viz. the Gospels. Issues
of history and truth do come up in dramatic ways in other books of
the Bible – particularly Exodus for adherents of Judaism, and in
general the historical books of the Old Testament and the Book of
Acts in the New.

The overt reason for my selectiveness is that I wish to consider
those texts which give an account of the life and death of Jesus of
Nazareth.

THE TEXTS AND HISTORY

The first issue to be identified concerns the relation between text and history. A central point to be noted about the text (or better texts), which we are considering is that they are part of a set of scriptures. Without wishing to argue through the plethora of issues sometimes tendentiously referred to as the Intentionalist Fallacy, I should want to assert that for a text to have, by whatever means, the status of Scripture, is for it to have 'ideally' a certain set of relationships to the reader.

Scriptures in the end have to do with the beliefs and practices of their intended readers. That is their *raison d'être* They are there to be the focus of teaching and meditation, to guide, to reinforce, even to be the occasion of the inauguration of belief. Their role is to guide, and on crucial matters to define, the perimeters of the Tradition, and to do so for each believer. Now it is a matter of common recognition that different strains of Christianity each accord differing weight to the Scriptures, but there is no disagreement about their status as the primary authoritative source about the origins of Christianity, nor about their continuing role as, in at least some sense, authoritative today. Let us not be sidetracked into that argument, but retain rather the general agreement about their unique status in the tradition.

It is necessary now to make a brief intellectual excursion in order to draw a broad distinction between the differing ways in which beliefs can be related to history. I can do this most clearly by using two examples which I have used elsewhere, and the following paragraphs are from my *God, Jesus and Belief*:

In Rome in 1617, during the building of St. Peter's, some relics were found which were believed to be fragments of the True Cross. In honour of the occasion Monteverdi wrote and arranged the first performance of a particularly beautiful five-part motet. It is doubtful whether anyone now alive believes that these relics were fragments of the True Cross; it is even doubtful whether these relics still exist. Monteverdi's motet, however, has been preserved and is still performed regularly. The historical belief which was the occasion of its composition is now discredited, yet the music is no less delightful, nor at all diminished in quality or value.

106

Sometimes, what we value especially highly is connected in one way or another with particular historical beliefs. Sometimes the connection is such that we may come to see these historical beliefs as mistaken without changing our valuation or regard for whatever it is that we connect with the beliefs. In such cases we may say that the historical belief is *externally related* to the attitude, evaluation, or belief that tends to accompany it: that is, the historical belief may be severed or cast off without substantial loss to its erstwhile companion. The case which I have just quoted is an example of the sort of relationship which I have in mind.

Let us consider a different sort of example. In a foreword to his book *Culloden*, John Prebble writes: 'The book begins with Culloden because then began a sickness from which Scotland, and the Highlands in particular, never recovered. It is a sickness of the emotions, and its symptoms can be seen on the labels of whisky bottles' (Prebble 1961: 10). The sickness, or attitude, or set of attitudes, of which Prebble speaks, shows itself in sentimental and highly coloured views of Scotland, and particularly of those parts of it which lie to the west and north of a line drawn from Glasgow through Stirling and Perth to Aberdeen. One of its roots is certainly Sir Walter Scott's imaginative and gifted story-telling. Its result is a kind of patriotism on the part of some Scotsmen and a romanticizing on the part of transatlantic descendants of Scottish emigrants. Part of these attitudes is a set of historical beliefs which are by and large false: for example that all the clans, except the traitor Campbells, rose as soon as Prince Charles raised his standard; that men went willingly, even eagerly, to support the Jacobite cause; and that Culloden was a last gallant and glorious stand against the ruthless overpowering odds of the Duke of Cumberland's war-machine. That the Duke of Cumberland could be ruthless is more than probable; otherwise the rest is a tissue of fantasy, as Prebble's book clearly demonstrates.

To see the fantasy for what it is, to see the historical beliefs as quite unfounded, is, if not to destroy, at least radically to alter the sentimental romanticizing: in Prebble's terms, it is to diagnose the sickness as a sickness, and to lay the basis for its cure. In this instance the historical beliefs are *internally* related to the complex of attitudes, beliefs and evaluations in question. To see these historical beliefs as false is to alter substantially one's relationship to, say, one's native land.

(Sutherland 1984: 142–4)

The *interim* conclusion which I draw from this is that in the interpretation of these texts there is an interesting duality of alternative approaches. On the one hand there are those who would argue that the historical content of Christian belief is in fact minimal or non-existent, and that by implication the reading of these texts is not significantly affected by the truth or falsehood of any *prima facie* claims. Paul Tillich committed himself to such a view when he wrote: 'Historical research can neither give nor take away the foundation of the Christian faith' (1953–64: II, 130). On the other hand, there are those who argue that the historical content of Christian belief is an essential and central element of that belief, that the authoritative source for that historical content is this collection of texts, and that therefore if the historical content were factually seriously in error that would be most significant indeed.

It is difficult to find as clear a statement of the dichotomy as this, since even those who violently reject the former are not happy with the latter as the alternative. They would rather see an uninterrupted spectrum of possibilities moving from the one to the other. This is largely because of the fears expressed, for example, by van Buren that: '. . .the Christian [would] be at the mercy of the historian, so that if historical judgment were to repaint the picture of Jesus, the character or content of faith would have to shift with the historical reconstruction' (1963: 124–5).

Whatever may be the case with regard to the historical content of belief, it is worth while reminding ourselves that the historical content of texts covers a wide spectrum of cases – that the Gospels do not face these problems of interpretation alone.

ANALOGIES OUTSIDE THE SCRIPTURES

There is a wide range of analogies from secular writings which provide both a broader context from which to comment on the Scriptural cases and a distancing from those cases. These literary near and not so near neighbours raise related, but in certain important respects different, questions about the attitude which we take to the historical content of texts.

Consider the following range of cases – it could be more extensive and more subtle in its classifications, but it will suffice to indicate how widespread is the issue of history and truth in texts.

(i) Some works are self-confessedly historical or biographical. At one crude level they stand or fall by their historical accuracy, though the relationship to history is *much* more complex than that. Examples are Peter Ackroyd's magnificent *T.S. Eliot* or Alan Moorhead's *History of the Russian Revolution*. This latter is a most important and interesting case in that it destroys the myth about the origins of the revolution and Lenin's part in it, by showing Lenin's collusion with the German high command (much later Solzhenitsyn's *Lenin in Zurich*). The difficulty which a pre- (and possibly post-) Glasnost Soviet leadership has with these is that the accepted mythical account of the origins of the Russian revolution is challenged both by the historical work and by the novelist's re-presentation of history. Such historical challenges to the myth are also implicitly challenges to the ideology of Leninism which traces its origins to these historical events.

(ii) There are other works which are again self-confessedly historical novels or biographical novels e.g. Mary Renault, *The King Must Die*; Walter Scott, *Rob Roy*; Olivia Manning, *The Balkan Trilogy*; William Golding, *Rites of Passage*; Gore Vidal, *Lincoln*. Now each in its own way offers to the reader an historical backdrop which the reader either validates from other sources/experience, or takes on trust. The question, however, is whether the historical content is quite incidental to the worth or value of the novel in question. Is the history *only* mood or background or context? Or does the author and therefore reader make greater demands on it than that? It may be that different judgements should be made about each of these cases, but if Vidal were to miscast Lincoln as on the Southern side in the Civil War, the novel would lose credibility, though it might still have curio interest. But why? I am inclined to think that Walter Scott did significantly misrepresent the character of life in the Highlands, but his stories seem not to suffer as a result.

(iii)   I mention in passing the example of the drama-documentary,

109

that most beguiling of broadcast dramatic forms, but of course it also exists as text. There are many forces at play here. Not least in importance is the fact that such drama-documentaries play upon the ambiguity of form: on the one hand they interest and beguile as constructed or dramatized representations of 'reality'; on the other they interpret or wish to inform us about segments of history by, apparently at least, representing history to us. The membership of this class is perhaps even more elastic than that of the others so far distinguished. Examples range from the television presentation of *Kathy Come Home*, to the dramatized *Trial of the Chicago Six*, and to a version of a play given a specifically historical context e.g. John McGrath's production of Arden's *Sergeant Musgrave's Dance* with a cast of soldiers, alive and dead, who have served in Northern Ireland. The variation here is from examples such as *Kathy Come Home* which focus upon a fictional but firmly typical and representative character, to *The Trial of the Chicago Six* which deals with historical and still living individuals. There will be an appropriate variation in the types of historical criteria applied, but there is no doubt that there is here the representation of segments of history and that therefore historically-based criteria must play some part in the evaluation of the work.

(iv) There is a further range of examples, of which I shall give two from the vast literature of spies, in which questions of fact and accuracy arise, though I suspect that they have more importance for some than others. Apparently one of the skills demonstrated in Ian Fleming's James Bond novels is Fleming's detailed knowledge of type, calibre and performance of firearms. However I am not convinced that his novels would be any more or less worthy of attention if he had made the slip of substituting a non-existent 7mm Mannlicher for a real 9mm Mannlicher.

However I suspect that for many the bewitching puzzlement of John Le Carré's spy stories would lose something of their savour if it were thought that Le Carré knew as little of the workings of international espionage as most of the rest of us. (Why else publicize so well, prior to the publication of *Little Drummer Girl*, Le Carré's visit to the secret sanctuary of Arafat in a PLO camp?) These, however, are specific cases where one of the attractions of the novels in question to the reader is that they may incidentally provide the reader with factual insights. These cases, especially Le Carré's, clearly are close in the spectrum to (ii) above.

(v)   A very different set of examples concern novels which at least include, but often explicitly make predictions about the future. The futuristic science fiction novels of Jules Verne, or Arthur C. Clarke grow in stature as their implicit but apparently unlikely predictions turn out to be near the truth. On the other hand, the fact that 1984 as a date has come and gone without Orwell's 'prophecy/threat' being fulfilled in no way diminishes our response to the novel. That, however, is not unconnected with its continuing historical plausibility as to what might happen.

In each of the above cases historical accuracy is more or less relevant to a reading and an evaluation of the text. The response of a reader who was unaware of the varying levels of commitment to historical content would be diminished. By way of raising explicitly the question of narrative I should like to mention one further class of writing in which the role of history is quite distinctive, but in a sense of 'history' not yet properly explicated.

(vi)   The interpretation, but also the creation of narrative, of either a human life or indeed of human history on a grander scale. Examples include Edwin Muir's *Autobiography*, Gibbon's *Decline and Fall of the Roman Empire* and Tolstoy's *War and Peace*. Clearly this is also an elastic category.

Muir's *Autobiography* is, as we learn from the title of its first published form, an attempt to create the Fable from the Story. It is a reading of a single human life as a fable rather than as a chronicle. It achieves this by shaping a narrative and it does so by attempting to see what meaning lies in these dry chronicled events.

Gibbon's *Decline and Fall*, as in other examples of a certain band of historical writing (cf. Hume's *History of England*), also shapes a narrative out of history in the attempt to shape, find and create a meaning from these different dry bones.

Tolstoy's *War and Peace* is, in certain respects at least, a companion piece to these. In narrating the life of Pierre Besukhov and Prince Bolkonsky in the context of Napoleon's invasion of Russia, Tolstoy explores meaning – the place of the individual on the canvas of history.

In each of these instances history, whether of an individual or indeed of a civilization, is narrated and questions beyond the empirical are tackled. The tackling of the latter are not fortuitously related to the former. That we are dealing with history is in varying degrees important and introduces a degree of historical vulnerability to the answers given to the wider questions.

I shall not attempt to summarize points to be made from these many examples for that would be like trying to 'summarize' a landscape within which events take place, or a backdrop which is to be seen as the setting for a play. They are, in Wittgenstein's phrase, 'examples assembled as a reminder' – for one thing to remind us that the intersection of history and truth and the interpretation of a text is not a problem unique to the Gospels or even the Bible.

There are, however, some differences also, which is why these are near neighbours and not identical twins; and it is to these differences which I now turn.

RELIGIOUS TEXTS

What I wish to explore briefly is the peculiar or distinctive role claimed by the Christian Scriptures, and particularly by the Gospels. The text is at least in part what it is because of the content which it is believed, and indeed professes, to have.

(i) A set of Scriptures within a theistic religion claims some absolute status and importance for its content. Thus the Gospels are not just 'good news' they are the Good News. They provide the history of the events, but not just as a chronicle, rather as interpreted (in that sense 'narrated'). Thus they compare in this specific respect with works of history. If they have blundered historically then they are in deep trouble. However, unlike a work of history they cannot simply be shelved as 'the best so far', or 'brilliant but flawed', or 'overtaken by advances in historiography or archaeology'. If they diminish in status so does the Good News which they proclaim. (Compare the attachment which different sets of believers have to different sets of scriptures e.g. *The Book of Mormon* or *The Divine Principle*.)

(ii) The Gospels, like the Bible as a whole, are taken to be an account of, in James Barr's phrase, 'God's confessed action in history'. Now this is a comparatively modern and largely Protestant manner of speech, but it illustrates further the role

112

which these texts have in the unfolding history of Christianity. Not only do these texts 'reveal' these particularly important events in history – 'God's actions' – they are so revealed under the fiat or guidance of God. The disruption implied by a suggestion that the historical claims can be falsified is far from trivial. There is here a close comparison to be drawn between a historical challenge to the official or revealed account of 'God's acts in history', and the type of challenge to Soviet orthodoxy to be found in Solzhenitsyn's *Lenin in Zurich*.

Further, however, and this is a key to how the Gospels and the Bible are read and demand to be read, the events recounted are not ordinary historical events, they are 'unique' in some non trivial sense. The comparability here, which is limited, is perhaps with Muir's *Autobiography* or Tolstoy's *War and Peace*. But in those cases the uniqueness has to do with ordering, with the narrative structure. In the case of the Gospels, this is part of the story but not the whole of it. There is the further uniqueness that this is God's story – a story of 'God's confessed action in history'. Now *that* is a claim to an order of uniqueness quite unprecedented in these other texts – provided, that is, that the notion of uniqueness being canvassed is intelligible.

(iii)   To expand this further, a uniqueness is claimed for Jesus which is not a relative uniqueness but an absolute uniqueness. Thus the Jesus of the Gospels is not compatible with the Jesus of the Koran. In Christianity he is *the* Way, *the* Truth, *the* Life: in Islam he is but one prophet amongst others. The writers of both *The Book of Mormon* and *The Divine Principle* imply in different ways that Jesus does not have the absolute uniqueness of being God's final revelation.

The nature of the claims to uniqueness and finality for the figure of Jesus is however both theologically contentious and theologically complex. In a piece of theological heterodoxy (Sutherland 1984) I have argued that the acceptability of the claim of Jesus' uniqueness is non-contingently related to the success and persuasiveness of the portrayal of Jesus as a uniquely, indeed perfectly, good man.

There are some important literary analogies and disanalogies. Thus Melville's Billy Budd portrays goodness as does Dostoevsky's Alyosha in *The Brothers Karamazov*. Dostoevsky however had greater ambitions than Melville for he believed (or at least set out in search of the Holy Grail), that perfect goodness could be (uniquely?) portrayed. In setting himself such a literary task in, for example, *The Idiot*, he self-consciously compares what he was doing to what is to be found in the Gospels.

Dostoevsky's letters of that period tell a tale of literary audacity qualified by critical uncertainty. To his close friend, the poet Makov, he wrote, 'I have long been haunted by a certain idea, but I was afraid of making a novel out of it, because the idea is very difficult and I am not ready for it . . . This idea is – *to create a wholly beautiful character*. There can, in my opinion, be nothing more difficult than this . . .'. In a letter written on the next day to his niece Sofia, he made the explicit connection which undoubtedly occurs to today's readers: 'The main idea of the novel is to present a positively beautiful human being . . . There is only one positively beautiful character in the world – Christ'. The idea of beauty here is moral, rather than purely aesthetic, and indeed one translator has delineated Dostoevsky's problem as that of 'the representation of a truly perfect and noble man'.

The difficulty facing Dostoevsky the novelist, is, in part, as he realized, the problem of incarnation – or at least one aspect of it. His comment on the Fourth Gospel contained in this same letter to his niece is a vivid illumination of his conception of the literary task upon which he was engaged: '. . .the appearance of this boundlessly infinite, beautiful person [Christ] is of course an infinite miracle in itself (the entire Gospel of St John is full of this thought: he finds the whole miracle in the Incarnation alone, the manifestation of the beautiful)'. It would be shortsighted indeed to dismiss this as piety tending towards sentimentality. It is, rather, the admiration of one writer for another. What Dostoevsky recognizes in the writer of the Fourth Gospel is what literary professionalism has taught him in one agonizing page after another: the manifestation of beauty, of moral perfection (for that is what he understands by beauty) is infinitely hard to achieve – 'the whole miracle', he agrees, is 'in the Incarnation alone, the manifestation of the beautiful'. It is the particularization of the beautiful, of goodness, indeed the very idea that goodness and beauty should be, or could be particularized (or 'incarnated'), which causes him to marvel.

(Sutherland 1984: 152–3).

Interestingly (and, I believe, inevitably) he failed. However, if Dostoevsky failed to portray perfect goodness, goodness particularized and incarnated, what hope have the writers of the Gospels? Yet such a unique, incarnated goodness was their aim. That aim was made even more difficult to fulfil by setting constraints accepted by neither Dostoevsky nor Melville – the constraint of simultaneously portraying a human being who is part of our history and who shares history with us.

CONCLUSION

The texts called the Gospels pose both writers and readers with formidable, perhaps even insoluble problems, some of which I have sketched. These problems relate in part to the role which history plays in them, though also to other issues e.g. the difficulties of the portrayal of goodness, let alone perfect goodness.

These texts have analogies with other texts which have varying degrees of historical content. I gave some examples. However, there are dramatic differences which are a consequence of the claims to absoluteness and uniqueness implicit in the texts.

Troeltsch's three principles of critical historical enquiry illustrate well the difficulties which beset the interpretation of texts that seek to combine the contingencies of historical content with some form of absoluteness or uniqueness.

(i) Principle of criticism – historical judgements claim only a greater or lesser degree of probability and are thus in principle revisable.

(ii) Principle of analogy – we must presuppose that our own experience is not radically dissimilar to the experience of past persons; this implies no 'unique' events.

(iii) Principle of correlation – all events are inter-connected.

The problem of Christian belief, with which theologians are still grappling, is that it involves historical beliefs but does not accept the consequent historical vulnerability. This affects the relation which the reader has to these texts for the texts were intended to create such belief via the definitive account of a particular segment of history. Alternatively, if one focuses upon the goodness of Jesus, as portrayed in the Gospels, as providing a means of giving authoritative status to those texts, then the difficulties faced by Dostoevsky in providing a 'narrative of perfect goodness' are sufficient warning of rocks and possible shipwreck ahead.

Chapter Six

'TALES ARTFULLY SPUN'

ROGER TRIGG

I

Much enlightenment can be obtained by viewing the Bible as literature, and interpreting its various components in terms borrowed from the field of literary criticism. Emphasis on 'myth', 'narrative' and 'story', for example, is often made in contemporary theology, and connections made between biblical criticism, and the interpretation of texts as such. Yet there are dangers in such a course. Michael Dummett has alleged that an appeal to literary genres has slowly degenerated into what he terms 'an unconscious mechanism for allowing the exegete to adopt what opinions he chooses while formally progressing to acknowledge the truthfulness and inspiration of the New Testament writings' (1987b: 560). Dummett is particularly concerned with the Gospels. He points out that literary genres normally rest on widely known conventions, while he considers that the habit has grown up of assigning the Gospels 'to a genre to which there is no evidence whatever, or even any plausibility in supposing, that contemporaries understood these or any other writings as belonging'. Dummett believes that the reason for this is 'to ascribe to them a sense consonant with the exegete's opinions without branding them deliberately deceptive'.

At first sight the Gospels are, or at least claim to be, accounts of what actually happened at a particular time and place. Luke, for example, takes pains to date the events he is portraying. Whether he is accurate is one question. What seems harder to doubt is that he wants to be accurate. Yet much of what he writes, not least the birth-story at the beginning of the Gospel, seems hard for so-called 'modern man' to accept. How then should a Christian theologian react, if he wants to keep his religion in contact with what is taken by his contemporaries to be knowledge? Dismissing the Gospels as unhistorical is too drastic. After all, it would be a bold Christian (though there are such) who would claim that it does not matter whether Jesus actually existed or not. Accepting them at face value, however, involves accepting the Virgin Birth, miracles, the Resurrection and so on as literal events. While this is surely the traditional Christian position, it sits uneasily, it might seem, with the assumptions of twentieth-century science. It can be alleged that it is 'unscientific' to accept that the events should have occurred, as portrayed. The spell of Hume's scepticism is still powerful. We have no experience of such things ourselves, so why, we are challenged, should we accept on trust what others say about them.

The stage is set for the advocacy of a middle course which would enable us to revere the Gospels and gain inspiration from them without having to take the details too seriously. Such a course has, it might seem, proved very successful in the interpretation of parts of the Old Testament. The 'myth' of Adam and Eve can still teach us about the human predicament, about the origin of sin and the nature of human responsibility, without us having to worry about where the Garden of Eden actually was. The story can carry power, without needing to claim historical truth. We can even still read it with reverence and with profit, while being full-blooded neo-Darwinians.

It is perhaps not surprising that so much emphasis in biblical criticism has been put on the way which the Gospel writers selected and constructed their material, and on the effects they wanted to produce. In this way, our attention is directed from *what* they say to how they say it, from questions about the possible truth of their accounts to seemingly more manageable issues concerning the way in which the faith of the early Church was expressed. Thus Schubert Ogden expresses a recurring theme in modern theology when he says that 'our only sources for Jesus are at best secondary and, in their controlling concern, witnesses of faith, not historical reports' (Ogden 1982: 54). His argument is that the traditions conveyed by the gospels can be compared to a historical drama. The controlling concern, he alleges, 'is not to provide information about the past, but rather so to make use of historical material as to say something significant to the present'. This position owes much to Existentialism, and Bultmann is a theologian who embraced it eagerly.

Ogden makes much of the fact that we can have no independent access to Jesus, except as he is portrayed in the Gospels. We have to rely on the earliest Christian witness still available to us. His conclusion is that there can be no distinction between Jesus as he actually was, and Jesus as he is represented as being in what Ogden terms 'the earliest stratum of witness' (55). The historical facts of Jesus' life must then recede into insignificance, compared with what Ogden takes to be the important question of 'the meaning of Jesus for us as he still confronts us in the present' (59). Even the basic stratum of witness is 'witness of faith and not historical reportage'. Reports which are apparently historical must be viewed as expressions of faith in the significance of one who was believed to be 'the decisive re-presentation of God'.

Ogden's emphasis is significant. He moves our attention from the person Jesus actually was, to the person he was believed to be by the earliest Christians. Indeed Ogden's point is precisely that no distinction can be drawn between these two. We are invited to share the reactions of the first witnesses, but are left with no way of wondering if these reactions were justified. Because it is alleged that we cannot have independent access to the historical Jesus of whom the Gospel writers speak, we are left with the fact of their faith and what Jesus meant to them. Yet this is in danger of proving too much, as an argument. Any claim to truth can be similarly discounted. What I say I see in a room is merely a report of my perceptions, not of the room, it may be suggested. The account in a newspaper of some happening is merely the way a reporter reacted to the situation. The television news bulletin merely shows a cameraman's or producer's selection of events. Everything is always, it seems, described within some frame of reference, and can owe as much to the frame as to the nature of what is described. This form of argument is in fact often used to show that there is no objective truth, and that all is relative. It is a typical move by sceptics that can undermine all claims to knowledge. In history, in particular, it effectively removes us from all contact with the past. At most, we have access to the interpretations made by historians. As a specific argument, therefore, concerning the writers of the Gospel, it is of doubtful value. Just because the writers wrote from the standpoint of faith, it does not automatically follow that what they said was not independently true, and may even be assessable on ordinary historical grounds.

Ogden's move, in the tradition of Bultmann, is of great significance since it transfers attention from the events described to the way in which they are described. The shift from the Jesus of history to the Jesus of faith means that the manner in which faith is expressed becomes relevant. If, on the other hand, we are primarily interested in the actions of the historical Jesus, concentration on the literary effects intended or achieved by the Gospel writers must be of secondary importance. This cannot be so, if we regard the Gospels as above all conveying the faith of their writers. The focus of our attention then has to be on the Gospels as historical drama, rather than as history.

The theme of the faith of the Gospel writers evoking faith in the reader is allied with the repudiation of the New Testament as a straightforward historical document. Those who still wish to cling to a Christian faith have to find another category in which to place it. Literary criticism, coupled with the notion of the Gospels as a special form of literature, then becomes relevant. Yet how could what appears to be history, whether accurate or not, be interpreted as being in fact something very different? The characteristic answer to this question is that we are wrong to impose modern criteria on documents written in a very different age. Modern conceptions of historical writing, it is alleged, should not be read back into what was written for a different purpose. We should not assume the identity of our world with that of the first century AD, believe that our respective ways of thinking are similar, or even think that we are still the same kind of people. A chasm that is almost unbridgeable thus seems to yawn between New Testament times and our own day.

It is significant that this type of argument quickly brings us to a relativism that stresses how each society can only be understood in its own terms. The problem is then how we from the standpoint of one society can even begin to understand those who lived in what appear to be such different circumstances. Once again a sceptical argument can prove too much. It could not merely show us why we should not assume the standards of our own society in our interpretation of the writings of an ancient society. It may prove that there can be no point of contact whatever between the two societies. However that may be, there is a clear link between the desire to emphasize differences in understanding between ourselves and the inhabitants of the New Testament world, and the tendency to see the New Testament as literature, or a collection of pieces of literature, rather than as primarily an historical document. David Jasper writes:

> Both Jesus and the New Testament which testifies to him are of their own time. The man and the literature necessarily conform to conventions and a culture which is not our own.
>
> (Jasper 1987: 13)

Jasper continues by suggesting that 'our notion of "history", which is built upon a careful and unprejudiced collation of factual evidence, would have meant little to the writers of the Bible'. Because society now is simply different, he claims, neither Jesus nor Paul can be just re-created and made to work for our time as they worked in first-century Palestine. He prefers to describe the New Testament as 'mythical literature rather than as history' (14). Its purpose is a form of sacred history rather than anything conforming to modern notions. He concludes: 'Such sacred history is much more clearly related to the art of fiction than we have been used to believe,and much more open to the methods of literary analysis'. A relativism separating our time from that of Jesus, and asserting that he and we are different kinds of people, is thus explicitly linked with a desire to interpret the New Testament with the methods of literary criticism. The result is that the New Testament can be taken seriously, while we do not have to be too concerned whether the events portrayed actually happened or not. Jasper can portray Matthew as wishing to establish Jesus in his place in salvation history while at the same time denying that 'Matthew would have understood our modern anxiety to get the facts right, or our modern distinction between fact and fiction' (15).

Jasper enlarges on his description of the New Testament as mythical literature, by defining myth not as something false but 'as something collectively motivated which draws together the great central values of a culture, or a faith'. Thus a myth can be important and in some sense 'true', without necessarily having to be viewed as historically accurate. The latter notion imposes modern standards of precision on an age which allegedly did not appreciate such niceties. The connection between the New Testament and the world it describes is not a literal one. The writing is not descriptive. Instead, as Jasper puts it, 'its language, of metaphor, symbol, and myth has produced imaginative fictions which demand an imaginative response' (95).

II

The same emphasis on the distinctive character of the New Testament, and the error of taking it to be straightforward historical writing, is made in a variety of contexts. It is usually coupled with assertions about the differences between the world of the New Testament and that of today. The effect is often to contrast the thought-forms of the ancient world with the rational, scientific approach that supposedly animates the present age. David Jenkins, Bishop of Durham, for instance, attacks those who take it for granted that 'writers of the New Testament must have supposed that they were giving what we call accurate and historical reports when they preached, recollected and wrote down the stories about Jesus'. Claiming that this is a simple mistake, he maintains that the stories were intended to convey 'the dynamic truths about Jesus and his and our relationship to God'. They were told in good faith in ways which would make sense to those around them. Jenkins stresses the great differences that existed 'between thinking and feeling about truth and the world (and indeed ourselves) before the scientific and industrial revolutions and after them' (Jenkins 1987: 26–8).

The conclusion that can be drawn from this is that one can apply what Jenkins refers to as 'modern critical principles' to biblical stories and find 'differing layers of historicity, myth, legend, and sheer embroidery'. Yet all this need not call into question 'either the total good faith and credibility of the writers or the validity and authenticity of their witness'. What they say may not be true by our standards, it seems, but that does not mean they were lying. It is just the result of their having different standards of what constitutes truth. As Jenkins puts it in colloquial terms: 'They are simply doing it their way' (27). Their ways were not our ways. A strong doctrine of relativism could not be more succinctly stated.

Jenkins pursues this theme by stressing that the Gospel stories should not be viewed as history. They expressed a faith in Jesus and were written to provoke faith. As he says: 'The stories are products of faith and preaching of faith'. It is significant how the literary characteristics of a story then become much more important. Putting the Gospel accounts into such a category rather than that of history means that we come to the texts with different expectations and judge them by different standards. It is, though, possible to make the categories seem more distinct than they are. Accurate history can still be great literature, while stories can themselves still be literally true. They can tell us what actually happened, even if they still make a powerful appeal to our imagination.

Jenkins's purpose, however, is to make a distinction between the Gospel stories and history as it is viewed today. He is convinced of the distance between ancient and modern understanding. He says firmly of the writers of the Gospels that 'their world was not our world' (37). In fact, this notion of living in different worlds is a favourite one in many intellectual disciplines nowadays, ranging from social anthropology to the philosophy of science. To take an example from the latter, Thomas Kuhn has put forward influential views about the role of theories in science. When there is a fundamental change, or revolution in science, as in the change from classical to quantum mechanics, scientists' views about which entities constitute the world change; Kuhn is able to say that 'after a revolution scientists are responding to a different world' (Kuhn 1962: 110). Whatever the rights and wrongs of this position, its consequences are clear. Scientific theories are incommensurable. That means that there is no way of translating one into the terms of another, because they posit different entities. Scientists thus live in self-contained worlds created by their particular theories, and cannot understand one from the standpoint of another. To take a favourite example, used by Kuhn, and also by Wittgenstein, you can see the drawing of a duck-rabbit as a duck or as a rabbit, but not both at once. What counts as true depends on the conceptual scheme with which one is operating. Our understanding, too, is conditioned by our concepts. Only something like a revolution can alter the way we see and reason about things.

It is fascinating to reflect how relativism has even attacked the heartlands of science, so that it becomes problematic how far science can claim objective truth, or indeed whether the notion of scientific progress, according to which our knowledge can steadily increase, is still possible. Those who approach the Bible in the spirit of Jenkins, however, do not seem plagued by such doubts.

They may use similar forms of argument, talking of different 'worlds', and the consequent difficulties of understanding. They may even talk of revolution in thought. They do, though, seem to take it for granted that science sets the standards of truth. The problem becomes how far the stories of the New Testament can withstand the searching examination of minds trained after the so-called scientific 'revolution'. The assumption is that they cannot if they are literally claiming what they appear to be saying. Jenkins says of Mark's story of Jesus healing an epileptic boy (ix 14–29): 'The story is not important for its historic, still less for its scientific, descriptive accuracy. It is important for its message'. He takes it for granted that our views are and should be conditioned by the criteria of modern physical science, and that the people of New Testament times were radically different. We should, therefore, not bring our concepts to bear on the passage, but shall see its meaning for us, regardless of whether the events actually occurred. We are invited to share the faith of the writers, even though, as Jenkins says, 'their way of understanding the epilepsy need be nothing like ours'.

Jenkins does accept that the story of the epileptic boy is based on a real incident, but he believes it also reflects the impact made by Jesus on those who became his disciples. He considers that our conceptual scheme – the assumptions and manner of our thought – is so different from that of the first disciples, that we are wrong to judge what they wrote in terms of what we take for granted. Our respective worlds are so different, it seems, that it would be misleading to interpret what they say in terms appropriate to our world. As Jenkins remarks: 'The faithful, believing and trustworthy writers of these Gospel documents simply did not share our concern for our types of either historical or scientific statements. They could not – nobody had thought that sort of thing up' (Jenkins 1987: 37).

We have a situation where conceptual schemes – and hence apparently whole worlds – diverge so much that contact between them is put at risk. After all, if, according to Kuhn, the holders of one scientific theory will find it difficult to grasp what the holders of another mean, how much greater difficulty will there be in stepping from our scientific age to what is alleged to be a pre-scientific one. The problem is not just that standards of accuracy and precision derived from science may not be usefully applied. It becomes one of how we can get a grip on the thought processes of those in such an alien world at all. The greater the alleged differences between the world of the first century AD, and ours, the greater the difficulty of translating. We become so locked in our own self-contained conceptual scheme that it must seem impossible to get out of it. Either we use our own categories of thought, or we cannot think at all. In fact, attempts to mitigate the 'unscientific' character of the New Testament stories by appeal to cultural differences can prove too much. Those who try to do so, as we have seen, do not wish to dismiss the New Testament as irrelevant or unintelligible. They wish to preserve its truth, at least in some manner, by invoking the categories of literature. Because it is unscientific, it has to be literary. Then the stories, or myths, can still challenge us and have a message for us, because they engage our imaginative sympathies in the way that all great literature does. Instead of history, we are confronted by historical drama. Instead of literal description, we have stories.

This way of looking at things, including the very distinction between the scientific and the literary, is itself a product of our scientific culture. It is itself imposing an alien way of thinking on to the New Testament. If the latter is genuinely rooted in a world so different from our own, then *any* form of modern understanding applied to it will misrepresent its content. Indeed from a religious standpoint, the whole exercise is particularly pointless. If the people of the New Testament were so utterly different from ourselves, what was relevant to their needs is irrelevant to ours. Any religious message emanating from its pages would be pointless in our world, even if it could be made intelligible.

The practice of history and even the possibility of the translation of ancient languages, depend on the assumption that there are major points of contact between what may seem alien worlds. The New Testament writers did live in the same world as us, in a very real respect. They confronted the same reality, and shared the same human nature, with much the same hopes and fears, desires and needs. They may not have possessed modern gadgets (though it is possible to underestimate the technological achievements of Roman civilization). That does not mean, though, that they were an alien species. These may be assertions, but if they are contested, it must mean that any understanding of any society different from our own becomes impossible. It is indeed a favourite ploy of some scholars to show in great and intelligible detail just how different some other culture is from our own. Yet the very fact that such an exercise is possible at all proves the similarity between the alien culture and our own. We have to realize that we are all humans living in the same world.

If we start with the assumption that people are always similar, whatever the superficial differences, the question must arise whether the writers of the New Testament must have had a radically different understanding of what they were doing from anything we normally envisage. Were they really, as has been alleged, so indifferent to questions about accuracy? Were they dealers in myths and stories rather than historians? Did the fact that they wrote because of their faith mean that they had to be blind to questions of truth and falsity, as we understand them? There are clearly no answers that can automatically be given to these questions. Much must depend on the authors' intentions, and one way of responding is to see if they possessed concepts which would enable them to make the necessary distinctions. Whether what is written is actually true or not, and whether it is *good* history are separate issues. The point is whether they were trying to write what we could regard as history, or whether they would be unable to grasp the distinction between what was historical and what was not. I am not arguing that if we reject relativism, the New Testament writers *must* be seen as trying to write a true account of real events. The point is that they may have been. We have no right to assume that they were so distant from us intellectually that there could be no point of contact. Indeed as I have argued this thesis is double-edged in that, if it succeeds, it must remove their writings totally from our comprehension.

III

The distinction between myth and claims to truth, and between poetry and history are not modern ones, but arose in the ancient world. They are in fact clearly enunciated in texts dating long before the New Testament. Aristotle, for example, in the ninth chapter of his *Poetics* denies that the difference between poetry and history has anything to do with whether either is written in verse or prose. He argues that 'the true difference is that one relates what has happened, the other what may happen' (1451b). He suggests that poetry is more philosophical and more serious than history. Poetry expresses the universal, and history the particular. His conclusion is that the poet (or 'maker') is a maker of plots (*muthoi*) rather than verses. A 'myth' may thus portray what is universally true, rather than an event that has to be real.

The word *muthos* (or 'myth') is a favourite one with ancient authors, and is often associated with the work of poets. Plato makes Socrates remark that someone who wants to be a poet should make *muthoi* and these are contrasted with *logoi* (*Phaedo* 61b). Socrates goes on to say that because he was not very good at inventing stories he would make use at that point of Aesop's fables (*muthoi*). Similarly in the *Republic* (II, 376e), Plato makes a distinction between *logoi* and *muthoi*, when he is talking of the role of stories in education. After saying that *logoi* could be true or false, he uses the term *muthoi* to refer to what is false. He asks: 'Do not you understand that we begin by telling children fables (*muthoi*) and the fable is, taken as a whole, false, but there is truth in it also?' He goes on to advocate censorship of the 'makers of myths' so that children would be moulded by the stories in ways Plato thought desirable. Something that was false could still have a beneficial effect if it portrayed what would set a good example.

Another example of what was obviously a regular contrast between a *logos* and a *muthos* comes in Plato's *Protagoras* (320c) when Protagoras asks whether he should put his point in terms of a *muthos* or a *logos*. In other words, should he tell a story or present a reasoned argument? He decides it would be pleasanter to tell the story, and he recounts the myth of how Prometheus stole fire and gave it to mankind. A similar distinction was often drawn, and even self-confessed historians were aware of the difference between the art of poetry and the duty of the historian to find out exactly what happened. Thucydides claimed to be an accurate historian, and he repudiated anything that spoke of myth. He apologized (I, 22) that his work would be less attractive because it did not traffic in fables. Instead, he asserted that his account was based on eyewitness reports and subjected to the most severe and detailed tests possible.

The history of Greek thought was in fact very much the growth of the realization that all claims to truth, and all arguments, can be rationally assessed and criticized. A *logos*, as opposed to a *muthos*, was precisely something that claimed truth, and because of that was itself open to challenge. No doubt, the distinction derived in part from notions of claims being tested in a law-court. Evidence could be assessed and eye-witness reports given special weight. A *logos* aspired to survive such scrutiny, whilst a *muthos* was precisely the type of fable that would never even be considered in such an arena. Story-tellers could please their listeners or bore them. Their *muthoi* could provide wholesome examples. They were not, however, the kind of thing that could be rationally examined. *Logoi*, on the other hand, were supposed to withstand criticism, and if they did not, they would have to be given up.

What, though, it might be asked, has all this to do with the New Testament? First, it demonstrates that ideas of precision and accuracy, and of the difference between historical and poetic truth, did not suddenly appear after the modern industrial and scientific revolutions. Unless we are to be totally locked up in our own period of history and unable to understand those who lived in other periods, we must recognize that distinctions making sense to us also made sense to the ancient Greeks. Once we allow the corrosion of scepticism to creep in, we undermine the possibility of history. Whilst we would be foolish not to recognize some differences between ourselves and our predecessors, the very recognition of difference only makes sense against the background of a fair degree of similarity.

Just, though, because some ancient philosophers and historians made important distinctions, does this mean that we can assume that the same ones would be familiar to the writers of the New Testament? This is clearly a large question. Involved with it is the whole issue of the influence of Hellenistic ideas on New Testament authors. Yet there are straws in the wind, apart from the not insignificant fact that the New Testament was written in Greek, as the common language of the Eastern Mediterranean region. The notion of an eye-witness was of great importance in a Greek court as in any court of law, and the New Testament stresses that its accounts rely on eye-witnesses of the events described. We have only to think of St Paul's list of those who had seen the risen Lord (I Cor. xv 3) to realize that truth of a literal kind is surely being claimed. St Paul is referring, so to speak, to those who would be prepared to give evidence on the matter under cross-examination in a court of law. Indeed that is precisely what he says, when he concludes that if there is no resurrection, 'we turn out to be lying

witnesses for God'. A similar emphasis is made in the first
Christian sermon when St Peter preached of the Resurrection of
Jesus, 'of which', he said, 'we are all witnesses' (Acts ii 32).

There are times too when the contrast between *muthos* and what
is true is explicitly drawn. For instance, in II Timothy iv 4 we read
of those who turn to myths and away from the truth. Indeed in the
very same passage, the word used to refer to Christian teaching is
logos. This juxtaposition of *muthos* and *logos* occurs at other points in
the New Testament. In I Timothy iv 7–9, after Timothy is told to
have nothing to do with godless myths, fit only for old women, he
is then given a 'logos' on which he is told he may rely. Similarly, in
the passage from which I have taken my title, we read:

> It was not on tales (*muthois*) artfully spun that we relied when we
> told you of the power of our Lord Jesus Christ and his coming;
> we saw him with our own eyes in majesty, when . . . there came
> to him from the sublime Presence a voice which said: 'This is my
> Son, my Beloved, on whom my favour rests.' This voice from
> heaven we ourselves heard; when it came, we were with him on
> the sacred mountain.
>
> (II Peter i 16–18)

Here is the contrast between relying on 'myths' and being actual
eye-witnesses, and sure enough the myths are also contrasted with
a reliable *logos*. We are told that 'all this only confirms for us the
logos of the prophets, to which you will do well to attend'.

These examples are taken, of course, from the Epistles rather
than the Gospels themselves. It is, however, natural that the latter
are not going to waste time reflecting on the status of the truth they
proclaim. They wish to proclaim it. The Epistles, however, are able
to indulge in such theological reflections, and claim the truth of
what is given in testimony. It can be contrasted with what is told
in order to suit people's fancies.

The issue we are confronting is not whether these claims to truth
are justified or not. They should be subjected to the utmost
scrutiny and criticism. The point is that the authors themselves
would not have objected to that. Indeed, they expected it. They
were on the witness-stand and were prepared for cross-examination.
This implies, indeed, that they would have been horrified if their

129

claims were consigned to the world of myth, however politely defined. They believed that they were claiming truth. What they said, they believed was reliable and worthy of acceptance by all people everywhere.

The inhabitants of the Greek and Roman worlds were not unaware of the difference between truth and falsity, or the difference between asserting truth and telling a story. Just because they were not using the criteria of twentieth-century science does not mean that their claims can be re-interpreted. Assuming that truth can only be assessed in terms of what is taken to be knowledge in *our* society is dangerous. Identifying truth with what is held true at any given moment involves us again inexorably in a form of relativism. No gap is allowed between what is believed to be true (even by us) and what is true. Yet this in the end reduces rather than enhances the status of modern science. It becomes merely the outlook of a particular society at a particular time, and its claims to be a path to truth become somewhat tarnished.

Relying on the assumptions of modern science as a way of undermining the claims of people in other societies at other times is perhaps a sign of how we are unable to detach ourselves from our own prejudices. The standards of the scientific laboratory are always inappropriate for testing anything connected with religion. By definition science is concerned with the workings of the physical world. If it is alleged that these do not exhaust the nature of reality, and if the experience of people points to the existence of anything transcendent, reiterating the prejudices of science is merely a massive begging of the question. For example, if an account is given of an apparent miracle, some may argue from a scientific viewpoint that miracles cannot happen and that therefore this alleged one did not. Yet if eye-witnesses persist in what they claim, and if their lives are even changed as a result, mere allegiance to the principles of science may not be enough. It would seem sensible, instead, to test the veracity of the witnesses in every way we can. In other words, we should turn from the criteria of the laboratory to that of a court of law.

Even from a modern point of view, questions about the reliability of what is claimed, and the task of establishing the truth of a particular matter, can naturally remind us of a legal rather than a scientific context. This is particularly so when something controversial is claimed and a case has to be proved beyond all reasonable doubt. Those who adjudicate in modern courts know full well that the kind of proof aimed at is not the proof of a scientist, let alone of a mathematician. Because what is being dealt with are particular events that may never be repeated, judgment must be made after all available evidence has been properly tested, and witnesses cross-examined by lawyers representing each side.

This is precisely the model that the writers of the New Testament seem to have in mind. The very notion of being a witness conjures up the idea of taking the witness-stand and being cross-examined. Is it at all strange that Luke should insist (i 2) on the importance of what had been handed down by those who were eye-witnesses of the events in the Gospel? Indeed is it a coincidence that the word he uses for what the New English Bible translates at that point as 'Gospel' is *'logos'*, the word that is so often contrasted with *muthos*, and that clearly carries with it the implication that it can be rationally tested?

The law-court analogy does not just demonstrate how inappropriate it is for us to turn to the assumptions of modern science. Our understanding of the nature of the task New Testament writers are engaged in will be affected. They should not be regarded as writing from the standpoint of a pre-scientific world view and hence in need of re-interpretation in our terms. They make extraordinary claims, but are willing to face any cross-examination and for their claims to be tested by all rational means. They are like advocates presenting a legal case. This certainly means that their writings are pieces of advocacy, and as many ancient writers knew full well, the skills of rhetoric were needed in a court more than anywhere else. Indeed Plato grumbled that a clever lawyer could convince a jury, whichever side he was arguing for (*Theaetetus* 201a); it would be just good fortune if he persuaded them to bring in a correct verdict. Plato significantly contrasted this with the position of an eye-witness who would possess knowledge of the facts of a case and could not therefore be persuaded. He was highly suspicious of rhetorical skills for this very reason. People could be too easily swayed by them.

For Plato what mattered was knowledge of the truth. The writers of the New Testament would surely have agreed. They are presenting a case, and it is legitimate for us to take note of the manner in which they do it. They are undoubtedly trying to persuade their readers of the truth of what they are saying.

Nevertheless, they themselves passionately believe it. Literary skills must for them come second to the prime task of communicating what they see as truth. They may have been mistaken, but it does them no service to pretend that they were really not claiming that people had actually witnessed the events as described. When David Jenkins claims that a story can be important for its message, rather than its descriptive accuracy (1987: 37), what he says could not be acceptable to any of the Gospel writers. They believe an event carries with it a particular message because it actually happened. They were able to select the happenings which they regarded as of particular significance, and so it is not surprising that their accounts can be seen as having several layers of meaning.

To suggest that an account (or *logos*) can carry a meaning even if it is based on lying or mistaken witness is not in the spirit of the New Testament. We may wish to reject parts of what is written. What we cannot do is to suspend our belief in what actually happened and still be guided by the 'message' of the putative events. Keeping the message of a story while denying its truth, is to treat the accounts as *muthoi* and not *logoi*. It is like trying to hold on to the grin while the Cheshire Cat has long since departed.

Chapter Seven

'IN THE SERMON WHICH I HAVE JUST COMPLETED, WHEREVER I SAID ARISTOTLE, I MEANT SAINT PAUL'

(attrib. Revd William A. Spooner)

DAVID JASPER

I

The right thing in speaking really is that we should be satisfied not to annoy our hearers, without trying to delight them: we ought in fairness to fight our case with no help beyond the bare facts: nothing, therefore, should matter except the proof of those facts. Still, as has been ... said, other things affect the result considerably, owing to the defects of our hearers.

(Aristotle, *Rhetoric*, III, 1404a)

It is no bad thing for a lecturer to establish a certain authority of manner, if possible, in the early stages of his delivery since, thereby, the gravity of form might carry more easily with it whatever substance may be implied. It may, of course, be the case that the assertion of superiority by the suggestion that your listeners' understanding is defective is neither amiable nor particularly effective in the face of an academic, critical community such as yourselves – but perhaps we can smile together since I, too, am a member of that community, isolated for a moment (as all of us are, from time to time) for praise or blame in order that the community as a whole may sharpen its wits and reassure itself that we may be a community, forged perhaps upon the sense of alienation of each of its members, but a community still.

I have begun by briefly exploring the given relationship – in rhetorical criticism termed the *aptum* (see Lausberg 1960: II, 54ff. and 258) – between the three fundamental terms of an argumentation: the relationship between speaker and speech content, between speaker and audience, and between speech content and audience. I suggest that in so far as the question of both the interrelation and interdependence of form and content (*res* and *verba*) is here raised, the *aptum* is the crucial hermeneutical issue (see Lausberg 1960: I, 45 and II, 1055–62; also Wuellner 1976: 342). The situation is granted further complication by the confusion which is recognized in the title of my paper – and not peculiar to William Spooner – that what we say and what we mean may be, consciously or unconsciously, two quite different things. As we struggle to clarify the *aptum* of speaker-audience, and the *aptum* of the audience-speech content, the textual situation in which all meet contains within itself a wilful undercurrent of argumentation, recognized perhaps in the structuralist distinction between 'deep structure' and 'surface discourse', in the discovery of paradigmatic patterns embedded in the syntagm of the surface discourse (see Detweiler 1980: 9–10). But let us not assume that this is a twentieth-century discovery, for classical rhetoricians were discussing the same issue as the *intellectio* by the writer concerning the nature of the *quaestio* and the *status* or *stasis*, that is the underlying key-issue, before he carries out or enacts (*actio*) the surfacing *causa* (see Wuellner 1976: 333).

With this in mind, and before giving specific attention to a New Testament text, we should consider in some detail the nature and purpose of rhetoric. Though Erich Auerbach (1953: 39ff.), and after him G.B. Caird (1980: 183–4), have sought to distinguish the New Testament writings from the spirit of rhetoric, I rest upon the universality of Aristotle's purpose in writing the *Rhetoric* to describe a phenomenon which is a universal facet of human experience (see Kennedy 1984: 10–11). And in what I shall argue, though the terms may remain, to a certain extent, those of classical rhetoric, their use may be radically adapted as rhetorical criticism of the New Testament is recognized as the necessary, indeed vital, counterpart of hermeneutics as inquiry, not only into the art of understanding and appropriating meaning, but into the very fundamental questions of theology itself (see Klemm 1987: 443–69). '*Rhētōr*' might be defined as 'a man skilled in speaking who addresses a public audience in order to make an impact upon it' (Dixon 1971: 2); 'rhetoric' as 'argumentative composition' (Whateley 1832: 6), 'that quality in discourse by which a speaker or writer seeks to accomplish his purposes' (Kennedy 1984: 3), or 'reflection on the role of style in the art of persuasion' (Klemm 1987: 443). Aristotle, we may recall, distinguished three categories in the arts of language: logic, rhetoric and poetic. Very briefly, 'clarity' and the ability to persuade and change our opinions are the functions of logic and rhetoric. Poetic, on the other hand, has 'distinctiveness' rather than 'clarity', and by moving beyond the realms of 'ordinary' speech, does not seek so much to persuade as to invite us to use our imaginations (see Jasper 1987: 30–1).

In short, rhetoric is concerned with persuasion, and concerned therefore with the exercise of power, the establishment of authority. Even in Wayne Booth's classic study *The Rhetoric of Fiction*, which avowedly ignores 'fiction used for propaganda or instruction', the criticism is concerned to explore 'the author's means of controlling his reader' (1961: Preface). By rhetorical means and 'invention' – the treatment of the subject matter, the use of evidence, the argumentation, and the control of emotion – power is asserted which establishes a situation, or changes it, and in the relating of form and content in a biblical text it is the creative synthesis of the specific formulation with the content of a pericope that makes it a distinctive and powerful composition.[1] It should be clear, therefore, why classical rhetoricians were so insistent that goodness is a necessary prerequisite of the true orator (see Dixon 1971: 4ff.). Never far away is the anxiety that rhetoric may be used by the wicked man as a tool for manipulation to his own evil ends. And, yet more disturbingly, in Plato's *Gorgias* and *Phaedrus*, we move nearer to the suspicion that the evil lies in rhetoric itself – a vaunted art of deception, a contrivance and falsification of great power. Indifferent to truth and morality, rhetoric must be subordinated according to Plato, to dialectic, whose province is definition and division in the ceaseless search for truth.

Against this subordination, Aristotle makes his counter-claim in the very opening sentence of the *Rhetoric*: 'Rhetoric is the counterpart (*antistrophos*) of Dialectic. Both alike are concerned with such things as come, more or less, within the general ken of all men and belong to no definite science' (1354a). The two studies in other words, fit together, each the legitimate equal of the other in discipline and intellectual rigour. But did I say Aristotle? Or did I mean St Paul? For it is my contention that in the New Testament we have erred grievously in our failure to heed Socrates, since in the New Testament, so obsessed with theology, we are playing with power in the ultimate degree, and rhetoric is in its element, playing its subtle games with a freedom that eludes authorial or even rational demands.

As we come to the New Testament where is the locus of power which drives its rhetorical machinery of persuasion? One answer, a familiar and comfortable one (though fraught with its own danger), is suggested by a distinguished New Testament critic with a particular sensitivity to Early Christian rhetoric. In the Introduction to the 1971 reissue to his formative work, *Early Christian Rhetoric*, Amos Wilder writes:

> What is crucial . . . is that all such manifold particularity in the language and the language events – in the various genres, voices and images – requires a corresponding rich structure in Reality itself, in Being itself.
>
> (Wilder 1971: xxx)

This 'ultimate mystery', then, is cast outside the text, relieving it of responsibility and defusing the crucial meeting point between the elements of rhetorical interplay – the *aptum* – in a typical escape. But in the fabric of the compositional structure of early Christian rhetoric wherein is located the drive to power? One thing seems to be clear – that the argumentative nature of religious literature demands a methodology that can give an account of the nature and effects of argumentation (see Wuellner 1976: 350; also Georgi 1971: 124–31). Modern scholars of rhetoric seem to be generally agreed that at the heart of religious rhetoric, quite distinctively, lies authoritative proclamation and not rational persuasion (see Kennedy: 1984: 6 and 104–7). But the consequences of this absolute, rhetorical demand have not been properly recognized. Most radically, and disturbingly, such rhetoric is operative within the Gospel of Mark in which language it seems, tends towards an absolute claim to truth without evidence and without recourse to logical argument.

The tone is set in the first few verses – assertive, absolute, pitched without compromise. We may compare Jesus' initial proclamation of the gospel in Mark with the version in Matthew. There the call to repentance is delivered in a form which classical rhetoric would term an *enthymeme*: '*Metanoeite, ēngiken gar ē basileia tōn ouranōn*' ('Repent, for the kingdom of heaven is at hand' Matthew iv 17). In the enthymeme a supporting reason is always given. In Mark, however, the gospel is purely proclaimed, not as an enthymeme, but as four authoritative moments: the time is fulfilled, the kingdom of God is at hand, repent, believe in the gospel (Mark i 15). Indeed, as Professor Kennedy has noted, the enthymeme is very largely absent from the Gospel of Mark, which stands beside Matthew almost bare of argumentation, its radical rhetoric stark in its assertion of authority and mysterious, threatening, confusing power.

In consequence it is not sufficient, it seems to me, to conclude with Kennedy that 'Mark is seemingly addressed to devout Christians who want a written account of the sayings and deeds of Jesus in simple terms that they can understand and use in their life and worship' (1984: 98). Such claims for simplicity just do not match the rhetorical claims of the Gospel's narrative, which proclaim to us as Frank Kermode so powerfully stated in *The Genesis of Secrecy*,

> that stories can always be enigmatic, and can sometimes be terrible. And Mark's gospel as a whole – to put the matter too simply – is either enigmatic and terrible, or as muddled as the commentators say this passage is (Mark iv 10–12) . . . Mark is a strong witness to the enigmatic and exclusive character of narrative, to its property of banishing interpreters from its secret places.
>
> (1979: 33–4)

The 'Messianic Secret'; 'say nothing to anyone' (Mark i 44); the muddled confusion of the disciples; 'they began to beg Jesus to depart from their neighbourhood' (v 17); 'Get behind me, Satan!' (viii 33); the boy in the linen shirt (xiv 51–2); *'ephobounto gar'* (xvi 8). Are these the simple terms of a gospel proclaimed to be understood and used in everyday life and worship?

According to Eusebius (1976: II, 15; see also Kennedy 1984: 104) the Gospel of Mark arose out of a request by churches which had been founded by St Peter for a written text of the gospel which they could use after Peter himself had left them and moved on. In other words, this Gospel was conceived as an address to an already established Christian community, to convinced Christians. If this is so, it seems to me to be crucial, for I want to suggest that the rhetorical demands of this text have developed out of a newly-established community wishing to assert its identity and sense of mutual interdependence by an act of self-entextualizing – asserting the 'content' of its being in the 'form' of a rhetorical construct which both realizes and enacts its necessary moment of power and authority.

I suggest further, and drawing upon the insights of a remarkable essay by Donald Pease entitled 'Critical Communities' (1987), that two models may be proposed as illustrative of the formation of such a coherent group with the necessary internal strength and energy.

(a) The group which derives its cohesion from the power exerted by the threat of alienation of each member of the group. The rhetoric of the defining text enacts a 'discourse of repression' (Pease 1987: 95) in which the conditions of alienation are recognized by each individual who, by virtue of the common text, retreats into the false security of a group powerfully bound together by their specific, furtively repressed, anxieties.

(b) The group organized by the logic of what Sartre called a 'group-in-formation'. In this model each member acts in a situation of mediation to every other member of the group, his position being 'a context for reflecting on the common project that draws him in relation to the rest of the group' (Pease 1987: 101; compare Sartre 1976: II, chap. 1). Thus, although difference becomes the basis for further development, the group project does actually become a means of both defining and developing each individual member. Is this the model in essence adopted by Paul to overcome the near-surrealistic picture of the church in Corinth (I Cor. xii 15ff.) as a community withering under the experience of individuals projecting themselves or alternatively feeling excluded through the lack of a powerful cohesive element in the rhetoric of their self-identity? (See also Bornkamm 1969: 195.)

II

Let me try to justify my use of this last term as I turn back to the Gospel of Mark, and apply to it my first model of critical community. In the terms of that model, the anxiety experienced under threat of alienation is produced in so far as the community is actually unwilling to admit any radical discontinuity in its appropriation of the gospel.

> To you has been given the secret of the Kingdom of God, but for those outside everything is in parables.
>
> (Mark iv 11)

For the group within there is no prior moment of destruction (deconstruction?). Instead, a more pervasive, more seductive strategy is assumed in the easier terms of simply opposing the new to the old, a procedure of modernization.

But the community thus self-constituted is betrayed by its own rhetoric, for the necessary repression required to assert continuity will reveal the threadbare ragged features of that which lies outside the power structures erected by the huddled community of lonely, frightened individuals. The ragged figure, in the necessary moment of ontological destruction, has not been recognized, the priority of its authority not insisted upon (see Bloom 1973: 9–10).

Of what, therefore, are they afraid? 'And they were filled with a great fear' (Mark iv 41); 'and they were afraid' (Mark v 15); 'for they all saw him and were terror-struck' (Mark vi 50) 'for they were afraid' (Mark xvi 8). Is it a rhetorical betrayal that lies at the root of this anxiety? In answer to this I adopt a rhetorical vocabulary which has been recently used to brilliant effect by David Klemm in an analysis of tropes in postmodern theological enquiry. Fascinated by this enquiry I began to wonder what would be the result of putting the Gospel of Mark through the same analysis.

Klemm concentrates upon the four master tropes of thought and discourse: metaphor, metonymy, synecdoche and irony (Klemm 1987: 446–7), ordered by Giambattista Vico in *The New Science* (1744), and re-established more recently by Kenneth Burke (1947), Hayden White (1978) and Paul Ricoeur (1985). The pattern moves from a primary *metaphorical* perspective on reality, to a *metonymic* analysis (described by Kenneth Burke (1947: 506) as the '*reduction* of some higher or more complex realm of being to the terms of a lower or less complex realm of being'), to the *synecdochic* reassembly of the elements of metonymic reduction, to an *ironic* dialectic as a reflexive comprehension of synecdochic integration. The last phase, of course, is crucial, in breaking down a false idolatry or rescuing discourse from merely gambolling over the abyss in playful, rhetorical irresponsibility. The pattern is, admittedly, a convention, but arguably rooted deep in biblical narrative and serving necessarily to remind us that understanding is lodged within our sensitivity to the linguistic practice of mediation between conceptual thinking and prereflective experience.

My contention is that our difficulty with the Gospel of Mark seen in terms of the first model of community, lies in the absence from its rhetorical pattern of the last of the four master tropes – irony. It is that absence of the ironic, of reflective comprehension and an ability to stand outside the rhetorical strategy, which flings the community which generated the text back upon itself in a frenzy of repressed anxiety and ultimate refusal to change.

'He would not permit the demons to speak, because they knew him' (Mark i 34). The possession of the interpretative key in Mark is demonic, because that immediately affirms a locus of power outside the claims of the entextualized community. The repression of the Messianic Secret, the repressive mystery of the parables (and even those 'inside' apparently fail to grasp the point 'for their hearts were hardened' vi 52), the blindness of the disciples, the blank fear of the women rushing out of the tomb – all combine to reinforce the authority of a group maintained by the anxiety engendered in each individual through rhetorical strategy. Dare one admit one's alienation from the fundamental relationship – the *aptum* – presupposed in xiii 14, '*ho anaginōskōn noeitō*' ('let the reader understand')? The phrase, of course, can be read in many ways – assuming a secret complicity between reader and author; the genuine ignorance of the author saying 'Make of that what you can'. But what does the reader understand? Only that a community is being assumed, and there is a knowledge which he cannot afford not to possess. What manipulation is being contrived here?

Scholars, of course, gleefully establish their own community by proposing answers to the riddle, proposing a background which will grant an origin to the mystery. But the mystery is the Sphinx which is met upon the road back to origins,[2] and the Sphinx is our anxiety. In the Gospel of Mark only the demons hold the interpretative key, while for everyone else there is only hardness of heart, the mystery, the secret or the fear which thrusts us away from the moment in the tomb. On the cross, the cry of dereliction –

why not dereliction? But that moment is most powerful to cast us back into the arms of the community and the God from whom in reality we are alienated. There *is* no interpretative key, only blankness, and if it were otherwise the power of the rhetoric would be loosened.

Frank Kermode (1979: 33) has suggested that 'Matthew took the first step toward reducing the bleak mystery of Mark's proposals', replacing Mark's *'hina'* (iv 12) with *'hoti'*. Luke, perhaps, goes even further than Matthew in the process of the domestication of the church's authority, adding argumentation and amplification to the bare Marcan rhetoric. Cleopas and his companion in Emmaus recognize the stranger who had walked with them in the eucharistic breaking of the bread (Luke xxiv 30–1), an interpretative key which opens to them the mystery of their encounter, and a key guarded closely within the comfortable and comforting domesticity of the church's sacraments.

No such domestic structure rationalizes the drive to power in the text of the Gospel of Mark. Failing entirely in the moment of irony which establishes the proper distance between God and the symbol of God – a necessary act of literary self-reflection – the Gospel declines to make any distinction between *priority* and *authority* (see Bloom 1973: 9) and, emptied of historical content, simply sets the new in opposition to what has become merely obsolescent. The authoritative claim of the Gospel is absolute, the apparent achievement in literary creativity of the ambition of Borges's Pierre Menard who proposed to write, word for word and line for line, *the Quixote itself.*

> My intent is no more than astonishing. . . . The final term in a theological or metaphysical demonstration – the objective world, God, causality, the forms of the universe – is no less previous and common than my famed novel.
>
> (Borges 1981: 66)

This isolation from what has gone before, not in terms of historical radical discontinuity, but rather of an absolute claim to authority, is a form of *kenosis*, an 'undoing' of the precursor's strength in order to isolate the moment of power repeated in the self (see Bloom 1973: 87–92). Priority is emptied, so that we are left amazed and asking, 'What is this?' *'didachē kainē kat' exousian'* (Mark i 27). Here is no Pauline *kenosis*, but a daemonic parody of it (one has always known that the demons held the interpretive key in Mark), humbling not the self but all precursors in a grand act of ultimate defiance: in the rhetoric of the Gospel to choose between the textual community or the admission of fear unto death. In Harold Bloom's discussion (1973: 92) of this moment we are reminded of Blake's cry to Tirzah:

> Whate'er is Born of Mortal Birth,
> Must be consumed with the Earth
> To rise from Generation free;
> Then what have I to do with thee?

III

In working thus with my first model of a critical community, the rhetoric of power in the Gospel of Mark, fearful of irony, leads us to a terrible Nietzschean vision of a church whose 'conscious misery is set up as the perfection of the world's history' (Nietzsche, quoted in Bloom 1973: 55).

But what now of the second model, the model of Sartre's 'group-in-formation'? As an image of a community struggling to assert its identity through an exercise in textuality, does this model illuminate for us more sharply and properly the terrible majesty of the Gospel of Mark? Having glanced at the worst, the significant point is to be made in the crucial absence from the rhetorical pattern of the Gospel of the moment of irony under the terms of the first model of the critical community. But is this also true under the terms of the second model?

I believe it is not, and the significance of this is to be recognized in an important revision of Professor Klemm's 1987 article, 'Toward a Rhetoric of Postmodern Theology', to which I have already made reference.

We need to be reminded of the nature of the second model. In such a group every member provides a moment of reflection based upon his difference from the other members of the group in their common task of the building of the whole body. The community thus becomes, in the activity of mutual reflection and self-reflection, an interdependent organism which also defines and encourages the task of each individual.[3] It is engendered and strengthened, therefore, by repeated acts of reflexive comprehension – in Klemm's terms by the final figure of irony. Furthermore, if, as we have seen, the first model of community, rhetorically structured upon the threat of alienation, is unwilling or unable to admit of any radical discontinuity, this second model of 'group-in-formation' both tolerates and welcomes the critical reaction, the moment at which ironic reflection recognizes the radical turn, the discontinuity which does not merely oppose the new to the old, but in a deconstructive spirit exhilaratingly collapses the dangerous edifices in the lumber-room of our inheritance. The shock may be profound, traumatic: '*Kai meta to paradothēnai ton Iōanēn ēlthen ho Iēsous*' (Mark i 14); 'Get behind me, Satan! For you are not on the side of God, but of men' (viii 33; I shall return to this passage of Peter's confession at Caesarea Philippi in more detail later); 'With men it is impossible, but not with God; for all things are possible with God' (x 27).

In rehearsing the fourfold rhetorical pattern of metaphor, metonymy, synecdoche and irony, Klemm identifies synecdoche (when the elements are reconstituted into a new figure) as marking the inbreaking of God from outside the linguistic structure. This moment of summation he applies to the conventions of biblical narrative and the theologies constructed from it (Klemm 1987: 447). I want to suggest that this moment of inbreaking into the linguistic structure can only take place *ironically*. And it is the element of irony which is precisely missing from that anxious, repressed model of community which I have hitherto applied to the Gospel of Mark: a community formed by a rhetoric of power which both alienates and dictates – a church outside of which there is no salvation, for there is indeed nothing but the threat of fear and the fear of nothingness.

May we, then, recover the ironic moment of divine reflexity in the Gospel, a moment which can only be grasped by a community whose defining rhetoric can embrace the shock of radical discontinuity? An essential attribute of God?[4] In his book *A Rhetoric of Irony*, Wayne Booth writes of such that

> In the kind we turn to finally, infinite but somehow stable, the ironist of infinities suggests that there is, after all, a Supreme Ironist, truth itself, standing in his temple above us, observing all authors and readers in their comic or pathetic or tragic efforts

to climb and join him. For such an ironist it is not so much the whole of existence that is absurd as it is mankind in the proud claim to know something about it. His works may in some respects resemble Beckett's: every proposition will be doubted as soon as uttered, then undercut by some other proposition that in turn will prove inadequate. The meanings are finally covert. But both the effort to understand and the particular approximations, inadequate as they are, will be worthwhile; the values are stable.

The picture of God or Truth as supreme ironist, incomprehensible and infinitely distant, may superficially resemble the picture of an impersonal universe that indifferently (and hence brutally) frustrates all human effort at statement. But the form of 'reading assignment' given by the two views is radically different. For the second, infinite ironies present finally a treadmill, each step exactly like every other, the final revelation always the same: *nada*. Since the universe is empty, life is empty of meaning, and every reading experience can finally be shaken out into the same empty and melancholy non-truth. But for the first, the universe, though deceptive, is infinitely, invitingly various; each flash of ironic insight can lead us toward others, in a game never ending but always meaningful and exhilarating.

(Booth 1974: 268–9)

It is upon this 'reading assignment' that we are now embarked, not on the dark road of melancholy non-truth, but on a journey which is always meaningful and exhilarating.

Consider the cry of the soldiers in the Gospel of Mark, uttered in derision of the Lord in bondage.

And they clothed him in a purple cloak, and plaiting a crown of thorns they put it on him. And they began to salute him, 'Hail, King of the Jews!' And they struck his head with a reed, and spat upon him, and they knelt down in homage to him.

(xv 17–19)

In the context of the Gospel, as Wayne Booth has pointed out (1974: 28–9, 91–2), there is a double irony; the irony of the soldiers railing against their victim, and the irony of the Gospel against the original ironists. And it is this second, 'literary', irony which recognizes the fundamental stability cutting through the instabilities

144

of interpretation and military game-playing: that the forlorn, unlikely figure is, in fact, the King of the Jews. Furthermore, this generation of ironic pathos effects a binding together of the community of those who are brought to perceive the essential truth of the situation in the context established by the text.

The strength of the irony depends upon the radical rhetoric of Mark. In the Fourth Gospel, elaboration weakens the irony and changes the whole point.

> Pilate also wrote a title and put it on the cross; it read, 'Jesus of Nazareth, the King of the Jews'. Many of the Jews read this title, for the place where Jesus was crucified was near the city; and it was written in Hebrew, in Latin, and in Greek. The chief priests of the Jews then said to Pilate, 'Do not write, "The King of the Jews", but, "This man said, I am King of the Jews"'. Pilate answered, 'What I have written I have written'.
>
> (John xix 19–22)[5]

Finally, Booth has noted, the community of readers united by its grasp of this stable, radical, irony in Mark is larger and with fewer outsiders, than any that could be built upon a literal statement of beliefs. Such ironic form binds by its pathos and its generation of sympathy – a sympathy which is humanly felt even in the unbeliever who would retreat from any straightforward affirmation that Jesus was the King of the Jews, the Messiah, the Son of God.

And so, by this rhetorical device we have relocated the moment of power, not in the drive of the community to exert its influence by the threat of alienation, but in the demand of a stable point which lies outside the community and its intersubjective relations, a demand which draws forth sympathy and prompts self-reflection and reflection upon the common situation through the position of a mediatory figure, in the ironic, dialectical relation of negation and affirmation. It is upon this ironic moment, therefore, that our second model of community – a community realized as entextualized in the provision of the Gospel – that God's inbreaking is marked, definitively, upon the linguistic structure.

And the inbreaking and subsequent persuasive entextualization recognize a radical discontinuity in the formation of the group. Was this the Messiah of our hopes? This figure who engenders fear and perplexity, who hangs on the gibbet, a thing accursed? The experience seen as text is well described (I am not sure if there is not irony here!) by Harold Bloom: 'Most so-called "accurate" interpretations of poetry are worse than mistakes; perhaps there are only more or less creative or interesting mis-readings' (Bloom 1973: 43). The authority claimed within the ironic rhetorical moment admits, in one sense, a formal lack of distinction between priority and authority. In this it seems to be one within the pattern of the first model of community through which I approached the Gospel of Mark. What has gone before is abandoned in the creative mis-reading, the '*skandalon*' of the text. But it is a mis-reading, not an abandonment, a radical newness which does not derive its absolute claims upon us purely from within the conscious misery of its own textual perfection. It is a *kenosis* which is not simply an 'undoing' of prior strength in order to isolate the moment of power repeated in the self. Rather, it is the genuine, Pauline, *kenosis* which is utterly radical, daring a uniqueness which no other creative act of poetry or making could bear – for in poets mis-reading is an act of aggression whereby predecessors in the art are undone in a false display of individual talent and self-aggrandizement. In the greatest of all ironies, the mis-reading is found to be the true reading, a persuasive act achieved only by a self-emptying, an utterly powerful isolation on a turning point – the tree – when the past and the present are transfigured in the one true moment of poetry which achieves what all poetry aspires to, a timelessness which history cannot tolerate, but which changes history. In that moment of irony, the *aptum* is, for once, not a matter for rhetorical criticism to discuss, but remains beyond rhetoric in recognition and contemplation. In any other poet or text, it would be the moment of death in a supreme isolation and solipsism.

> Do nothing from selfishness or conceit, but in humility count others better than yourselves. Let each of you look not only to his own interests, but also to the interests of others. Have this mind among yourselves, which is yours in Christ Jesus, who, though he was in the form of God, did not count equality with God a thing to be grasped, but emptied himself, taking the form of a servant, being born in the likeness of men. And being found in human form he humbled himself and became obedient unto death, even death on a cross.
>
> (Phil. ii 3–8)

IV

I suggest that this latter reading of the radical Christian rhetoric of the Gospel of Mark requires us to recognize an early Christian community which was formed upon dynamics which are the same as those described by St Paul in I Corinthians xii in terms of the *body of Christ*. The community required its written gospel, perhaps in the first instance to compensate for the absence of St Peter (if Eusebius is to be believed), but more fundamentally because it required a text whose rhetoric would define it under the particular persuasion of an authority, recognized and exercised rhetorically.

The metaphor used by Paul of, in Günther Bornkamm's terms, 'a unified yet many-membered organism in which each member has its function and the whole could not remain alive without each' (Bornkamm 1969: 194), was a common one in the ancient world, and bears a remarkable similarity to our image of a community as 'group-in-formation'. As each individual in his or her uniqueness becomes a context for the necessary reflection upon the common project, so the group is not bound by the threat of alienation, but by a vital adhesion to a common task of mutual regard which both defines and ensures the well-being of the whole. For, 'if one member suffers, all suffer together; if one member is honoured, all rejoice together' (I Cor. xii 26).

Furthermore, such a community can only continue to exist under the central, formative drive of an ironic affirmation, which is also a denial, and can only be sustained in terms of a unique fulcrum of power with which each individual identifies, and yet which stands entirely isolated, a means of corporate identity; a crisis of authority which is also a promise of freedom. David Klemm describes the figure of this ironic affirmation:

> the figure of Jesus presents not only the meaning of authentic human being in faith but also the being of God. How so? The symbol not only presents me with the 'I' of faith as my own otherness but also discloses what it means for God to be God – namely, not to be aloof, impersonal deity but to be approaching each I with its own otherness (Scharlemann 1981: 134–41). Jesus, symbol of authentic faith, is symbol of God only through the cross of Christ – through Jesus' own denial that Jesus is God (see also Tillich 1953–64: II, 150–3). The symbol of God denies

that it literally is God and thus affirms itself as *symbol* of God. . . .
Jesus denies that he is God and yet performs the being of God.
(Klemm 1987: 464)

In the rhetoric of irony the dead-letter of literalism[6] is enlivened by
the literary which affirms an authentic faith. Power is asserted as
freedom only in bondage, and the premature celebration of the
messianic presence is in fact demonic, requiring – like the demons
in the Gospel of Mark who readily recognize Jesus – a peremptory
command to silence. Or, more dramatically in the Gospel, Peter's
too ready rebuke of Jesus' prediction of the sufferings of the Son of
Man (Mark viii 31–3) is immediately recognized as a Satanic
failure to understand the ambiguity of the presence of power in the
world of human affairs; that it requires a revolutionary subversion
involving a denial and a 'verbal' affirmation, not of God, but of
what it means for God to be God. The stable irony draws the
necessary gap between the symbol of God and God, for it is the
power of the symbol (the broken figure hailed, ironically, as King
of the Jews) to confirm the essential truth which can never literally
be seen – and if it were it would not be true. Drawn by its pathos,
which Peter wanted to deny, we come to affirm, in Booth's words,
'the immense sureties of interpretation that can be given an ironic
passage by a fully developed literary context like that provided by
Mark' (1974: 92).

It is precisely this affirming, hermeneutic dialectic, perceived
most radically in the Gospel of Mark, which allows us to perceive
at work in the Pauline community a 'transfiguration of politics'
(Lehmann 1975), which is brought about by a Christian rhetoric, a
rhetoric transformed by a radical shift of power and therefore in
the fundamental terms of argumentation. In this spirit we might
reconsider Romans xiii 1–10 as an exercise of power and a refusal
of power. The passage begins, 'Let every person be subject to the
governing authorities' (xiii 1). Quite literally, it seems, the Gospel
appears to demand of Christians complete submission to secular
authority as a matter of conscience. On the face of it the
community is denied the radical newness of life transfigured by
obedience to the crucified and risen Lord.

But, by now, we should be suspicious of the word 'literal'. As
Anders Nygren in his *Commentary on Romans* has reminded us, Paul
was anxious lest Christians become blindly enthusiastic about their

new freedom promised in the 'new aeon' so that they come to regard the order of life in the 'old aeon', which is still with us, with anarchic indifference. Bishop Nygren comments:

> Here Paul takes a most emphatic position against the fanatical view which makes the gospel into a law for society. . . . The two aeons do interpenetrate, but that does not mean that they may be arbitrarily confused.
>
> (Nygren 1949: 426)

The key word, it seems to me, is '*opheilete*' in verse eight (see also Lehmann 1975: 35–9), balanced between verse five ('one must be subject') and verse eight ('except to love one another'). The Greek verb has a double sense – 'owe' meaning 'being in debt', or 'owe' meaning 'being obligated'. In this double meaning as it is exercised in this passage can be recognized a Pauline rhetoric of irony, a reflective inbreaking into the community's self-perception whereby its reconstitution (the synecdochic moment) into a church of obedience is radically disturbed in the duality of *opheilete*. This new definition becomes, through its rhetoric and persuasive nature, both an exercise of power and a refusal of power in its reorganization of the crucial hermeneutic issue of the relationship between speaker, speech-content and audience.

Applied to the state *opheilete* is used in the first sense of 'being in debt'. Applied to the neighbour (*allēlous*) it is used in the second sense of 'being obligated'. The Christian should not be indebted to the state, but is obligated to the neighbour, to unrestricted love. Once this radical moment is acknowledged, one is caught in the powerful drive, fuelled by the linguistic tension between a negative, indifferent obedience and a responsible, energetic 'freedom in the spirit of which Christ's authority under God is already a foretaste' (Lehmann 1975: 38). The Church is continually stirred into radical reflection by that which, standing outside, necessitates and engenders its rhetoric, its entextualizing.

V

One of the most stimulating, perceptive, and provoking studies of the Gospel of Mark in recent years is Dan Via's *The Ethics of Mark's Gospel – In the Middle of Time* (1985). I refer to it finally because

Professor Via is a New Testament critic who is deeply appreciative of the ways of literature and sensitive to the proper and necessary integration of the manifold concerns of interpretation, in this instance literary criticism, biblical studies and constructive theological ethics. But I refer to it also because it seems to me that in his conclusion Via collapses the rhetorical dimension of this Gospel in favour of a critical systematic attempt to rationalize and conclude. He refers to William Wrede's long-established presentation of Jesus as both the revealed and the concealed Messiah.

> What Wrede calls contradiction I would call paradox: a logical tension that is yet believed to be necessary to account for reality as experienced. The phenomenon under discussion expresses itself in Mark as two related paradoxes. Revelation when given is still concealed: the disciple stands both before and after resurrection. When revelation does occur, human beings resist the existential entailments of what they know intellectually. These two paradoxes are intertwined in Mark: the full existential appropriation of what is known intellectually is prevented by the incompleteness of the revelation.
>
> The revealed/concealed motif is illuminated by our immediate text (Mark x 32–52) and has a bearing on the problem of Mark's use of the narrative form. That Jesus is revealed is seen in the facts that James and John know that he will enter into glory and Bartimaeus senses in him a wonder-working power which he then demonstrates. His true glory is concealed, however, in that it lies within and on the other side of suffering and death (x 33–4). The concealment is manifested in that James and John do not understand what Jesus' particular kind of glory entails for them (x 42–4), as is seen in their inappropriate request (x 36–7). Yet the disciples can at least understand intellectually what Jesus says about his coming fate, and they must have had some inkling of its implications for them. Otherwise why would they be afraid (x 32)?
>
> (Via 1985: 172–3)

This attempt to understand revelation as revealed/concealed, even within Via's discussion of its narrative mode, seems to me to be ultimately misconceived. For if approaching the New Testament through the terms and tropes of classical rhetoric is, as Professor

Kennedy claims (1984: 10), justified both historically and philosophically, then my enquiry in this paper has, I hope, indicated the
radical development of such rhetoric in the self-defining documents
of the early Christian church. Via's 'paradox' must be further
extrapolated from the single moment of a riddling motif to the
drama of a dialectical encounter enacted only in the pattern of a
revolutionary rhetoric. Here Kennedy is quite wrong when he
argues that 'Matthew and Paul make extensive us of the *forms* of
logical argument, but the *validity* of their arguments is entirely
dependent on their assumptions, which cannot be logically and
objectively proved' (1984: 17–18). Rather, the validity of the
arguments of Matthew, Paul, and above all Mark, is dependent
upon a literary necessity which denies the assumption that
validation is granted to textual authority by the presence/absence,
revelation/concealment of God, in its affirmation of the symbol of
God – a synecdoche comprehended and made powerful by irony.

On the one hand this may be a path to the sad, disappointed
agnosticism which awaits the brilliant insights of Frank Kermode
in *The Genesis of Secrecy*, and 'hot for secrets, our only conversation
may be with guardians who know less and see less than we can;
and our sole hope and pleasure is in the perception of a momentary
radiance, before the door of disappointment is finally shut on us'
(Kermode 1979: 145). Or, on the other, can a second *näiveté*[7]
rescue religious experience and the experience of the Church in
formation through an indirect, reflective, reflexive, creative adoption
of a rhetorical consciousness which is deeply aware that in text we
acknowledge our metaphorical perspectives, our fictions and our
interpretations. To conclude with the nicely-turned exhortation of
Wilhelm Wuellner:

since we are surrounded by a cloud of witnesses of rhetoricians,
linguistic analysts, structuralists, and others, let us lay aside
every weight imposed by priorities of traditional historical and
literary criticism, and by logical and dogmatic preoccupations
which cling so closely, and let us run with perseverance the race
that is set before us, looking to Paul [and the Gospel of Mark],
the pioneers and perfecters of the spirit of faith – the rhetoric of
faith argumentation [and radical Christian rhetoric].

(1976: 351)

NOTES

1 See also James Muilenburg 1969: 5. In this article, Muilenburg proposes a 'rhetorical criticism' as the next stage in consolidating the advantages and overcoming the deficiencies of form criticism.

2 See Bloom 1973: 36ff. on the Sphinx and the Covering Cherub.

3 See Pease 1987: 101. Pease in his essay is writing of a critical community of scholars. I am suggesting that the development of the early church, or churches, as communities wrought upon textual definition (in the necessary creation of the Gospels, Acts, the Epistles, Revelation), should be perceived in terms of a basically similar model.

4 We are properly reminded by Wayne Booth (1974: ix) that if, before the eighteenth century, irony was one rhetorical device among many, by the end of the Romantic period it had become something more like the grand Hegelian concept which, it might be said, underlies my present discussion. That may be so. But the Gospel of Mark remains one of the great ironic visions in literature.

5 Booth (1974: 28) points out that further elaboration of the episode in the Mystery Cycles weakens the irony yet more.

6 See S.T. Coleridge, *The Statesman's Manual* (1816; in Coleridge 1972: 30): 'A hunger-bitten and idea-less philosophy naturally produces a starveling and comfortless religion. It is among the miseries of the present age that it recognises no medium between *Literal* and *Metaphorical*. Faith is either to be buried in the dead letter, or its name and honours usurped by a counterfeit product of the mechanical understanding.'

7 The phrase, of course, is Paul Ricoeur's in *The Symbolism of Evil* (1969).

Chapter Eight

THE FOURTH GOSPEL'S ART OF RATIONAL PERSUASION

MARTIN WARNER

I

Now Jesus did many other signs in the presence of the disciples, which are not written in this book; but these are written that you may believe that Jesus is the Christ, the Son of God, and that believing you may have life in his name.

(John xx 30–1)

This sentence is normally held to conclude the main body of the Fourth Gospel, the twenty-first chapter that follows appearing to have the status and form of an epilogue. The presuppositions upon which this judgement rests must be discussed in due course, but for the moment let us consider what these verses tell us if taken at face value as the Gospel's closing statement.

First, they indicate that the work's main purpose is persuasive; thus if we follow the classic Aristotelian definition of 'rhetoric' in terms of the available means of persuasion (*Rhetoric* 1355b) we may say that the complex art it undoubtedly displays may properly be considered in the first instance in terms of rhetorical artifice – an art of persuasion.

Second, the first object of persuasion is 'that you may believe that Jesus is the Christ'. The oddity of this to a first-century Jew is masked to us by familiarity; given contemporary expectations of the Christ as inaugurating the messianic age, his arrival would be evident to all, and the application of the title to one who had been found guilty on a capital charge by the supreme Jewish court would have seemed extraordinary; the problem is adumbrated as

153

early as the Prologue: 'He came to his own home and his own people received him not' (i 11).

Third, the statement points us beyond the written text to the 'signs' which Jesus did 'in the presence of the disciples'; a selection has been made for persuasive purposes from a multitude of such signs, whose reality does not depend upon the written record – and the dual status of these non-textual items, their status as 'signs' and their being witnessed by the disciples, is presented to the reader (or of course hearer) as significant.

But, fourth, it is notoriously difficult to determine the status of the intended reader, for there is insufficient evidence to enable us to adjudicate conclusively between the variant readings here of an aorist and a present subjunctive of the verb for belief, between 'that you may come to believe' and 'that you may continue to believe', and hence between construing the declared rhetorical strategy as directed primarily to those who do not yet believe or to those who already believe. However, this ambiguity needs to be finessed a little for the evangelist elsewhere uses the aorist rather than present for the corroboration of faith (cf. Brown 1966: 2, 1057), a linguistic feature of the Gospel which is of a piece with its insistence on distinguishing between the levels of faith that may be evoked by signs.

At one level there are those who merely see the signs as warranting belief in Jesus' divine power, a level which is 'placed' early on in the Gospel: 'Many believed in his name when they saw his signs which he did; but Jesus did not trust himself to them' (ii 23–4). At another level there are those who see the true significance of the signs, which for the evangelist may be summarized in the term 'glory'. Where this latter type of belief may lead is gradually clarified until the closing sequence leads to Thomas' declaration 'My Lord and my God!' (xx 28).

This casts light on the final clause of the sentence: 'that believing you may have life in his name'. Not all who 'believe' in his name have 'life' in his name, but there is an internal relation between a certain sort of belief and a certain form of 'life'. The belief which the Gospel's art of persuasion is designed to evoke may have its propositional, intellectual, element but it appears to have a dimension beyond that.

Whether or not the Gospel is intended for those who as yet have no belief at all, it is certainly intended to help transform any reader or hearer who does not yet partake in the Father's 'glory' which the signs manifested, with the aim that such transformation may lead the unbelieving 'world' to at least minimal belief at which point, presumably, the way is open for the Gospel's dynamics of transformation to operate *ad infinitum*; in this sense, at least, the Gospel is essentially open ended.

But although open ended it has a discrete and strictly finite base: the signs that Jesus performed 'in the presence of the disciples'; this basis was announced at the start with the words 'we have beheld his glory' (i 14) and that this 'presence' and 'beholding' are not to be taken in senses which exclude the literal seems to be insisted on at the climactic moment of Jesus' glorification – his death (with its accompanying sign of water and blood): 'He who saw it has borne witness – his testimony is true, and he knows that he tells the truth – that you also may believe' (xix 35); this insistence is spelt out in the opening words of the first Johannine Epistle:

> That which was from the beginning, which we have heard, which we have seen with our eyes, which we have looked upon and touched with our hands, concerning the word of life . . . that which we have seen and heard we proclaim also to you, so that you may have fellowship with us; and our fellowship is with the Father and with his son Jesus Christ.
>
> (I John i 1–3)

II

It may be thought that with the invocation of the first Epistle the pressure of critical presuppositions lying behind my account has become intolerable, so at least a sketch should be given of them. Rhetorical criticism operates in the first instance on the received versions of the final redaction(s) of a text, and only seeks to break it up into the ur-versions generated by biblical form criticism where the final text needs such adjustments to render it coherent. To use fashionable jargon, the synchronic approach here takes priority over the diachronic. Whether or not sections of the Prologue originally formed part of an independent hymn, one is no more debarred from considering it in its present role than the widespread supposition that Romans i 2–4 forms a fragment of an early Christian creed has ever been thought to disable analysis of its role in Paul's own epistolary strategy. As Kennedy puts it,

> rhetorical criticism takes the text as we have it, whether the work of a single author or the product of editing, and looks at it from the point of view of the author's or editor's intent, the unified results, and how it would be perceived by an audience of near contemporaries.
>
> (1984: 4)

In theory one might expect considerable overlap with redaction criticism, which is concerned with the intent of the redactors, or editors, of a work, but in practice redaction criticism normally takes its start from form criticism and looks to the *Sitz im Leben* in which the fragments supposedly revealed by the latter were welded together to explain the nature and purpose of that welding; as Robinson remarks, 'one gets the impression that . . . the history behind the material is simply being reduced to the history of the community that shaped it' (1985: 251–2). Thus we are pointed to the need of the Johannine community 'to distinguish itself over against the sect of John the Baptist and even more passionately over against a rather strong Jewish community' (Meeks 1986: 145; see also Brown 1979) to explain the roles of the Baptist and the 'Jews' in the final redaction, a concern which can take the place of exploring their significance in the terms presented by the text itself.

Nevertheless, the contrast should not be over-drawn; no responsible rhetorical criticism can altogether dispense with issues of redaction, for the very notions of 'text' and 'coherence' which I have used are notoriously problematic. So far as the text is concerned, lower and higher criticism combine to show beyond all reasonable doubt that the narrative of the woman taken in adultery is no part of the Johannine account. The case of the final chapter (xxi) is more problematic; there is no external evidence of the Gospel circulating without it, and despite some differences there are strong linguistic and stylistic similarities with the rest of the work, but chapter xx appears to constitute an impressive conclusion to the Gospel and xxi reads like an addendum; if it is such, rhetorical considerations themselves impel one to ask about the *Sitz im Leben* of the addition.

For the purposes of this paper I shall treat the Fourth Gospel as an integral whole, save that I shall assume that the narrative of the woman taken in adultery is an interpolation and that chapter xxi is an addendum or epilogue added either by the evangelist himself or by a member of the Johannine circle who was powerfully influenced by the evangelist's thought and style. Since the first Johannine Epistle similarly bears a close resemblance to the body of the Gospel in doctrine, style and vocabulary, I shall assume that in this case also we have a document written either by the evangelist in different circumstances or by another member of the same tight circle, and which is therefore a relevant guide to the Gospel itself. By the 'evangelist' I mean whoever was the main shaping force behind the Fourth Gospel as we now have it, recognizing that the latter shows traces of some subsequent redaction.

From one point of view these critical considerations may be taken as 'presuppositions' or 'assumptions', but their logical status is more problematic than these terms may suggest. The attempt to insulate rhetorical criticism entirely from the more familiar forms of higher criticism is bound to fail, but this does not force the former simply to take as its assumptions the findings of the latter; rather, the different forms of higher criticism are in dialectical relationship. This may sound innocuous enough until one reflects that if this is so it becomes possible for rhetorical criticism to mount its own critique of the findings and perhaps even assumptions employed in form and redaction criticism. What Kennedy (1984: 3) irenically presents as merely 'an additional tool of interpretation to complement' the standard approaches may turn out to be radically disruptive; this paper may be read as a modest essay in such subversion.

III

The Fourth Gospel has an immensely complex texture and any brief account must inevitably fail to do it justice, but for present purposes it may be helpful to consider it cumulatively at four discrete levels: that of narrative, that of judgement, that of sign and that of transformation.

The first level of attention has received a bad press, from St Augustine's preference for typology in this Johannine *Tractatus* and even his commentaries *ad litteram* to the current Pelican commentary on the Fourth Gospel with its endorsement of Hoskyns and Davey's contention that

> the true understanding of the history of Jesus . . . cuts right across the chronological understanding of history. For this reason, in the interests of that history which has been seen to bear witness to God, it has to be detached from its chronological context and narrated non-historically since only so can justice be done to its theological significance. Even the chronological movement of Jesus from His Baptism to the Cross, which in itself, as a chronological movement, is theologically significant . . . has to be rid of any semblance of evolution.
>
> (Marsh 1968: 54; Hoskyns 1947: 126)

The underlying assumption appears to be that theological significance and chronological understanding are antipathetic to each other, but this raises both philosophical and theological problems.

From a philosophical point of view it needs to be pointed out that narration of itself involves significant succession ('he remembered his parachute and jumped out' is significantly different from 'he jumped out and remembered his parachute') and hence the diachronic reading of a narrative cannot be reduced without remainder into an achronic reading. Indeed, the function of narrative appears to be precisely 'to extract a configuration from a succession' (Ricoeur 1981: 278) – to bring together the sort of pattern or configuration in which we can find significance with the simple occurrence of events. History, myth and fable all in this way participate in the fundamental character of narration, thus when Bultmann (1925) insisted that in Johannine studies we should be less concerned to explicate concepts than to perceive the function of myth, that religious myths are not to be reduced to theological categories, he was (*inter alia*) taking account of the essentially chronological element in narration which classical logic firmly excludes (though the development of tensed logics may have a role to play here).

Of course one may take the Platonic route of insisting that only the eternal is of ultimate significance and the temporal order is mere appearance; the narrative level is only for those who cannot achieve wisdom or *gnosis*. It was in this spirit that Nietzsche

ironically characterized Christianity as 'Platonism for "the people" '.
(1966: Preface, 3) But this raises theological problems for, as
Hoskyns and Davey concede, the Fourth Gospel presents history as
being capable of bearing 'witness to God' and a 'chronological
movement' can be 'theologically significant'; since the whole New
Testament revolves round certain events seen as salvific it could
hardly be otherwise, and it is the general perception of Christianity
as being grounded in narrative that gives point to Nietzsche's
epigram. The affirmation of the Prologue that 'the Word became
flesh and dwelt among us, . . . we have beheld his glory', taken
together with the sequential account of that 'dwelling' and
'beholding', indicates that the sequential mode of narration is for
the evangelist indeed appropriate to 'the true understanding of the
history of Jesus'. No doubt, Hoskyns, Davey and the Pelican
commentary do not really wish to deny this; the history has still to
be 'narrated', but it must be narrated 'non-historically', and
although they insist that the narration 'has to be detached from its
chronological context' they avoid the self-contradiction of requiring
non-chronological narration. Quite what is being claimed once
these qualifiers are given their full weight is far from clear, but the
passage at least gives rise to the suspicion that their obscure claim
that 'a true understanding of the history of Jesus . . . cuts right
across the chronological understanding of history' is being used
equivocally; on the one hand to suggest in good Platonic manner
that human experience should not ultimately be understood in
chronological terms, and hence that such mundane issues as
chronological accuracy in narration are irrelevant, but on the other
to indicate merely that conclusion when the Platonic support
becomes theologically embarrassing.

However this may be, if one refuses to allow oneself to be
distracted from the text by a Platonizing theology one finds not
merely a strong line of narration in the Fourth Gospel, but one that
reveals significant development (whether or not this counts as
'evolution'), not only in the deepening belief of the disciples but
even in Jesus' own understanding of his role. A full analysis of this
process has been given by Robinson (1985), so a brief sketch will
suffice.

Jesus first appears accepting baptism at the hands of John the
Baptist, a Qumranic figure who identifies himself with the 'one
sent before' of Malachi and Jesus with the 'Son of God'. Malach

speaks of the 'terrible day' when 'the Lord whom you seek will suddenly come to his temple . . . but who can stand when he appears?' and accordingly, after his ministry has been precipitated by his mother, Jesus' first planned action is the cleansing of the Temple. At the start of his ministry it appears that he saw his role in the judgemental and national terms set by Malachi and the Baptist, apparently accepting Nathaniel's apposition: 'Son of God', 'King of Israel' (i 49). However Jesus breaks with the Baptist when he finds himself being compared with him, moving through Samaria where his outreach extends beyond that of the Baptist which was limited 'to Israel', to Galilee where the second sign inaugurates a healing ministry – more concerned to 'give life' (v 21) than to judge – declaring that 'the testimony which I have is greater than that of John' (v 36); the impression given is that of a shift in Jesus' understanding of his ministry from Malachi's 'terrible day' to Isaiah's 'acceptable year'. This is not a simple repudiation of the early picture for, we are told, John 'has borne witness to the truth' (v 33) and through their response to Jesus men do indeed 'come into judgement' (v 24); rather, it represents a deepening of the original understanding.

Nevertheless, the role of Third Isaiah's messianic liberator also proves inadequate, and its dangers become apparent after that foretaste of the Messianic Banquet, the Feeding of the Five Thousand, when the people try to 'take him by force to make him king' (vi 15). The sequel is Jesus' off-putting discourse about his flesh and blood being the heavenly food and drink required for eternal life, and the consequent disillusion of 'many of his disciples' – of those who had merely seen Jesus' signs as warranting belief in his divine power. To Jesus' challenge 'Will you also go away?' Peter speaks for those at a deeper level of faith, 'You have the words of eternal life; and we have believed and come to know that you are the holy one of God' (vi 67–9). The division adumbrated in the Prologue between those who 'received him not' and those who 'received him' sharpens from now onwards. Before the feeding Jesus declared that 'the Son gives life to whom he will' (v 21) but now he speaks of giving life only by giving his own life, and this is a theme that continues to the end of the ministry (cf. x 10–11). This final transition in Jesus' self-understanding moves from Third Isaiah's anointed one to the Suffering Servant of Second Isaiah; that once again it is a matter of deepening rather than simple repudiation is made clear by the fact that the imagery of being 'lifted up' which is soon to be identified with crucifixion is to be found as early as the conversation with Nicodemus, though there the Old Testament reference makes it clear that it is to be understood in terms of healing (iii 14; cf. viii 28, xii 32). There will indeed be liberation, indeed glory, but the way of glory is the way of the Passion (xiii 31), and to many disciples the expression of this new insight is 'a hard saying' (vi 60) – indeed, the theme of Judas' betrayal is here broached (vi 70–1) as if its underlying cause was his inability to accept Jesus' new understanding of his role.

From now on the die is cast and everything begins to flow inexorably towards Jerusalem and death. Making clear that his time is running out, Jesus makes three attempts on the capital, but his healing and associated preaching incur the hostility of the religious leaders who see him as a national danger, and after the raising of Lazarus he is a proscribed man. During that final tense interim Greek proselytes ask to see him and Jesus takes this as an indication that 'the hour has come for the Son of man to be glorified', as if the purpose of this final visit to Jerusalem was to enable the light of the world to be revealed to the Gentiles, and his final public teaching uses language which expresses his sacrificial understanding of his role in terms of the universal imagery of death and renewal in nature, evocative of the Mysteries: 'unless a grain of wheat falls into the earth, and dies, it remains alone; but if it dies it bears much fruit' (xii 20–4). Thereafter, he performs the acted parable of footwashing to bring home to the disciples the new understanding of 'lordship' as service, and completes their instruction – with his command 'to love one another as I have loved you', his promise of the Paraclete, and his concluding prayer to the Father with its concern both for the disciples and 'for those who are to believe in me through their word' (xvii 20). Through the treachery of Judas, Jesus is then arrested, interrogated and crucified as 'King of the Jews'.

The narrative then breaks off until early on the first day of the week when Jesus' body has disappeared, though the grave-cloths remain virtually undisturbed; the beloved disciple interprets what he sees correctly and 'believes', though without a full grasp of all its implications (xx 8–9), and after his departure Jesus himself appears to Mary Magdalene. That evening he appears to the disciples gathered behind locked doors, shows them his hands and side, and declares 'As the Father has sent me, even so send I you' (xx 21). In the light of the narrative so far this might seem a daunting commission, but he who had promised the Paraclete and whom the Baptist had at the outset proclaimed as 'the Lamb of God, who takes away the sin of the world' (i 29) now breathes on his disciples with the words: 'Receive the Holy Spirit. If you forgive the sins of any, they are forgiven; if you retain the sins of any, they are retained' (xx 22–3). Thomas was not with the other disciples at the time and is sceptical of their report, but eight days later he is with them when Jesus again appears and offers physical proof of his presence; Thomas responds with 'My Lord and my God!' Jesus comments 'Blessed are those who have not seen and yet believe', and the evangelist concludes by pointing this remark at the reader, 'these are written that you may believe that Jesus is the Christ, the Son of God, and that believing you may have life in his name' (xx 31).

IV

If this account of the narrative level of the Fourth Gospel is even approximately correct it places the readings of a number of influential scholars in a very odd light. Accounts of the Johannine Christ as a 'God striding over the earth', not genuinely human but a 'stranger from heaven' with 'ichor' rather than blood in his veins, radiating an aura of divinity the evangelist terms 'glory' (Käsemann (1969); de Jonge (1977); see the discussions in Bornkamm (1986) and Ashton (1986: 8–9)) owe more to theological and scholarly preconceptions than a careful reading of the text. Instead we have what would have seemed to a classical rhetorician to be sophisticated uses of *ēthos* and *pathos*. The Gospel develops the appeal of Jesus' character through a narrative which approximates to the mythopoeic shape of a quest; commissioning, progressive deepening in the understanding of the task required, followed by action, betrayal, death and – through death – ultimate victory; as we move through the successive layers of comprehension of what it is to be 'King of Israel' we learn to trust Jesus' integrity and authority and that of the evangelist as witness to it, and when the action proper starts the contrast of the healing and self-sacrificial love of the protagonist with the narrow sympathies and *realpolitik* of those who condemn him reinforce the credibility, the *ēthos*, of Jesus, as the affirmation of eye-witness status does of the evangelist. But such a tale clearly also arouses emotional reactions, *pathos*, for such opposition, rejection and betrayal can arouse sympathy and a willingness to attempt to understand. But in classical rhetoric there is a third essential element, that of *logos*, the rational argument found within the discourse, and at the narrative level we have been considering there is little room for this. If the Fourth Gospel is to be considered as attempting a *rational* art of persuasion, we need to look further, from the level of narrative to that of judgement.

Despite all that *ēthos* and *pathos* can do, the evangelist is faced with the fact that the one whom he wishes to commend as the Christ not only failed to fit the expected categories and in any obvious way alter the course of history, but was actually found guilty on a capital charge by the supreme Jewish court entrusted with upholding the revealed law of God; unless it can be shown that the charge was unjustified the whole persuasive strategy collapses, at least for a devout Jewish reader, and at the level of *logos* this is what the evangelist sets out to do. The narrative itself is designed to disarm the first difficulty by showing Jesus himself opening his ministry in terms of the standard expectations as enunciated by the Baptist yet moving beyond them, but the latter difficulty raises legal issues which the evangelist is concerned to meet on a legal level. Harvey's pioneering work has analysed the Gospel from this perspective and for present purposes it is sufficient to summarize his findings.

In brief, Harvey analyses the Gospel 'as a presentation of the claims of Jesus in the form of an extended "trial"' (1976: 17), paying attention to witnesses, procedure, charges, defence and verdict. As witnesses the evangelist first calls John the Baptist, who was 'sent from God . . . for testimony, to bear witness to the light' (i 6), and identifies the source of his evidence as 'he who sent me' (i 33). Next he calls the disciples who 'beheld his glory' (i 14) and subsequently became the founders of the Church but 'they had no pretensions to learning or influence. However impressive they might be to the . . . reader, they could hardly be introduced as a factor in any actual confrontation between Jesus and the Jews'. Once the action shifted to Jerusalem the case 'rested on the word of one witness only: Jesus himself' (Harvey 1976: 45) In such cases Jewish procedure allowed the claimant both to bear witness to himself, when his general credibility could determine the issue, and to 'call God to witness'; Jesus is represented as doing both, and the fact that the overall credibility of a self-testifying witness could have legal standing enables the evangelist to bring considerations of *ēthos* to bear at the judgemental level of *logos*. However, Jesus is represented as invoking the latter procedure in a highly provocative manner; accused of sabbath breaking he defended himself by claiming a special relationship between himself and God, and this was either true or blasphemous.

The main charges of Jesus' accusers, then, are sabbath-breaking and blasphemy, but the latter charge swallows up the former when Jesus invokes God's special authorization to override the sabbath regulations in specific circumstances, a prophetic authority 'which rendered the entire Pharisaic tradition obsolete' (Harvey 1976: 85); such a claim should either be acknowledged and the claimant obeyed, or rejected as false and the blasphemer punished. Typically Jesus is identified as a prophet in response to one of his actions (iv 19; vi 14; ix 17), and it is these that impress the Pharisee Nicodemus – 'no one can do these signs that you do, unless God is with him' (iii 2; see also vii 31); but for the evangelist Jesus' authority is more than just prophetic, he is God's agent in all respects – hence the title 'Son of God' (Harvey 1976: 89–90), 'the Son can do nothing of his own accord, but only what he sees the Father doing' (v 19) – and if God is responsible Jesus cannot be properly charged for his actions. As witness to himself for such a claim Jesus' status is, for the participants in the story, equivocal; to the Pharisees he is a law-breaker and hence unreliable, but to the man born blind his healing capacity is a sign that he is a god-fearer and therefore worthy of belief. What is required is secondary evidence, like the sign Tobias asked of his father to prove he was an accredited agent in a strange country (Tobit v 2; cf. Harvey 1976: 95–6); and this is indeed demanded 'What sign have you to show us for doing this?' (ii 18). Thus the 'signs' in the Gospel are typically presented as the occasions for belief or unbelief, and at the climactic one – the raising of Lazarus – Jesus expressly prays aloud 'on account of the people standing by, that they may believe that thou didst send me' (xi 42). Two other forms of admissible evidence also appear in the Gospel, corroborative support from scripture (cf. v 39, 46) and a divine voice (xii 28); but neither are presented as of themselves probative, for it is acknowledged that both types of evidence could be and were read in more than one way, and the main weight of the defence has to lie on Jesus' *ēthos* supported by his 'signs', hence the appeal to them in the Gospel's concluding words.

But the Gospel itself is a form of witness, and the status of the testimony of Jesus' disciples which had no standing at the time of the original confrontation becomes a central topic of the final instructions Jesus gave them after the last supper. As Jesus was the Father's agent so the disciples are appointed as Jesus' agents (xvii 18; xx 21), and like him they will perform signs, 'the works that I do' (xiv 12) (what the evangelist sees as signs Jesus calls 'works'), but in all this they will be supported by the Paraclete, the Holy Spirit, who will act as advocate and defender in 'that eternal "trial" in which, first Jesus, and then his followers, are inevitably involved before the judgement of the world' (Harvey 1976: 115), defending, accusing, guiding, teaching, inspiring and foretelling. The reader is thus drawn into this trial, and on similar terms to those who encountered Jesus; even supported by the Paraclete, the disciples may not be believed any more than Jesus was, but one who turns away brings judgement on himself.

> God may appoint and authorize witnesses to the truth, but their evidence may not be accepted. In the last analysis it is still the reader or the hearer who has to make up his mind whether Jesus is the Messiah, the Son of God.
>
> (Harvey 1976: 121)

V

In its persuasive strategy, therefore, the Fourth Gospel invokes witnesses to support Jesus' claim who were not present or did not carry weight during the crucial debates at Jerusalem, and re-presents the arguments of the parties in such a way as to bring out aspects that were lost on the original judges, but at the heart of this 'retrial' lie the *ēthos* of Jesus (together with that of the evangelist as witness guided by the Paraclete) and the testimony of the 'signs' which Jesus did. These latter are indeed integrated both with each other and into the ongoing narrative, but before we can consider how this is done we must consider more particularly what the signs signify; here the standard rhetorical categories fail us, for what is required is not so much analysis in terms of rhetoric as of poetics.

There is no space here to do the issue justice but it can hardly be ignored, since it has been regarded as one of the great riddles of Johannine scholarship for over sixty years. Bultmann's statement of the problem is still the *locus classicus*; for him the *Grundkonzeption* of the Gospel is to be found

> in the constantly repeated proposition that Jesus is the emmissary of God (eg. xvii 3, 23, 25), who through his words and deeds brings revelation. He performs the works given him by the Father, he speaks what he has heard from the Father or what he has seen in his presence. The man who believes is saved; he who does not is lost. But there lies the riddle. What precisely does the Jesus of John's Gospel reveal? One thing only, though put in different ways: that he has been sent as Revealer.
>
> (Bultmann (1925); trans. Ashton 1986: 7)

The clue to the solution, of course, is given in Bultmann's very formulation – that the revelation is 'put in different ways'; the assumption that one can neatly separate form from content appears to be perennially attractive to theologians (we noticed earlier Hoskyns and Davey insisting on the separation of narrative form from theological content), but the characteristically parabolic and imagistic form of Jesus' teaching strongly suggests that such an assumption with respect to his language is at least no less crass than it is in literary criticism. As Meeks has remarked, 'it is symptomatic of the impasse in NT hermeneutics that we have as yet no adequate monograph on the Johannine symbolism as such' (Meeks 1986:143).

But before we consider the symbols or images we should consider the signs. Here much work *has* been done and C.H.Dodd's classic account of the first half of the Gospel as 'The Book of Signs', in which he links sign with interpretive discourse, has done much to illuminate the first half of the Gospel; his conclusion that these first twelve chapters constitute 'a great argument, in which any substantial alteration of the existing order and sequence would disturb the strong and subtle unity which it presents' (389) is widely shared, though in the thirty-five years since he wrote a number of adjustments to his account have been suggested; his proposal to describe the second half as 'The Book of the Passion' is more problematic, and Brown's suggestion (1966) of 'The Book of Glory' is greatly to be preferred – using a Johannine term and integrating the Resurrection narratives into the whole.

The starting point must be that the evangelist begins by counting the miraculous signs, and narrates seven in some detail: changing water into wine (ii 1–11), healing the official's son (iv 46–54), healing the paralytic (v 1–15), Feeding the Five Thousand (vi 4–14), walking upon the sea (vi 16–21), healing the man born blind (ix) and the raising of Lazarus from the dead (xi). It is not wholly clear how far the sevenfold pattern is important to the evangelist, and the uneven distribution of these signs raises problems if we try to treat them as structural, but taken together they seem to provide a suggestive pattern, as Temple (1945: 33) has pointed out, through the different ways in which they exemplify Jesus' role; the initial transformation signifies the radical nature of the new beginning brought about by the Word becoming flesh, and the first healing is made possible simply because the official trusts Jesus and begs help for his son – these signs present, as it were, the nature and condition of entry into the new era; the remaining signs exemplify Jesus as restorer, nourisher, guide, light and finally, with the raising of Lazarus, life. Dodd uses the hints provided by the signs with their associated discourses to organize the first twelve chapters into another sevenfold pattern, more evenly distributed and with life as the key theme: the new beginning, the life-giving Word, bread of life, light and life: manifestation and rejection, judgement by the light, the victory of life over death, and finally life through death: the meaning of the Cross. This is not the place to examine these analyses in detail, but the above sketch serves to show that the signs and themes of the first part of the Gospel have a suggestiveness which Bultmann's formulation tends to mask.

However there is, notoriously, another apparently sevenfold pattern, the *egō eimi* or 'I am' passages where Jesus uses the predicate nominative formulation to speak figuratively about himself as 'the bread of life' (or 'living bread'; vi 35, 51), 'the light of the world' (viii 12; ix 5), 'the door of the sheep' (x 7), 'the good shepherd' (x 11, 14), 'the resurrection and the life' (xi 25), 'the way, and the truth, and the life' (xiv 6), and 'the true vine' (xv 1, 5). Each of these images is many-sided and it is probably appropriate to look for a strict progression through them, especially as they are not marked out by the evangelist as a seven-fold

167

fold sequence; rather, it is more appropriate to see them as flowing into and complementing each other according to imagistic rather than conceptual rules. The most closely related may be used to illustrate the general point; in chapter x we have first the image of the shepherd entering by the door, then Jesus' identification of himself as the door by means of which the sheep go in and out, and finally his self-identification with that true shepherd who used the door and calls his sheep to him. This parallels the later teaching after the last supper when Peter asks Jesus where he is going and offers to follow even to death; Jesus declares that he goes 'to prepare a place for' his disciples and Thomas asks how they can 'know the way', which evokes another of the *egō eimi* sayings, 'I am the way, and the truth, and the life' (xiii 33–xiv 6); ' "following Jesus" does not mean . . . merely imitating him or accepting a similar fate: it is to go *by means of him*' (Meeks 1986: 158).

This shifting of the terms of discourse is characteristic of Jesus' language as recorded by the evangelist. After the five thousand are fed the people seek Jesus, find him in Capernaum and ask 'When did you come here?' – he replies 'You seek me, not because you saw signs, but because you ate your fill of the loaves' (vi 25); similarly, when the Jews ask 'Where is your Father?' he responds with 'You know neither me nor my Father; if you knew me, you would know my Father also' (viii 19); again, when Peter asks 'Lord, do you wash my feet?' Jesus replies 'What I am doing you do not know now, but afterward you will understand' (xiii 6–7); finally, when Pilate asks 'Are you the King of the Jews?' the reply comes, 'Do you say this of your own accord, or did others say it to you about me?' (xviii 33–4). Nuttall's commentary on this latter specimen of discontinuous dialogue is worth quoting:

> When Jesus is asked if he is the king of the Jews, he answers neither yes or no but instead asks a question of his own. When he is asked what he has done, he answers not that question but the earlier one with the mysterious 'My kingdom is not of this world'. Even so, he skips one logical stage; to make the logic fully explicit he would presumably have had to say something like 'I am a king, yes, but not of the Jews or of anything earthly'. The logical ellipse seems to trouble Pilate and he asks, seeking confirmation, 'Art thou a king, then?' and hears in answer the words 'Thou sayest that I am'.
>
> (Nuttall 1980: 129)

Of the passages instanced Nuttall comments that they represent not only a strategy for 'seizing of the initiative' but also 'a technique of deliberate transcendence'.

> Jesus' (non-) answer implies that their assumptions in asking the question were all wrong, that they were thinking on the wrong plane. Yet, note, he could have told them this and yet preserved the form of a direct answer. . . . But of course such an answer would not have quickened the minds of his listeners anything like as effectively as the answer he chose.
>
> (Nuttall 1980: 131–2)

It is this process of imaginative demand that appears to be operative not merely in Jesus' dialogues, but in the images he uses, and the signs he performs; it is little wonder that the Bultmannite quest to pin down 'What precisely does the Jesus of John's Gospel reveal?' proves so elusive. However, at the close of Jesus' instruction to his disciples, immediately before the final prayer, he provides a comment on the whole procedure:

> I have said this to you in figures; the hour is coming when I shall no longer speak to you in figures but tell you plainly of the Father. . . . I am leaving the world and going to the Father.
>
> (xvi 25–8)

This should be taken together with the almost immediately preceding 'when the Spirit of truth comes, he will guide you into all the truth; . . . he will take what is mine and declare it to you' (xvi 13–15). Since 'He who has seen me has seen the Father' (xiv 9), the implication appears to be that his disciples will ultimately be so transformed through the power of the Spirit that they will grasp what he has been revealing to them without the need for the language of imaginative demand, its figures and signs. For the readers signs are still necessary, thus the evangelist records a selected few so that they may similarly be transformed, guided into all truth, and 'believing you may have life in his name' (xx 31). As Meeks remarks:

> the signs in John place their observers in a situation where more

and more is demanded of them until they are forced to accept or to reject an unlimited claim.

(Meeks 1986: 153)

But the promise of the Gospel is that for those who accept it and 'believe', a transformation is possible – a grafting into the true vine which is at once the way, the truth and the life. This claim represents the final level at which the Gospel should be considered.

VI

What I have called the level of transformation bears striking similarities to that soul-raising, elevating or 'anagogical' sense of Scripture familiar to the medieval exegetes but long since neglected; when one reflects that in their Schools this type of reading was to be prepared for via the literal, moral and typical senses while I am treating the transformative level as the conclusion of the series narrative, judgement and sign, the analogies are more than striking. This is the reverse of an embarrassment; the Scholastic schematizations were grounded in the Patristic exegetes and it has often been noted that commentators like Origen thought in ways similar to those of the Fourth Evangelist (e.g. Lampe 1969: 176); it is not unreasonable to find the accounts of the Gospel by the intellectual progeny of Origen considerably more 'sympathetic and valuable' than many of those by the followers of Bultmann.

However Bultmann himself is another matter for, although the existential apparatus in terms of which he attempted to account for the transformative effects of Scripture is seriously flawed, he saw the need for such an attempt. And despite the barbarous Heideggerian terminology he pointed with some precision to the heart of the transformative process in the Fourth Gospel:

Being-in-the-world (or 'of' the world) is thought of as a quality of human existence. To be man is *to be world*. This 'being-of-the-world' is 'being from below', 'being in sin' (viii 21–24), because it is being without God. The apparent freedom of the world is only the abandonment of the world to itself and is therefore bondage to sin (viii 31–34). Of course, this quality of being world only acquires the character of *sin* through the fact of revelation. 'If I had not come and spoken to them, they would have no sin' (xv 22–24; cf ix 39–41). *The real sin is unbelief* (xvi 7f.). . . . [Sin is] to hold fast to being-world when confronted by the revelation which puts in question the world in its 'being as world'. . . . Through the *event of revelation*, therefore, *two possibilities* become actual for the world.

1. To be world in the new sense of *remaining* world. To press down the seal on fallenness; deliberately to appropriate it, to cling firmly to one's self.

2. Not to be world, not to be 'of the world'; and thereby in a new sense to be 'out of' the world – really outside it, no longer to belong to it (xv 19, xvii, 6, 16).

(Bultmann 1969: 169–70)

The resort to Heideggerian categories reflects Bultmann's belief that the ancient ones can no longer speak to modern man; nevertheless, it may legitimately be wondered whether the invocation of somewhat dated and radically 'deconstructible' German metaphysics represents a significant advance in either accessibility or credibility. However this may be, I suggest that the Fourth Gospel's categories are drawn from the Wisdom literature and that it is to these rather than to more recent analyses that we should first look.

The Wisdom perspective is present from the start when 'the Word became flesh, and tabernacled among us' (i 14, RV margin), thereby evoking the Wisdom of *Ecclesiasticus* (xxiv 3–8, AV) which 'came out of the mouth of the most High' and for which 'he that made me caused my tabernacle to rest . . . in Israel'. The Johannine *Logos* appears to have roots both in the Wisdom or Word of the Lord of the Old Testament and in Greek philosophy – a synthesis already pioneered by Philo – and the capacity of the term to reach out beyond the Hebrew thought world becomes important when the public ministry of the Word become flesh reaches its climax in the arrival of the Greeks to 'behold' it; nevertheless the Hebrew understanding is always the starting point, as the conclusion of the Gospel makes clear in its use of first the Jewish title 'Christ' and only then of the more open 'Son of God' in its specification of the content of the belief to which it witnesses. The presence of Wisdom motifs in the Fourth Gospel is, of course, a commonplace; more specifically, several surface resemblances with the book of Job – a prologue in heaven, the literary form of an extended trial, a theophany at its heart, a final submission to the Divine presence – are obvious enough; but more fundamental than any of these, I suggest, are the dynamics of transformation in Job which provide an important clue – both though similarities and through differences – to those of the Fourth Gospel.

I have provided a detailed analysis elsewhere of the persuasive art of the author of Job, together with its claims to be designated 'rational', and for present purposes I shall make use of those findings. The book represents a clash between two types of Wisdom; on the one hand there is that of the Comforters, which fits the conventional patterns of theological reasoning and which Job himself rejects; on the other is a radically subversive pattern which emerges through the interplay between the development of Job's confrontation of the Comforters, the Lord's confrontation of Job, and the form of Job's submission.

> The work presents a picture of human development in such a way that it is possible for the reader to judge its credibility; this development culminates in an experience of the numinous which integrates its various strands and leads to a conviction of the presence in the midst of innocent suffering of a God before whom it is . . . appropriate to repent rebelliousness. . . . This aspect of the work stands or falls with the psychological credibility of the pattern. If it is credible, then it shows how a man can be brought by experience to such beliefs, and to the extent that Job's experience appears to the reader to resonate with his own it enables him to see how they could resolve his own perplexities. . . . But however much such a faith might resolve one's own perplexities, it cannot be accepted if it is self-contradictory or otherwise refuted. Thus the author both tests it against the wisdom of orthodoxy, showing that in terms of faithfulness to the facts it is a better account, and sets out to guard against the charge of inconsistency.
>
> (Warner 1989: 148)

Analogously, as Bultmann (1969: 168 and 182) points out, in the Fourth Gospel we are presented with the world of sound human wisdom confronted by a liberating form of knowledge of the truth that is only possible 'if you continue in my word' (viii 31–2). The reader is invited to enter into that liberation ('you will know the truth and the truth will make you free') through making his own the transforming experiences of the disciples which are themselves mapped on to the progressively deepening understanding of the protagonist himself, from a comparatively 'external' vision of judgement to a fully internalized perception of the glory of God in and through innocent suffering; 'Now is my soul troubled. And what shall I say, "Father save me from this hour"? No, for this purpose have I come to this hour. Father, glorify thy name' (xii 27–8). This pattern is itself placed, like that of Job, in a wider cosmological setting where the Word of the Prologue is transformed into flesh when 'that which *was* crossed over into *becoming*' (Kermode 1987: 445) in order that those who 'believed in his name' might have 'power to become children of God' (i 12); that is, to become one with that 'Son of God' in whom the final sentence of the Gospel bids us 'believe' so that we 'may have life in his name' (xx 31).

Such a transformation is not to be achieved without cost, and one way of bringing out some of the tensions which provide the dynamic for reconciliation at the psychological level is to look at Johannine writings where they are not so well integrated as in the Gospel itself. The first Johannine Epistle, whose status as a witness to the Gospel I touched on earlier, oscillates somewhat uncomfortably between, on the one hand, 'he who commits sin is of the devil' or 'this is the antichrist, he who denies the Father and the Son' (iii 8; ii 22), and on the other, 'if we confess our sins, he is faithful and just, and will forgive our sins' or 'beloved, let us love one another' (i 9; iv 7). For simplicity let us use terminology associated with the traditional belief that the evangelist is to be identified with John, son of Zebedee, the beloved disciple who took Mary into his own home, and let us also be traditional in supposing the Boanergean tendencies of the *Magnificat* to be by that time purged through suffering; then we may term the first voice the judgemental, son of thunder, Boanerges voice (Mark iii 17), and the second the Virgin Mary voice; much of the Epistle may profitably be read in terms of the dialectic between these two voices. (For an illuminating dramatization of this theme, see Francis Warner 1983: 1, vi.) In the Gospel itself the Baptist provides the Boanergean pole, which is not repressed but rather sublimated into 'For judgement came I into this world, that those who do not see may see, and that those who see may become blind' (ix 39) – 'those who see', of course, being the representatives of ordinary human wisdom. In the final acted parable the footwashing presents disciples and readers with the reversal of ordinary human values that true sight reveals and the final teaching places it as an outworking of the 'new commandment' of the Virgin Mary pole – 'love one another; even as I have loved you' (xiii 34). Despite the teaching, Peter has still to internalize the reversal of values when he cuts off Malchus' ear, 'Put your sword into its sheath; shall I not drink the cup which the Father has given me?'; it is only through the experience of denial, repentance and restoration that, as the Epilogue tells us, he becomes ready to 'Feed my sheep' (xxi 15–19).

Job's response to the voice from the whirlwind is complete submission; Peter has to learn to submit not merely to Divine power but to Divine humility – 'If I do not wash you, you have no part in me' (xiii 8) – and the Gospel itself is concerned to show us that the Divine glory is most fully exemplified in self-sacrifice: 'The hour has come for the Son of man to be glorified. Truly, truly, I say to you, unless a grain of wheat falls into the earth and dies, it remains alone; but if it dies, it bears much fruit' (xii 24). It is a message of universal scope, available to the 'Greeks', but it is learned through suffering ('now is my soul troubled') and overturns ordinary human wisdom. From this perspective, though, one can make sense of the great images – we enter into the form of life in which this is intelligible through the door of the sheep, an experience so profound that it is a form of rebirth or resurrection through one who is himself way, resurrection and life, needing in this unfamilar terrain a good shepherd to guide us by the light of the world into an understanding of the truth which he exemplifies, strengthening us with life-giving bread for the journey whose goal is to become one with the new pattern of life, internalizing it and fully grasped by it, as branches once grafted in may become one with the true vine. Similarly, the signs show the radical nature of the new pattern; the condition of entry to it through concern for others and trusting belief, and its marks of restoration, nourishment, guidance, illumination and new life. At its heart is that paradox of the cross as glory, witnessed to by the risen Christ to whom Thomas responds 'My Lord and my God!' (xx 28); like Job, he worships.

But the differences from the the Old Testament book are as

illuminating as the similarities. For the Wisdom writer the historicity of his account was of no importance – the book's appeal is to a certain pattern of experience which it presents in such a way as imaginatively to evoke and develop it; to the extent that it succeeds it has persuasive power, and that persuasion's title to be called 'rational' turns both on that credibility and on the work's ability to avoid incoherence and falsification by the facts of human experience. The Gospel goes further; its transformation of values is more radical and can therefore only be sustained by that which transcends the facts of human experience and the forms of wisdom to which a Nicodemus can have access:

> No one has ascended into heaven but he who descended from heaven, the Son of man. And as Moses lifted up the serpent in the wilderness, so must the Son of man be lifted up, that whoever believes in him may have eternal life.
>
> (iii 13–15)

The focus, therefore, is on a particular historical moment when 'the Word became flesh and . . . we . . . beheld his glory' (i 14), and it is that same historical individual to whom the Baptist bore witness who declared 'unless you eat the flesh of the Son of man and drink his blood, you have no life in you' (vi 53). Both the particular and the more general claims are remarkable, and we have seen that witnesses and signs were required to reach even the first stage of belief – those very signs on which the evangelist relies at the close to draw the reader into belief and so into 'life in his name'. So concerned is the Gospel with the reliability of that which it tells of Jesus' doings 'in the presence of the disciples' that it explicitly claims eye-witness authority (i 14; xix 35; xxi 24), and there is reason for this concern.

In his discussion of Jesus' oral 'technique of deliberate transcendence' Nuttall argues that 'the gaps in Jesus' dialogue imply a transcending complement, a super-nature'; further, on the Gospel's own terms 'not even an exceptional man like John the Baptist can give true light, only the supernatural can irradiate the natural. But, we are told, this indeed happened and the evangelist can tell us the superhuman words of the superhuman man.' We need, therefore, to know whether these words are Jesus' own or the evangelist's.

If we choose the first interpretation, or indeed a modified version of it whereby the words of Jesus could have been believed by John to have been Jesus' own, our course is easy. . . . But if we choose the second, and suppose that John is in any degree ingeniously constructing this transcending dialogue of Jesus, then at once . . . both his argument and his good faith are in ruins.

(Nuttall 1980: 134–5)

Of course he concedes that the evangelist 'may not have had even the concept of accurate verbatim quotation. At least, it is a pretty safe rule that no Ancient ever quotes another accurately. Plato's quotations from Homer are always perfectly metrical, perfectly Homeric but rarely if ever impeccable' (140), but unless the style of transcendence is Jesus' own and the content and context of the conversations and discourses something more than invention, then the evangelist or his sources are in 'hideous bad faith' (141). However unfashionable it may until recently have been, there is point in Westcott's concern to show that the beloved disciple not only could have been but probably was an eye-witness to Pilate's interrogation of his prisoner (1908: 2, 279) and his wrestlings with the conflicting evidence about such a possibility in the conversation with the woman of Samaria (1908: 1, 147). And such concern with eye-witness credibility is, as we have seen, explicit in the Gospel itself as an integral part of its *ēthos,* with its centrality to Johannine theology witnessed further in the opening of the first Epistle.

At this point, as I warned earlier, rhetorical criticism becomes subversive of much traditional higher criticism, with its tendency to reduce 'the history behind the material . . . to the history of the community that shaped it' (Robinson 1985: 251–2). For Bultmann *'the true way of making present* the historical fact of Jesus is . . . not historical recollection and reconstruction, but the *proclamation'* (1969: 177), yet this is an antithesis unknown to the Gospel with its culminating appeal to the signs which Jesus did 'in the presence of the disciples' as part of its proclamation. Bultmann attempts to cut the level of transformation free from the levels of narrative, judgement and (in some degree) sign, but this is to evacuate the rhetoric of its persuasive power. If the narrative is treated as invention, the witnesses who point to a correct judgement discarded as irrelevant, and the signs regarded as pious fictions, the *ēthos* of the work is totally destroyed and its *logos* gravely weakened; we are left with a legend of considerable *pathos* but little more. The Gospel itself, of course, claims much more; it does not pretend that the signs can compel assent, for many of those who witnessed them themselves failed to 'believe the works' (x 38); the proclamation cannot be empirically verified. But it does not follow that it cannot be falsified, and the whole persuasive strategy of the Gospel depends on its being subject to rational controls at the levels of narrative, judgement and sign.

The language of verification and falsification is indeed misleading here, but not because issues of truth and falsity are irrelevant; rather because the procedures for judging are so complex and subtle. In the modern era Pascal pioneered an account of the way Job-like appeals to authenticity can be integrated with patterns of reasoning we have learnt from the Greeks, in those cases where 'the principles are so intricate and numerous that it is almost impossible not to miss some' (*Pensée* 512, and see Warner 1989: chap. 5); this sort of handling of a cumulative case he termed '*finesse*', as distinct from the deductive geometric pattern which was favoured by Descartes and which lies behind the standard accounts of verification and falsification. More recently Anthony Quinton, in opening Warwick's Centre for Research in Philosophy and Literature, defended 'the notion embodied in Pascal's *esprit de finesse* or Newman's illative sense, the kind of . . . accumulative procedure by which a mass of sensitive responses are precipitated into a philosophical belief' (Quinton 1985: 21). It is in terms such as these that we should consider the credibility of the 'proclamation' of the Fourth Gospel. The belief which the Gospel's art of persuasion is designed to evoke is ultimately transformative, but it is not without its intellectual element; the believer of integrity must be able to grasp why the Sanhedrin's verdict of guilty on the capital charge of blasphemy is to be rejected. It is only by taking as an integrated whole the four levels of narrative, judgement, sign and transformation that we can fully grasp that exemplification of the art of *rational* persuasion which culminates with the words:

> Now Jesus did many other signs in the presence of the disciples, which are not written in this book; but these are written that you may believe that Jesus is the Christ, the Son of God, and that believing you may have life in his name.

Chapter Nine

THE WORLD COULD NOT CONTAIN THE BOOKS

MICHAEL EDWARDS

I

The Fourth Gospel is concerned with many matters that we think of as literary: with beginning and ending, for example, with writing and rewriting, with interpretation, with the relations between narrative and history, story and people, words and the Word. We may find it convenient to believe that this presents the evangelist with problems, in his announcing of religious truth. Perhaps, however, the problems are for us; and he certainly seems to have pushed further in these areas than other writers, even providing a model for what occurs elsewhere, so that we can learn a great deal by following him carefully.

John's Gospel begins, as one knows, in the beginning. So, for that matter, do the others. Matthew opens with a 'book of . . . generation' about Jesus according to the Authorized Version, or a 'table of . . . descent' according to the no-nonsense New English Bible, but what he offers in the Greek is a 'book of genesis'. He repeats exactly the initial words of the second creation story in Genesis ii 4 (and the reprise at v 1) as translated in the Septuagint. Since his Gospel has been placed first, a book of genesis ushers in the New Testament – the narrative of the new creation – as it does the Old. His serial use of the word *egennēsen* ('Abraham *begat* Isaac; and Isaac *begat* Jacob', etc.) also recalls the series of *egeneto* ('and *there was* light', 'and *it was* so') in the first creation story of Genesis i. Mark's first word is *Archē*, as in Genesis, and his opening phrase: 'The beginning of the gospel of Jesus Christ, the Son of God', may be an interpretative expansion of the opening phrase of Genesis: 'In the beginning . . . God'. Even Luke begins with a reference to those who were with Jesus 'from the beginning' (*ap' arches*), though his description of them as 'eyewit-nesses . . . of the word' (*tou logou*) can only resonate when we have read John.

Matthew and Mark may well have already related the *genesis* or the *archē* to Jesus. John does so more famously, and also more comprehensively. His exordium: 'In the beginning was the Word, and the Word was with God', is a more daring intervention than Mark's in the Greek text of Genesis, since it explains God's 'saying' the world ('God said, Let there be light', etc.) in terms of the Word of God and thence of the man Jesus. Yet this is only the start of John's quest for origin. He also returns to the very first act of creation: 'Let there be light', so as to suggest that there too Jesus was present, since 'In him was . . . the light' (i 4). As the Word was within the saying, so the Light was within the light; as its source, perhaps, as the 'true light' (verse 9) of which physical light is a sign. And in a different way he returns, surely, to the Spirit. In Genesis i 2, the *pneuma*, that is, the Spirit, or wind, or breath, of God, moves over the water; in John i 32–3, the *pneuma* descends and remains on Jesus as he is being baptized in water. It even does so 'like a dove', possibly as a reminiscence of the same phrase added to Genesis i 2 in Jewish tradition.

As soon as he commences writing, John reaches for the language of the commencement, for the light of origin, for the Spirit hovering over genesis. He travels to the beginning of the world, to the moment, incidentally, when, by a triumphant grasping of a rule in Greek grammar which requires a neuter plural to govern a singular verb, he can say that the original multiplicity was a unity, that *Panta. . .egeneto*, 'all things was made'. And he also travels to the beginning of the scriptures; as writer, he makes contact with the beginning of 'the writings'. To penetrate to the world and the word of the beginning is a desire which haunts poetry in particular, and which roves through some of our greatest poems, through *Paradise Lost*, *The Prelude*, *The Waste Land*. It is always frustrated, and the vanity of our condition is nowhere more evident than in the distance between John re-writing and creatively interpreting the beginning of the Hebrew Bible and Eliot re-writing the beginning of *The Canterbury Tales*, likewise at the beginning of his own work, only to distort it. Of course, John may not literally return to genesis and deny history, but his confidence to go there in words comes from his realization that he has known the Beginning as a person. He has heard the Word, he has seen the light of origin, he has touched the source of 'all things'; he has received the Spirit. It is not even a question of rediscovering Eden, for in the company of Jesus he has voyaged beyond.

Even he, however, cannot sustain the beginning, any more than could the writer of Genesis, and he too enacts the Fall. In Genesis one is surprised by the speed with which one is hurried from creation and the garden to the act of disobedience: the loss of origin takes just over two chapters. In John's Gospel it takes five verses, for the reference to the primal light in the Word is followed immediately by: 'And the light shineth in darkness; and the darkness comprehended it not' (AV), or 'has never mastered it' (NEB). The darkness into which the Genesis light now shines is evidently, as the succeeding verses show, that of a fallen world, and John returns quite vertiginously to our present experience, to reveal the condition of ignorance and ill will from which we are obliged to consider the flawless beginning. He is also making clear, or rather, he presumably takes it for granted, that his writing, however (as we might say) self-conscious, and powerfully imaginative, is impelled by an urgency which is spiritual. For the conflict between light and darkness is not a poetic vision to be contemplated but an activity in which we are involved. The Gospel will continually refer to it – in Jesus' words, for instance: 'I am come a light into the world, that whosoever believeth on me should not abide in darkness' (xii 46) – as to a matter of choice, of life, and death.

And doesn't he present Jesus as actually offering the beginning, as coming from origin and making origin available here and now? It is not only that everything Jesus says is words from the Word, though that in itself is no small affair. He also brings the light of Genesis, and the Spirit. And one can go further: what he offers – himself – is in excess of the beginning. To know the Word is more than to hear God's words or to live in a world said by him. To see the Light is better than to see light, since a more intense 'light has come into the world' (iii 19) than came originally, so as to illumine the earth. By stressing Jesus' declaration: 'I am the light of the world' (viii 12) on the first word, one marks his relation to the initial light, and one learns how and where to look. Similarly, when Jesus after the resurrection 'breathed on' the disciples (*enephusēsen*) for them to receive the Spirit (xx 22), he was clearly recalling the action of God in Genesis when, having formed the man from the dust of the ground, he 'breathed into' his nostrils (*enephusēsen*) so as to make him a living creature (ii 7); yet to be regenerated is greater than to be generated, and the disciples are given far more than was given to Adam.

At the end of his Gospel, as at the beginning, John sweeps the reader back into Genesis. But the movement is not retrogressive and nostalgic. The act of re-writing is also an act of transformation, which corresponds to the ternary movement of the world: from creation to fall to a more splendid re-creation; from birth to death to a profounder rebirth. I discussed these and other awesome triads of experience in *Towards a Christian Poetics*. In *The Great Code*, Northrop Frye claims that the 'entire Bible, viewed as a "divine comedy", is contained within a U-shaped story. . . one in which man. . .loses the tree and water of life at the beginning of Genesis and gets them back at the end of Revelation' (1982: 169). But it is not merely a question of 'getting back' to where we were, after all that labour and sacrifice. The end is more than the beginning, and after the fall the rise is higher. A graphic representation of it would be not a U but something like this: √. The shape of things, and the shape of literature in both its comic and, I would argue, its tragic dimensions, is a tick; which comes as quite a surprise, but seems strangely, laughingly, appropriate.

John's story is longer than those of the other evangelists, since it begins even earlier than Adam. As a narrative interpretation of history it is, of course, like theirs, exclusive, and one of its curious and defining features is that it makes persons in the real world the effects of narrative, and, specifically, of writing. In the case of Jesus this is to a certain extent obvious and familiar. He realizes the Jesus-types of the Old Testament (Joshua, David, etc.), re-living and climaxing the stories of others, whose lives become thereby part of *his* story. As Messiah, he fulfils the Messianic prophecies. It is worth noticing, nevertheless, that both type and prophecy occur and are accomplished within the Gospel itself. Lazarus is a type of Jesus through being a man who returns from the dead and emerges from a tomb. John seems careful to mention in both cases the cloth (*soudarion*) which binds the head (xi 44 and xx 7). The cynical words of Caiaphas: 'it is expedient for us, that one man should die for the people' (xi 50), are an unwitting prophecy of Jesus' death and of its substitutionary meaning. Remarkably, the raising of

Lazarus and the high priest's prophecy take place within a few verses of each other, as if John, in modelling his narrative, is focusing attention on Jesus' role as the enactment or re-enactment of event and of statement. It is presumably no coincidence that the further focus is on death and resurrection, so that even more essential matters are also in view.

One can also benefit by looking closely, even now, at the continual references to Jesus as a man 'written about' (i 45). And think of the way in which John the Baptist first alludes to him. He does not say, 'He that cometh after me is preferred before me', but 'This is he of whom I spake, He that cometh after me is preferred before me' (i 15). He uses the same formula fifteen verses later: 'This is he of whom I said, After me cometh a man which is preferred before me'. (This occurs on a 'next day' following an unspecified one: the Gospel makes a series of quiet, breath-taking, moves from God in the Beginning to the successiveness of our quotidian reality.) No prophecy is involved; it seems that the evangelist wishes to establish from the start, and quite ordinarily, that Jesus is preceded by words, and that when he appears he does so as a kind of incarnation of them.

I used the metaphor because it came to mind, but it is, of course, apt, since, according to John, Jesus *is* the Word, and the Word became flesh. This gives a quite other volume to the idea that words precede persons. For after all, John the Baptist too is, as it were, an effect of words. The first thing that anyone says to him in the gospel is, 'Who are you?' (i 19), and having replied, to this most radical of questions, that he is not the Christ, nor Elijah, nor 'the prophet', he answers finally: 'I am the voice of one crying in the wilderness'. He is a quotation (from Isaiah), the actualization of a text; he is what has been written of him. He has been made, like 'all things', through the Word of God, but also in response to the human and, John would say, inspired words of an Old Testament writer.

He is also someone who occurs in a story. I have suggested, again in *Towards a Christian Poetics*, that to figure in a story is a fundamental desire: to see one's life, that is, as teleologically shaped, by another hand, so that its beginning, middle and end form into significance; and that many narratives present even their characters as being aware of the desire. I cited, among others, Malory's *Tale of the Sankgreal*, where the knights, in seeking 'adventures', are looking to be gathered into a story-world, and Sartre's *La Nausée*, where Roquentin attempts to become 'the hero of a novel' in despair of a world 'unnecessary' and godless. John the Baptist is just such a hero, and knows it. His meaning derives from words given to others many generations before; his story, that of 'the precursor', pre-exists him. The evangelist clearly assumes that, at least in the case of certain elect individuals, who would also include Peter and himself, person derives from story as being follows from words. (One is reminded of Aristotle's assertion in chapter 6 of the *Poetics* about the precedence of plot over character.) John the Baptist is narrated by God, spoken by the Word.

Before thinking further about this preposterous notion (I use the word etymologically), one should consider that events too, no less than persons, are produced by writings and by words. Familiarity as well as scepticism make it difficult for us to be amazed at the assertion that, for example, hostility to Jesus comes about so that 'the word [the *logos*] might be fulfilled that is written' in the law (xv 25). The New English Bible here is rather loosened from the original Greek, but it does make the point with some vigour: 'this text. . .had to come true'. Whatever we think of it, a doctrine of prophecy involves words preceding events, and one remembers that for John, after all, the Word precedes everything. As God speaks things into being, so events occur, after a lapse of time, to fulfil their words. All the New Testament writers hold the doctrine, but John is the one who, through his vision of the pre-existing, creative Word, accounts for it most profoundly.

Perhaps this is why he so diversifies the play between word and event. He is very far from limiting himself to the classic case, where an event in Jesus' life is said to correspond to a text in the Old Testament. For instance, the text may be quoted before the event is recounted, as when Jesus recites a passage from Psalm xli as referring to his betrayal (xiii 18) in advance of Judas betraying him (chapter xviii). Or the disciples fail to recognize the word in the event at the time, and only do so some while afterwards, as when Jesus rides into Jerusalem on an ass's colt 'as it is written' in Zechariah (xii 14–16). Above all, Jesus' own words are also shown to be fulfilled. He claims that if the Temple were destroyed he could raise it again in three days; after the Resurrection the disciples realize that he was speaking of his body. They 'remembered that he had said this unto them; and they believed. . .the word [the *logos*] which Jesus had said' (ii 19–22). His words take on the status of a kind of spoken Scripture. They are even fulfilled within the Gospel itself, from one chapter to the next. In chapter xvii he prays: 'those that thou gavest me I have kept, and none of them is lost' (verse 12); in chapter xviii, when he himself is arrested but the disciples are allowed to go free, this is said to take place so that 'the saying [the *logos*] might be fulfilled, which he spake, Of them which thou gavest me I have lost none' (verse 9).

John is clearly organizing history into a constraining literary form, whose inordinate ambition is to relate heaven to earth, then to now, generation to generation, lives to lives, things said on one day to things done on another. He saturates his text with teleology and significance. He is also one of four writers doing this, each of them apparently summoning history to arrange itself according to a slightly different perspective. A natural response would be to conclude that they are groping around, or blithely ignoring, a non-verbal event, namely, the life of Jesus, and glossing it with their own private and extrinsic interpretations. Our job would be to struggle through the fables to the facts. However, the demonstration of the facts by the use of evidence according to proper method could never rise to the quite different level of the meaning of the facts. Empirical history can tell us what *happened*, but it cannot tell us, in this case at least, *what* happened. A more contemporary response would be that any event is already textual, always-already interpreted, so that the notion of a plain event unadorned with language and ideology is a mirage: beyond our hermeneutic scrutiny, literally nothing happened. The life of Jesus could only exist, or only be observed, in the glosses of the evangelists, and any meaning attaching to it would be that which their writing creates and bounds.

One might also take them at their word (though there is no argument that could persuade one to do so), in which case it becomes clear that they have already mastered the second view, and that the implication of history and story is not a discovery of modern narratology and historiography but a biblical commonplace. What distinguishes their doctrine, and makes it unacceptable to anything short of faith, is the assumption that history, or at least salvation-history, is already elaborated as narrative, by a more than human story-teller who writes events as humans write tales. John is neither failing to report 'what actually happened' out of a preference for the telling of pious lies; nor is he unconcerned with the correspondence between what he says and events outside what he says. He sees events as being in intricate relation with other events and with words, through typology and prophecy, and he structures his work so as to show the relations which he wishes to emphasize. We have no cause to be wary of his 'art', since his art is surely to perceive the relations and to declare them, much as John the Baptist, when saying of Jesus: 'Behold the Lamb of God' (i 29, 36), is perceiving him as the antitype of the Old Testament sacrificial lamb. As John the Baptist has the assurance to by-pass a merely empirical report (say, 'Behold Jesus of Nazareth'), so John the evangelist can show relations to previous scenes and statements from the conviction that the relations actually exist.

The narrative plan, John might say, is God's, since God has plotted our salvation in a story-shaped history and history-shaped stories. And one sees that this sophisticated notion, in a work which constitutes a model for the closest relation of narrative to event, is actually quite familiar, and that the activity it describes goes by the name of providence. What gives John's Gospel an extra hermeneutic depth, however, is precisely the fact that his theme is the Word. Jesus is the focus of a story which had been, in part, already told, in the Old Testament, and which is being continued as John writes it; but he occupies that position as the Word itself, as the source of the world and of language, as the creative centre from which both events and words derive, and in which they meet.

In certain other stories whose theme is partly story: the *Commedia*, *The Canterbury Tales*, *A la recherche du temps perdu*, the author's disclosure of himself is carefully placed and highly charged. As the author of a book about the fundamental story of history, John identifies himself not by name but, appropriately and movingly, as 'the disciple whom Jesus loved'.

II

The beginning of John's gospel is an explication of the opening of Genesis, and also much more. The ending too is full of writerly interest. There seem, in fact, to be no less than three endings.

Chapter xx closes with a reference to itself ('this book') and to what might have been written, and with an exhortation to the reader:

> And many other signs truly did Jesus in the presence of his disciples, which are not written in this book:
> But these (*tauta*) are written, that ye might believe that Jesus is the Christ, the Son of God; and that believing ye might have life through his name.

Chapter xxi reads like an afterthought, or an addition by someone else. It begins by attaching itself to the conclusion: 'After these things. . .' (*tauta*); recounts further actions of Jesus following the resurrection; and ends with a hint about hermeneutics, to which I shall return. Two final verses are appended, possibly by a third writer. It is as if the gospel does not need to finish – finishing is no problem – hence the exhilaration of the very last verse:

> And there are also many other things which Jesus did, the which, if they should be written every one, I suppose that even the world itself could not contain the books that should be written.

The writer, whoever he is, re-writes the ending of chapter xx in a visionary leap which is so much more than the 'hyperbole' of the commentators. The Gospel, like the Synoptics, is already a crowded compendium of tales, which are encompassed, not in an epic, or a decameron, but in a short story of about forty pages. The tale of Nicodemus in chapter iii, so full of theological teaching and also of human and narrative suggestion, takes up at most some four hundred words. Biblical narrators in general are, of course, masters of brevity. The ending then opens to the possibility of a quasi-infinity of books. Isn't this the New Testament's reply to a passage in the Old equally concerned with writing? Ecclesiastes, the work known for its refrain: 'Vanity of vanities, all is vanity', concludes with a statement which is similarly hard-eyed: 'of making many books there is no end; and much study is a weariness of the flesh' (xii 12). There is a writer's sadness here, before the plethora of writings, the redundance of the world – an unlimited anxiety of influence – to which writers like Montaigne and Eliot seem to have responded and which they knew in their own work. As against this seeming curse of endlessness, the conclusion of John's Gospel imagines, on the contrary, the blessing of an endless number of books, all derived from a single life. The perspective is no longer that of the fallen world but of the world redeemed. The writer's good fortune is in his subject: at the origin of the world and of words is the Word himself, and the potential infinity of books is a function of the infinite Word. Here is Erasmus' *copia* with a vengeance.

If the *Essays* or *The Waste Land* are the epitome of the sorrow of the text, John's Gospel is the epitome of the joy of the text. One contemplates it with longing. It is also, moreover, both finished and not finished, it closes without imposing closure, and this combination of completion and inexhaustibility, of fulfilment and possibility, is aesthetically, one may think, highly desirable. It also corresponds to the work of Jesus, which the Gospel describes as likewise complete and yet incomplete. Many similar statements culminate in the famous cry from the cross: 'It is finished' (xix 30); yet the final verses concern unfinished business (the destinies, as we shall see, of Peter and of John himself), and the whole Gospel, like the others, is presented as the culmination but also as the beginning of a story which is still in process, and whose further writing is to take place partly in the lives of its readers. The ending directs attention, first, to books, and thereby, as in Dante, or Malory, or Proust, to the book we have been reading, though not as an art-work but as a 'writing' to be believed and acted on. It equally directs attention to the world, which is shown as unable to contain the stories of Jesus, rather as it could not contain Jesus himself. The creation, in both cases, is too small for the Word, and the world as a living space is called into question. Once again, the reference is by no means exclusively literary.

Nevertheless, as an act of 'witness' the Gospel is overtly an act of writing. It starts with a quotation, and its first words are a re-working of the first words of the Bible. It begins with the beginning, and it ends with an allusion to endlessness. It opens with the Word and closes with books. (In the Vulgate, *libros* is the final word.) And doesn't John's confidence as a writer, by which I mean, in this connection, his willingness to bring his writing activity to the fore, derive precisely from the fact that the Word itself is his theme? In the Christian perspective, all writing, and indeed all life, are related to the Word, and John is the writer who declares the fact and who, if one may put it this way, takes most advantage of it, and inspires his continuator or continuators to do likewise.

His text, moreover, is itself self-reflexive. I realize the danger of regarding John through our own half-lights, of grappling him to what interests us. We cannot know exactly how he conceived of himself as a writer, and it may just be that the writer most celebrated for having composed his words in the dimension of the Word was less self-aware than, say, Joyce, burlesquing the Word in *Ulysses*. That he saw no link between the *logos* and his own *logoi* is, however, hard to credit, and one can at least speculate that in writing 'In the beginning was the word' at the beginning of his own words, and without any distinguishing capital for 'word', he is thinking of his own beginning, reflecting on the primacy of the word in all that he is about to write, and sharing the excitement of going back to origin and finding there, at the source of all things, and 'with God', the medium of his own craft.

John's Gospel is the ultimate of all literary works, where language aspires beyond itself. And even apart from that speculative psychology, the very text of the Gospel reflects word against word. For one of its most evident yet still elusive features is the fact that Jesus himself is self-reflexive: the Word speaking words. In John's Greek version of his sayings, he sometimes speaks *rhēmata*, but the Logos also tells the disciples that the *logos* which they hear comes from the Father (xiv 24), that they are clean by virtue of the *logos* which he has spoken to them (xv 3), that they must remember the *logos* which he has said (xv 20). The Logos claims himself to keep the *logos* of the Father (viii 55), and he brings the relation of word and Word to perfection in actually declaring to the Father, in the course of his prayer in chapter xvii: 'thy *logos* is truth' (verse 17).

The word of God is ultimately the Word of God, and God's words are spoken by God's Word. His word is truth, and his Word is the way, the truth, and the life (xiv 6). John's words too are written in that light, as he involves himself in the rather formidable business of putting words together. He also involves the reader, by making the vision marvellous but also uncomfortable, and by forcing one to realize just what is involved. For as we encounter the Word, we are also faced, continually, with Jesus' fierce and old-fashioned views about the scriptures. He even asks at one point: 'If ye believe not [Moses'] writings, how shall ye believe my words?' (v 47). This is constraining enough already, without the further thought that to be able to believe his words we also have to believe John's writings. Perhaps John has invented all this, and supplied Jesus with words that Jesus never spoke. And yet: is Jesus divine, or isn't he? Is he the Word, or not? So much follows from an affirmative reply, and the worldly-wise evasion of 'neither/nor' looks less manageable than it is usually taken to be.

Jesus, moreover, really does do things with words. Words for John, a Hebrew, are more than means of communication, or instruments of self-expression. They are active, they are presences; they can 'clean' (xv 3), they can 'remain' in a person (v 38), they can be 'kept' (e.g. xiv 24). They belong to the same world as his 'truth', which, far from being a Western abstraction, is something one 'does', and has for its opposite not only falsehood but the practice of 'evil' (iii 20–1). Jesus' words have the power of the Word: he commands Lazarus to come out of the tomb (xi 43) much as God creates light by saying it into existence. In the course of the first story told of him, the calling of the disciples, he changes Simon's name, less dramatically, to Peter, the Rock (i 43). This suggests yet another re-writing of the opening of Genesis, since Adam's first action is to name the animals (ii 19), while the first action of the new Adam is to re-name a man: the Word is thereby associated with both the divine and the unfallen human language. It also suggests that at the heart of the Word there is a delight in wordplay. And it leads to the second story, the marriage at Cana, where Jesus changes water into wine, not by pronouncing a magic formula but by telling the servants, prosaically, to fill the jars and draw the liquid (ii 7–8). John's Gospel, like the Synoptics, presents Jesus as someone who changes the world (turning blind men into seeing men, for instance), and whose power of change is endless, a doorway to possibility (the multiplying of the loaves and fishes). By placing the transformation of the water soon after the transformation of a name, John is perhaps intimating the role of language itself in the Re-creation.

The words of Jesus are all referable to the Word: they brim with authority but also with mystery. Hence, no doubt, the number of times that John shows people puzzling over his words, and repeating them. Here, for example:

189

Then said Jesus unto them, Yet a little while I am with you, and
then I go unto him that sent me.

Ye shall seek me, and shall not find me: and where I am,
thither ye cannot come.

Then said the Jews among themselves, Whither will he go,
that we shall not find him? will he go unto the dispersed among
the Gentiles, and teach the Gentiles?

What manner of saying [of *logos*] is this that he said, Ye shall
seek me, and shall not find me: and where I am, thither ye
cannot come?

(vii 33–6)

Jesus reiterates his words in the next chapter, to the same response
(viii 21-2), and then both reiterates and transforms them much
later for the benefit of the disciples. They too respond by quoting
him:

Then said some of his disciples among themselves, What is this
that he saith unto us, A little while and ye shall not see me: and
again a little while and ye shall see me: and, Because I go to the
Father?

They said therefore, What is this that he saith, A little while?
we cannot tell what he saith.

(xvi 17–18)

In *The Art of Biblical Narrative* Robert Alter has remarked that the
narrators of the Old Testament tend to avoid indirect speech,
preferring to give the actual words spoken (1981: 67). This
highlighting of *logos* finds its explanation in the nature of God and
in the nature of Adam, and its greatest moment in these 'obstinate
questionings', these repetitive broodings over the words of the
Word.

The final brooding is by John himself, and it occurs at the end.
Peter asks Jesus what will happen to 'the disciple whom Jesus
loved' and is told: 'If I will that he tarry till I come, what is that to
thee?' (xxi 20-2). On the basis of this reply (this *logos*), says the
evangelist, the rumour spread that the disciple would not die; 'yet',
he continues, 'Jesus said not unto him, He shall not die; but, If I
will that he tarry till I come, what is that to thee?' In repeating
Jesus' exact words, he is not issuing a scholarly caveat, I take it,

190

in the manner of a modern historian. He is perfecting the shape of a narrative, where, since the Word is beginning and end, *logos* is present in the first verse and the last. He is directing attention to words at the close of a book about the Word, and drawing us into an awareness of their reverberation. And he is bringing to a head the series of allusions throughout the gospel to words being fulfilled in ways which had not been expected. His point, surely, is that a saying is not understood, and perhaps cannot be, until it is fulfilled. Indeed, he reinforces the thought by reporting another saying of Jesus in the immediately preceding verses. Peter had already been told his own future, in phrases which could not have been entirely perspicuous at the time: 'When thou wast young, thou girdedst thyself, and walkedst whither thou wouldest: but when thou shalt be old, thou shalt stretch forth thy hands, and another shall gird thee, and carry thee whither thou wouldest not' (xxi 18). The saying can then be interpreted: 'This spake he, signifying by what death he should glorify God', because in this case the prophecy has already been realized and its significance revealed. The implications are clear: by the juxtaposition, John hints that our interpretations of unfulfilled prophecy are subject to error – he provides an example of probable error – and that in the meantime, in a world made by the Word, we have words, and that we should adhere to them.

There is another detail here for the narrative pattern. John ends his Gospel with the statement of a hermeneutic principle concerning unfulfilled words, having begun it by offering the interpretation of words which had been fulfilled, by taking the references in Genesis i to speech, to light and to spirit, and applying them to Jesus. He begins with a retrospective truth and, after a final instance of this in the death of Peter, he ends with a prospective truth, which issues the reader out of the book and into the world. It is a world poised, like the conclusion of the Gospel, between the Resurrection and the final End: the world, indeed, of the meantime.

It is in this world that we confront the hermeneutic problem, as I discussed it in relation to narrative. In a fallen world meaning cannot be taken for granted; we look for a truth that is self-evident, or at least finally clear, but what we see is the filtering of the twilights, the coruscations of Hermes. A youngish man is crucified (if he was), along with hundreds of others, and the New Testament writers try to make something of it. John in particular, in alleging that he was the Word, spins out a discourse of great complexity around a series of utterances purporting to be divine. If the event really does have the significance which the writers assign to it, it cannot be merely an instance of the problem: it displays and centres the problem, and shows why it exists. The crucial meanings will demand something more than openness, determination, honesty, and that something, or so the argument goes, is not exactly in our control, since it is faith, grace. John's is the Gospel, in fact, where Jesus is presented, especially in chapter vi, as having disconcerting views of the matter. His parables also involve his hearers notoriously in not understanding him, in being deliberately excluded from meaning: as in Mark (iv 11–12) and Luke (viii 10), he speaks to the crowd in dark sayings for the express purpose of preventing them from seeing the truth and being converted (xii 39–40). They are not ready for him, or he is not ready for them, and they can only make themselves available to his teaching by a complete change of heart. (It is a pity that Frank Kermode should have assumed, in *The Genesis of Secrecy*, that the exclusion is permanent, as if the blinded cannot be given sight.) As a method of persuasion, this is precisely not what we are expecting.

The first thing Jesus says in the Gospel, and these are the first words of the Word, is, 'What are you looking for?' (i 38). One only has to study the history of Christendom, or one's own history, to know that our replies range across the whole gamut of our own wants. What we are looking for determines what we find. And what we see, or hear, depends on what we are; as Jesus says to Pilate: 'Every one that is of the truth heareth my voice' (xviii 37). He has already said elsewhere that he is himself the truth (xiv 6), and there is terrible comedy when honest Pilate, thinking that it is Jesus who is on trial, responds by asking the fundamental hermeneutic question: 'What is truth?' not realizing that the Truth is staring him in the face.

Secular writers naturally assume that there is a human condition, with its problems, which can then be applied to Christianity. Christian writers, sadly, often seem to make the same assumption, as if God were unaware, absent-minded, not in control. If Christianity is not adventitious, however, and it is, of course, a very large 'if', the problems of the human condition are those which the Bible has diagnosed, and questions of truth and method are already adumbrated in the biblical texts. John's Gospel does not allow the reader to disengage himself, in the way that, say, Northrop Frye does at the end of *The Great Code*, by presenting the Bible as offering imaginative 'vision' (1982: 230) rather than demanding belief. It even defines the belief required. It is a narrative, and it forms part of a library not of philosophical works but of other narratives, and poetry, and drama. It declares that the Son of God is the Word, not Reason, or the vague Ground of our being. It shows that the Father is not a god of propositions, of dogmas to be believed in, but of actions, and of words to be believed.

III

The Gospel of John begins in the beginning and ends with a reference to the end, specifically to Jesus' second coming. It opens with a quotation from the opening of the Old Testament, and closes with a wondering surmise about all the works which its subject could engender. In its relation both to reality and to writing, doesn't it present itself as, quite simply, the book?

Like Montaigne, like Eliot, the evangelist was faced, as he began to conceive his Gospel, with a multiplicity of texts; but far from appalling him, they constituted 'the writings', that is to say, a body of work to which he could give his full allegiance and which was, moreover, unfinished. Along with the other writers of the New Testament, he re-writes the Old and thereby completes it, by reconstructing it in its true meaning around the focal theme of the now manifested Messiah. His Gospel is unique, however, not simply in commencing with a piece of literal re-writing but in its ambition to rework and to accomplish not the core of the Scriptures but their totality. His aplomb, in assuming them from the beginning, in interpreting them whole, comes from the realization that they all lead to one book, which it is his privilege to compose, since he has been given the one subject: Jesus as the Word, which fulfils and absorbs them. His Gospel is at an opposite extreme from *The Waste Land*, and yet comparable in confronting the whole of a literary past, and in being astonishingly different from any other work.

John is at the centre of the activity of re-writing, towards which all literature tends. One might even think that he gathers the other three Gospels already written, though not so as to depreciate or to exhaust them: here above all 'there is no competition'. His Gospel is *the* book for reasons which free it from literary arrogance. It is certainly not the supreme book as perfect artifact to be held against a world contingent and void of meaning, like that which Roquentin projects and Sartre achieves in *La Nausée*. Nor on the other hand is it the comprehensive book as model of an ordered and meaningful world itself understood as the 'Book of Nature', in the manner of Dante's *Commedia*. It is a work of quotation which joins the beginning to the end by recounting the adventures of the Word. When Dante gazes into the light at the close of the *Paradiso* he sees the scattered quires of the universe bound into a single volume; John binds into a single volume the hints and guesses scattered through the Hebrew Scriptures.

Its nearest analogue might be Ovid's *Metamorphoses*. Written in the same century as the Gospel, this too is a binding of the worlds and of time, and of the works of others, into a single work. It too penetrates to origin, and concludes with a prophecy and with a reference to itself. Ovid's concern, however, is to link the beginning of creation to his own life-time, through an unbroken series of tales, while the future envisaged at the close is that of his poem and of his fame. John draws everything into an extraordinarily potent and, in a way, repeatable *now*, in which the beginning and the end are both present at a moment in history, and walking in Palestine. The conclusions of the Gospel concentrate on the actions of Jesus on the earth ('And many other signs truly did Jesus . . .', 'And there are also many other things which Jesus did . . .'), on the mystery of the immediate future (the destiny of John), and on the intention of the Gospel, which is belief in the reader. It seeks to persuade us, but not by inviting us into a dialogue, or presenting itself for analysis: on the contrary, we are what is being analysed. It calls attention to writing but also to the need to respond. It moves without strain from what we should call literature to what we should call religion.

Chapter Ten

'TRUTH' AND 'RHETORIC' IN THE PAULINE EPISTLES

GEORGE KENNEDY

Among the most striking developments in the human sciences in the twentieth century have been changing views of the phenomena of language, widely though not universally agreed as carrying serious implications for our understanding of culture, philosophy, religion, literature, and even science. Simply stated, human society seems to be a network of codes consisting of inter-relating signs, and though there may be some ultimate grounding of reality in God, however defined, or in nature, within the codes themselves there are only signifiers referring to other signifiers in apparently circular patterns, much like words in a dictionary defined by other words in the same dictionary. Languages are arbitrary sets of signs, unable to achieve or preserve identity with referents. Their meaning is not reality, but in some strange way constitutes reality for us. As we try to look at other cultures, such as that of the late Hellenistic period and its cultural sub-set of Jewish and Christian communities, we encounter other codes. Their 'otherness' is cause for reflection; it is unlikely that we can expect to enter fully into understanding of them. At most perhaps we achieve some approximation of the experience, a kind of cultural translation through understanding of rhetoric, but coloured by our own assumptions and languages. This can pose a hermeneutical problem for orthodox Christians who wish to claim that the New Testament, as a text, is in some sense addressed to 'us'.

Human beings long for a grounding, a centre, a referent, or a principle of validation, and they have constructed elaborate systems of theology or metaphysics to that end, but these too are codes, capable perhaps at most of internal consistency: in the case of theology a transcendent, in the case of philosophy a rational

195

logos. Driven by human desires and fears, by a search for meaning in life and above all by the fear of death, religious and philosophical codes generate great energy, like that of a magnetic field or that induced in a closed circuit. This energy, expressed in language, is what has traditionally been described as rhetoric. Recently much effort has been going into trying to describe the rhetoric of religion and of the Christian religion in particular. The results have told us something about how the form of logical argument is adapted to reinforce religious proclamation, how moral force or personal passion can be transmitted through the linear flow of words to an audience, and thus how belief is experienced. In so far as we can approximate to the linguistic expectations of an audience in a given culture, rhetorical analysis can tell us something about how 'identification' – the key feature of rhetoric according to Kenneth Burke (1950) – was achieved and maintained, internally validating the code and creating solidarity within the sect.

Religious systems claim truth, often exclusive truth. They do so primarily by the authority given to the source of their sacred texts and by the authority and discipline of the institutions they build around themselves to preserve the truth as they see it. But they also readily adapt the resources of secular rhetoric, constantly reiterating their claims in differing contexts and seeking to bolster these with what evidence they can find. Probably the most powerful evidence is experience, at one level the personal experience of an individual, that the language of the religious code is consistent with reality as he or she has experienced it or desires to experience it. If it is indeed true that language has constituted reality in the first place, this is a circular process. At the level of the religious community personal experience is replaced by the collective experience of the group and becomes the claim that truth is authenticated by what we call 'history'. Judaism, Christianity, and Islam have greatly exploited this argument in their claims of God's intervention in history. If the claim can be maintained, the reality constituted by the code can be linked to a referent. If such a linkage can be made, seemingly transcending the arbitrary nature of language, exclusive possession of the truth can be asserted. Competing religious systems then can be dealt with in a variety of ways: as earlier, imperfect historical revelations, or as rhetorical codes generated only by human passion and lacking the confirmation of history. Marxism has similarly proceeded by claiming authenticity from history and by rejecting other rhetorics as 'ideologies'. But validation by 'history' takes place within language, is equally a phenomenon of a cultural code, and is thus also circular: the conceptions of historical reality of the Jews, of Paul, and of secular Greco-Roman society in the first century differ significantly, for example in their attitudes toward prophecy, the nature of a messiah, and the supposed interventions of divine beings in human events. They use different languages and imagery and even within a single language words take on different connotations. Yet each sees an external validation of its interpretation in 'fact'. A famous example is provided by Augustine's *City of God*, where pagan rhetoric about the sack of Rome is met with Christian rhetoric about the same event. 'History' becomes rhetoric.

Saint Paul's statements about 'truth' and his attitude to rhetoric can be examined as an example of this phenomenon, of a rhetorical attempt to claim external validation for subjective experience. 'Truth' (*alētheia* and related words) is not a locution Paul frequently employs – it came easier to the author of the Fourth Gospel – but it does appear thirty-odd times in his genuine writings. Though fundamentally experiential, 'truth' in the Pauline Epistles often has some relationship to what within our linguistic code is called 'historicity', not infrequently is in some opposition to the rhetoric of others, and in one context is associated with nature. Neither 'rhetoric' nor 'history' are part of Paul's vocabulary; they are 'our' approximations or translations of things he thought of differently: in the case of rhetoric, as word, power, truth, or conversely slander and lies; in the case of history as creation, law, prophecy, covenant, or a future coming. There were, of course, terms for history and for rhetoric available to him in the larger code of Hellenistic Greek, and his failure to use these terms may be viewed as a feature of his own rhetoric: a way of setting himself and his community off from secular society, much as modern fundamentalists avoid the language of science, sociology, and psychology.

If one reads the Pauline Epistles in their canonical order – something perhaps occasionally worth doing in understanding later reception of the New Testament – one meets reference to truth immediately in the first chapter of Romans. In a highly 'rhetorical' passage, a sustained invective against paganism, we read:

For the wrath of God is revealed from heaven against all ungodliness and wickedness of men who by their wickedness suppress the *truth*. For what can be known about God is plain to them, because God has shown it to them. Ever since the creation of the world his invisible nature, namely his eternal power and deity, has been clearly perceived in the things that have been made. So they are without excuse; for although they knew God they did not honour him as God or give thanks to him, but they became futile in their thinking and their senseless minds were darkened. Claiming to be wise, they became fools, and exchanged the glory of the immortal God for images resembling mortal man or birds or animals or reptiles. Therefore God gave them up in the lusts of their hearts to impurity, to the dishonouring of their bodies among themselves, because they exchanged *the truth* about God for a lie and worshipped and served the creature rather than the Creator, who is blessed forever! Amen.

(Romans i 18–25)

What can be extracted from this passage includes, perhaps, the following. First, there is in the passage an argument from nature. God's nature can be perceived in the things that have been made. This could be viewed as an anticipation of the later theological and philosophical argument for the existence of God on the basis of 'proof from design'. Its rhetorical amplification in the New Testament is chiefly to be found by implication in the parables of Jesus that draw an analogy from nature. Here in Romans it is proclaimed with some vigour, but not supported by argument or example. Indeed, there is perhaps a certain inconsistency in arguing that nature reveals the truth of God and then objecting to those who seek to worship the divine as present in the creatures of nature. This is met only by the assertion that they confuse the (visible) creatures of nature with the (invisible) Creator. The more powerful claim of validation is based on what can be described as an historical process noted by the apostle. That is to say, there is a movement from the creation, through a time when the truth was evident, to a time of futile thinking that led to the darkening of minds, and this in turn to claims of wisdom and to the exchange of the truth for a lie, followed by lust and moral degradation, invoking God's anger. Contemporary pagan society is regarded as demonstrating the truth of this degeneration. This account of history is interpretation, not fact, but has some appeal from its internal consistency and its breadth of view. In the claims of the pagans to be wise is an allusion to Greek philosophy, but also to the poetry and rhetoric associated with it, to the whole cultural code of the gentiles. Deceit, malignity, gossip, and slander are mentioned in verse 29, all pejorative terms for the rhetoric of somebody else. Paul's own rhetoric is implicitly set against this and is the truth validated by nature and history, but that validation exists only within his own ways of viewing events.

In Romans ii 2 we read that the judgement of God 'truly' (*kat' alētheian*) falls upon those who pass judgement on others. This might be paraphrased to say that God's judgement, as shown from historical experience, has fallen upon them and will continue to do so. In Romans ii 8 this is specifically cast as a prophecy for the future: 'for those who are factious and do not obey the truth . . . there will be wrath and fury'. Paul views it as a law of historical necessity. We shall return below to the relationship between 'truth' and prophecy. In ii 20 the 'law' is said to be the embodiment of knowledge and truth. The law is to Paul an historical reality; though it operates through language, its authority to him comes not from its rhetoric but from the source of proclamation and the witness of Old Testament history.

Romans iii 7 is a complex dialectical passage that contains a reference to 'God's truthfulness'. Paul is here seeking to maintain that God's promises have not been historically invalidated by the repeated failure of the Jews to keep the covenant. He can thus be said to attempt to refute possible objections to his understanding of truth. In Romans ix 1 the truth is 'in Christ', but the context again is an historical one where the advent of Christ as an historical reality has, in his own mind, cut Paul off, with sorrow and anguish, from his own historical connection with the Jews. Finally, in Romans xv 8, the old and new historic covenants are brought together: 'For I tell you that Christ became a servant to the circumcised to show God's *truthfulness* in order to confirm the promises given to the patriarchs'. Note again a connection between the truth and prophecy, this time one already confirmed.

Paul's claim in Romans – that the truth is known from past history and will be confirmed by future history – is generally consistent with his usage of *alētheia* in I and II Corinthians, where references to the rhetoric of his opponents, including here some other Christians, reappear as well. Thus in I Corinthians v 8 the unleavened bread of sincerity and truth are identified with the new Christian dispensation in contrast to the malice and evil of the past. In xiii 6, 'love rejoices in the right (*alētheia*)', and the passage continues with reference to past, present, and future. In ii 13, however, Paul imparts his teaching 'in words not taught by human wisdom but taught by the Spirit, interpreting spiritual truths to those who possess the Spirit'. Earlier in the same chapter (I Cor. ii 3–4) he had described his own rhetoric: 'I was with you in weakness and in much fear and trembling; and my speech and my message were not in plausible words of wisdom, but in demonstration of the Spirit and of power'. There is no historical note; the claim to validity resides in the meaning assigned to 'spiritual' (*pneumatika*), which is internal experience given the rhetorical force of faith (*pistis*). (On Christian adaptation of the rhetorical term *pistis* see Kinneavy 1987.)

In II Corinthians iv 2 Paul refuses to engage in rhetorical 'cunning' and will practise 'the open statement of the truth'; he proceeds to note how God has, historically, blinded unbelievers. What applies to history on the grand scale also applies to Paul's own life where 'truthful speech' is one of the items in a varied list of experiences in his career (II Cor. vi 7). 'Everything we said to you was true, so our boasting before Titus has proved true' (II Cor. vii 14): that is to say, its truth has been validated by the course of events. In II Corinthians xi 10 Paul's preaching of the truth of Christ is put in the recent past in Macedonia and in the future in Achaea. In xii 6 Paul's boasting (i.e. his rhetoric) would be speaking the truth, but he is kept from it by the actual (thus historical) experience of the thorn in his flesh. His references to 'boasting' are the regular way he refers to rhetoric, whether his own or others, actual or potential. When we come to the end of II Corinthians (xiii 8), 'we cannot do anything against the truth, but only for the truth', we can understand Paul to be saying that we cannot avoid the actuality of future history; we can only live in accordance with its reality. The validity of Christianity will be historically confirmed, for in Paul's cultural code prophecy has a secure place. It has been vindicated in the past and will be valid in the future.

References in Galatians (ii 5; ii 14; v 7) seem consistent with what has been noted in Romans and Corinthians, but Paul's emphasis on the validation of history differed from time to time in the context of his writing, and it is less evident in letters regarded as early or as late in his career. In I Thessalonians, usually regarded as the earliest of the Pauline epistles, his gospel has come to those God has chosen, 'not only in word, but also in power and in the Holy Spirit and with full conviction' (i 5). It is thus viewed as validated not by history but by an internal experience of faith. In Philippians (i 18), perhaps a late letter, Paul complains of opponents who proclaim Christ out of partisanship, not sincerely, but he claims to rejoice at the proclamation of Christ 'whether in pretence or in truth'. In Colossians (i 3–8), also probably late, the gospel, brought to that congregation by Epaphras, is 'the word of truth. . .as indeed in the whole world it is bearing fruit and growing'. Here it is again not tied to history, but to present reality as 'the grace of God in truth'.

After Paul's death, controversy about truth and rhetoric continued among his followers and their differing stances can be identified in the Pastoral Epistles and the Deutero-Pauline Letters. Frank Witt Hughes explores this debate in *Early Christian Rhetoric and Second Thessalonians* (1989). Validation of truth in history remained an issue. For example, future history is described in II Thessalonians ii 8–12; Satan is revealed as the arch-rhetorician who with his pretended signs and wonders will deceive those who refuse to love the truth, on whom God will then send a strong delusion. Another passage of prophecy implying the rhetoric of evil is found in I Timothy iv 2–4. In II Timothy ii 18 the deluding rhetoric of Hymenaeus and Philetas, seeking to show that the resurrection is already past, is attacked. Women are especially vulnerable to false rhetoric (II Tim. iii 6). In II Timothy iv 1–5, as the climacteric of history approaches, the faithful are urged to 'preach . . . convince, rebuke, and exhort', but the people will 'turn away from listening to the truth and wander into myths'. The author seeks to forestall by rhetoric the sophists of the future, but he is not very optimistic about the results.

If reality is in fact constituted by language, the perception of reality and of history will be differently constituted by people who use different languages, including (*heteroglossia*), different linguistic and social codes within a national language group. There are English-speaking people today for whom reality and history are still essentially constituted by the language of the Bible in some English translation; there are others, especially within the universities, for whom it is constituted by the language of science. Both, however, seek some criterion in historicity: for the former it is 'proof', for the latter usually a refutation of the doctrine of St Paul. A challenge for modern Christianity is to identify what in the 'Great Code' of the Bible (Northrop Frye's term) can be translated into modern codes and how. The code constituting reality for Paul included the phenomenon of inspired prophecy, to him authenticated by his understanding of past history and leading to his conviction that more recent prophecies by Jesus either were already (in the Resurrection) or would inevitably be authenticated in the future. The Resurrection is the one crucial 'fact' on which orthodox Christianity has had to insist to validate its truth, but at the same time an event for which historical evidence, even in the New Testament, not to say contemporary Roman sources, is far from satisfactory. Paradoxically (and paradox is a distinguishing characteristic of Christian rhetoric), this gives the Resurrection rhetorical power, for it can be read as a great metaphor of the mystery at the heart of religion: in Christian 'truth' everything is reversed from the world's standards.

It might be argued that for those who live in the modern scientific *epistēmē* there is also a sense in which the moral teachings of Christianity – brotherhood of man, love of neighbour, gospel of peace – have been validated by history. That is to say, the record of history can be viewed in a different rhetoric as the systematic betrayal of these principles, leading to continued disaster and culminating in such twentieth-century horrors as the First World War, the Great Depression, the Second World War, the Jewish Holocaust, Soviet aggression, international terrorism, and pollution of the environment. And New Testament prediction of deceptive rhetorics has certainly been vindicated. The historical confirmation of religion by God's intervention in history seems improbable and unnecessary within our dominant code. It can perhaps only be envisioned in the future creation of a Christian, neo-Christian, or post-Christian moral society.

EPILOGUE

Chapter Eleven

THE LANGUAGE OF ECSTASY AND THE ECSTASY OF LANGUAGE

CYRIL BARRETT

In this paper I wish to consider the language used by certain religious writers and speakers, such as the prophets, visionaries and mystics, including Jesus but not excluding Hindu, Buddhist, Islamic and other religious sages. The question I want to pose is: are these speakers and writers doing anything more than speaking or writing? In other words, is what they are doing anything more than playing beautifully with words and the images words conjure up? Is their speech and writing anything more than an ecstasy of language rather than a language of ecstasy? Are they not perhaps intoxicated by language, just as poets sometimes are? If not, how can we tell? Even if you say that it is poetic language, is this not an ecstasy of language, sound, if not fury, signifying nothing?

Let us take a few examples from the Bible and from the mystics. From the Song of Solomon:

> Your lips distil nectar, my bride;
>> honey and milk are under your tongue;
>> the scent of your garments is like the scent of Lebanon.
> A locked garden is my sister, my bride,
>> a locked garden, a sealed fountain.
> Your shoots are an orchard of pomegranates
>> with all choicest fruits,
>> henna with nard,
> nard and saffron, calamus and cinnamon,
>> with all trees of frankincense,
> myrrh and aloes,
>> with all chief spices

(iv 11–14)

or Psalm xix 1–4:

> The heavens are telling the glory of God;
>> and the firmament proclaims his handiwork.
> Day to day pours forth speech,
>> and night to night declares knowledge.
> There is no speech, nor are there words;
>> their voice is not heard:
> yet their voice goes out through all the earth,
>> and their words to the end of the world.

From the Revelation to John:

> Then I saw a new heaven and a new earth; for the first heaven and the first earth had passed away, and the sea was no more. And I saw the holy city, new Jerusalem, coming down out of heaven from God, prepared as a bride adorned for her husband; and I heard a great voice from the throne saying, 'Behold the dwelling of God is with men. He will dwell with them, and they shall be his people, and God himself will be with them; he will wipe away every tear from their eyes, and death shall be no more, neither shall there be mourning nor crying nor pain any more, for the former things have passed away.'
>
> (xxi 1–4)

This is all splendid stuff, but what does it mean? As visionary poetry or poetic prose, it is fine – among the finest ever written. But is it anything more than poetry? And as poetry is it anything more than an indulgence of language?

Before addressing myself to these questions I should make clear what I mean by 'ecstasy' and its relationship to poetry and religious language generally. The Greek word *ekstasis* (being put out of place, distraction, astonishment, a trance; see Liddell and Scott 1883), suggests an abnormal mental state. Indeed, it is technically used as a term for pathological states of frenzy and catalepsy. Religious ecstasy sometimes takes these forms. But it is not with this aspect that I am concerned. By religious ecstasy I mean such things as visions, rapture, insight into the mystical or transcendental. What I am particularly concerned with is the expression of these experiences in language. Not all religious language is the language of ecstacy. Nor is it all poetic. Deuteronomy could hardly be described as a great poetic or ecstatic work. Nor can most works of theologians. As for the mystics: John of the Cross was a poet. Others, though not necessarily poets, do seem to indulge in an ecstasy of language. Take Meister Eckhart and John Ruysbroeck. They are not visionaries in the narrow sense of describing visions; nor are they exactly prose poets; but they seem to be indulging in language.

> Thou shalt know him without image, without semblance and without means. − 'But for me to know God thus, with nothing between, I must be all but he, he all but me.' − I say, God must be very I, I very God, so consummately one that this he and this I are one *is*, in this is-ness working one work eternally.
>
> (Eckhart 1924: 247; Sermon XCIX)

> Now this active meeting and this loving embrace are in their ground fruitive and wayless; for the abysmal Waylessness of God is so dark and so unconditioned that it swallows up in itself every Divine way and activity, and all the attributes of the Persons, within the rich compass of the essential Unity; and it brings about a Divine fruition in the abyss of the Ineffable.
>
> (Ruysbroeck 1916: 'The Adornment of the Spiritual Marriage', 177; III, iv 39)

These utterances are, to say the least, odd. Some are simply obscure; some, though comprehensible at verbal level, make little sense; some are contradictory, or, at least, paradoxical. Two possible replies immediately present themselves. One is to say that what prophets and mystics say may be a beautiful use of language, but it is plain nonsense. Another is to say that, though it may appear to be nonsense, in fact it is a failure to express something adequately, but that at some time a more adequate means of expression may be found. I should like to get these suggestions out of the way first of all.

The most eminent proponent of the view that mystical, prophetic, religious utterance is meaningless is Professor Sir Alfred Ayer. In *Language, Truth and Logic* he has the following to say:

> We do not deny *a priori* that the mystic is able to discover truths

by his own special methods. We wait to hear what are the propositions which embody his discoveries, in order to see whether they are verified or confuted by our empirical observations. But the mystic . . . is unable to produce any intelligible propositions at all. . . . The fact that he cannot reveal what he 'knows', or even himself devise an empirical test to validate his 'knowledge', shows that his state of mystical intuition is not a genuinely cognitive state. So that in describing his vision the mystic does not give us any information about the external world; he merely gives us indirect information about the condition of his own mind.

(Ayer 1946: 118–19)

As an account of mystical or visionary experience this passage leaves something to be desired. But it will serve our purposes. I shall take up four points: that visionary and mystical utterances are not propositional; that they are not empirically verifiable; that they are not cognitive; that they are not about the external world but merely give us information about the visionary's condition of mind.

Given Ayer's understanding of what constitutes a proposition, his criterion of truth, and, hence, what constitutes knowledge, what he says is true. Indeed, he says clearly and succinctly, with the exception, possibly, of the second half of the last proposition, what visionary and mystical language is not. It is not propositional in the sense in which Ayer understands that term. As I wish to argue, this is precisely its nature, and anyone who thinks otherwise does not understand visionary and mystical utterance. Although it employs terms used in empirical discourse, its utterances are not empirically verifiable – that is, by perceptual observation. In that sense it is not cognitive, but that this is the only form of cognition is, at best, a presumption.

That visionary utterance does not give us information about the external world, if by that is meant the world of sensory experience, is also true. But then, that is not its purpose. It is not observational, much less scientific, or even historical, though it may sometimes be couched in historical terms. But that it merely gives us indirect information about the visionary's condition of mind seems to beg the question. It assumes that all utterances that are not about the external sensory world must reflect dreams, hallucinations, figments of imagination and suchlike. But that, again, is presumption. It may be true, but closer examination of the matter is called for.

It could be that by 'external world' Ayer meant nothing more than something independent of the condition of a person's mind, of his dreams, imaginings and fantasies. An item in it would not have to be an object in the physical world, verified by direct sensory perception. It might, perhaps, be apprehended by some sort of purely non-sensory or intellectual intuition, somewhat in the way we apprehend propositions of logic and mathematics and the more abstract principles of science. But I am certain that this is not what Ayer meant. He meant literally what he said: the external world of empirically perceptible beings. These are all we can *know*. The rest is fantasy.

This, of course, is sheer prejudice; how does Ayer himself know that there cannot be entities other than those observable by sensory perception? Nor can he verify the *principle* of verification by sensory perception. But this is not the issue. The real problem is how to communicate an experience to someone who has never had that experience. And, even if one can, is it the experience of anything and not just an experience generated by words and the images they evoke?

Here another distinction must be made, that between an experience and that of which it is the experience. We can experience shock, terror, fright, sudden joy and suchlike. These may not be experiences of anything other than the experience itself. We can be shocked at someone's behaviour, terrified of a fire, frightened by the sight of a scorpion, suddenly delighted by the sight of a sunlit spring landscape, and so forth. But we may also have these experiences without there being any apparent object independent of the experience. There may, indeed, be a cause of the experience that is independent of it, and of which we are not immediately aware – the blast of an explosion, an eerie sound, a sudden silence or a happy digestion. In so far as we are not aware of it, it is not the object of our experience. We simply are in shock, terrified, frightened, joyful, and so on.

We can say something similar of dreams, reveries, imaginings, fantasies and the like. They, unlike the experiences just mentioned, have an object of sorts. We dream *about* things which momentarily we take to be real; we imagine and fantasize about things which, for the most part, we know to be unreal – unless we are genuinely reminiscing. But though these experiences have an object, it is seldom more than tenuously connected with the external world of sensory perception.

Now, when we come to prophetic and visionary language we have these two problems to contend with. First, we have an experience that others may never have had. Secondly, we have its object.

I, so far as I am aware, have never had a prophetic or visionary experience. How then can I accept what the prophets and visionaries tell me? How can I distinguish them from poets, dreamers, weavers of beautiful words, charming tales, beguiling thoughts, to say nothing of charlatans and mountebanks? And, worse still, how can I have the faintest idea of what they are talking about, or whether they are talking about anything? Another prophet or visionary might understand what they are talking about and be able to distinguish genuine from false prophets. But what of the rest of us? The situation is difficult but not hopeless.

However, before answering these questions, I should like to turn the problem as stated by Ayer on its head. This move consists in conceding that prophetic utterances are not cognitive, any more than poetic, or metaphysical utterances, or utterances containing profound ethical experiences are. They are not only not empirically verifiable (i.e. by sensory perception), but that is their very nature. This is expressed by Wittgenstein by calling them 'nonsensical'. By this he means that they are attempts to go beyond the boundaries of language, to say the unsayable.

Let us first examine this suggestion in relation to poetry. Poetry, like prophecy to which it is closely related, is often expressed in propositional form. If it is empirically verified or falsified, however, this is irrelevant to it as poetry. That is to say, its status as poetry does not depend on whether it is empirically verifiable, much less whether it is verified. Keats's nightingale sang on the wing:

> Past the near meadows, over the still stream,
> Up the hill-side; and now 'tis buried deep
> In the next valley-glades:
>
> ('Ode to a Nightingale': VIII)

No nightingale sings on the wing, much less over 'still' (*sic*) streams. (Keats may have redeemed himself in the next line: 'Was it a vision, or a waking dream?'!) But the question of verifiability, of ornithological truth or falsehood does not arise. It is poetry; and, as such, is not in the business of giving accurate factual information. This is not to say that if it does give accurate factual information this might not, perhaps, add a tincture to its poetic value. But the point is that its poetical status does not depend on its being verifiable. Here is a piece of verse (my own):

> Autumn is on its way.
> The leaves are falling.
> In the shortening day,
> Someone will have to sweep them up.
> That is his calling.

This is probably empirically true, and certainly verifiable; but it is scarcely poetry. On the other hand, the following passages from Blake and Yeats are certainly poetry, but scarcely verifiable empirically, except incidentally – it is empirically true, for instance, that sunflowers follow the sun.

> Ah, Sun-flower!, weary of time,
> Who countest the steps of the Sun;
> Seeking after that sweet golden clime,
> Where the traveller's journey is done;
>
> ('Ah, Sun-Flower!')

and

> The Gyres! the gyres! Old Rocky Face look forth;
> Things thought too long can be no longer thought,
> For beauty dies of beauty, worth of worth,
> And ancient lineaments are blotted out.
>
> ('The Gyres')

How could you possibly verify these utterances empirically? To ask seriously whether sunflowers are seeking a golden clime where the traveller's journey is done or apply an empirical test to decide whether or not beauty always or regularly dies of beauty and worth of worth is patently ludicrous. Poetry and empirical verification belong to what Wittgenstein calls entirely different language games. The rules of truth and intelligibility are entirely different. This is not to say that the passages from Blake and Yeats are unintelligible and have no truth value. On the contrary. What it does say is that their intelligibility and truth value are not based on empirical evidence. More than that, one has to say that, though both Blake and Yeats make assertions, one about a 'sweet golden clime', the other about beauty, worth and lineaments, these assertions can be rejected as false, yet the poetry still stands. They remain poetic utterances, a wonderful weaving of words, images and conceits. Their status as poetry does not depend on their being taken seriously as assertions nor on what they assert being accepted.

Not so with religious utterances. These standardly have a referent: God. And their assertions have to be taken seriously. If they are not accepted, they may survive as poetry without ulterior significance or merely as a testimony to a profound experience (as in the Song of Solomon, many of the Psalms, and the Magnificat) which has no significance beyond itself. But, as such, like poetry, they tell nothing about the empirically verifiable. This is not to say a religious utterance does not refer to the perceptual world. But this is as a means of metaphorical, analogical and symbolical reference. Its empirical veridicality does not constitute it as a religious utterance. Far from it. Further even, possibly, than it constitutes poetry as poetry. Religious, like metaphysical and ethical, utterances are about the transcendental, that which may involve sense perception but goes beyond it or, at least, attempts to do so.

Wittgenstein said of religious, ethical and metaphysical utterances that they are inexpressible. And he is insistent that this is not simply because it is difficult to find a right formula of words to express what they are attempting to express. No formula of words could express what they are attempting to express. Ordinary language is designed to describe facts. What the prophets and mystics are talking about are not empirical facts, not about how the world is, but about an attitude to it which transcends it: a way of viewing objects and events and actions that cannot be empirically verified. This cannot be stated in ordinary language, any more than the utterances of poets can. Poetry cannot be translated into ordinary language: not even a prose poem or poetic prose. Much less can visionary language. As Wittgenstein says in answer to the objection that ethical value is relative, not absolute, since it is a fact, like any other fact, that, say, stealing is wrong:

> When this is urged against me I at once see clearly, as it were in a flash of light, not only that no description that I could think of would do to describe what I mean by absolute value, but that I would reject every significant description that anyone could possibly suggest, *ab initio*, on the ground of its significance. That is to say: I see now that these nonsensical expressions were not nonsensical because I had not yet found the correct expressions, but because their nonsensicality was their very essence.
>
> (Wittgenstein 1965: 11)

Wittgenstein abhorred theology, the attempt to turn vision and prophecy into a rational equivalent, and he considered that the proper way to convey ethical truths and insights was by biblical tales or parables or tales such as Tolstoy's *The Death of Ivan Ilyitch*, 'Does a Man Need Much Earth?', 'Master and Servant', 'Two Old Men' and 'Father Sergiy'.

Now, when Wittgenstein calls truly ethical and religious utterance nonsensical, he does not mean that it is mere gibberish or an indulgence of language for its own sake – a meaningless, if pleasing, use of language signifying nothing. What he is saying is (a) that its significance cannot be translated, because it does not state anything – it shows its meaning in its use of words, its structure and what it leaves unsaid; (b) that it is not a *report* of something beyond the reach of sensory perception, though it is an attempt, a desperate attempt, to reach beyond it, inspired by a belief that there is something there beyond our grasp.

Now, if prophetic utterance is not a report, inadequately expressed, of a 'vision' of the suprasensory, nor an indulgence of language, and yet, like ethics as expression of absolute value, represents an attempt to say the unsayable, to go beyond the boundaries of language, what, then, is it? I wish to suggest that, like poetry, visionary and prophetic language is not the expression of an experience *by means* of language but an experience in language. This, on the face of it, may not seem to do justice to the claims of prophets, visionaries and mystics who believe they are in contact with something that transcends language, as it does sensory experience. It smacks of indulgence of language. I hope to show that this is not the case.

In doing so, I wish to relate prophetic, visionary and mystical utterances very closely to poetry. It is no coincidence that the best and most revered religious and mystical texts, whether Hebrew, Christian, Hindu, Buddhist, Sumerian or Egyptian, are poetic, or that, to be recognized as a prophet in Old Testament times, one had to be recognized as a poet, a master and weaver of words. So let us first consider what the poet does.

The poet, as Sartre says in *What is Literature*, turns language upside down. He could be said to serve words rather than to use them as servants. This is what the prose writer does. He uses words, as Sartre says, to designate, demonstrate, order, beg, insult, and persuade. A word for him is merely a sign which signifies. It is quite otherwise with a poet. 'One might think', as Sartre says, 'that he is composing a sentence, but this is only what it appears to be'. What the poet is doing, in fact, is creating a 'phrase-object'.

> He is creating an object. The words-things are grouped by magical associations of fitness and incongruity, like colours and sounds. They attract, repel and *'burn'* one another, and their association composes the veritable poetic unity which is the *phrase-object*.

Sartre takes as an example the line from Rimbaud: 'Quelle âme est sans défaut?' He is not saying that no one is faultless. That is banal. According to Sartre he is asking an 'absolute question'.

> It is seen from the outside. . . . Its strangeness arises from the fact that, in order to consider it, we place ourselves on the other side of the human condition, on the side of God.
>
> (Sartre 1967: 8–9)

This may sound like an indulgence in language for its own sake. However, the opposite of using language for the purposes to which writers usually put it, as above mentioned, is not solely nor necessarily an indulgence of language. An indulgence of language, as I understand it, is a use of language and its imagery for no better purpose than to impress the reader or listener or simply because the writer is intoxicated with language. It sounds well, though signifying nothing. (I am not sure that the title of this paper is not an indulgence of language.) Certainly the language used by estate agents, travel agents, advertisers of all kinds, financial experts, connoisseurs of wine, and the past-masters of the art, politicians, is, for the most part, an indulgence of language, though not for its own sake. It is for profit, gain and self-advancement. To find indulgers in language purely for its own sake one has to turn to such poets as Swinburne and such manifesto mongers as Martinelli. Take Swinburne's 'Thy voice as an odour that fades in a flame' ('Hesperia') and Martinelli's *Futurist Manifesto*, published in *Le Figaro* on 20 February 1909:

> We stand on the last promontory of the centuries.... Why should we look back, when we want to break down the mysterious doors of the impossible? Time and Space died yesterday. We live in the absolute, because we have created eternal, omnipresent speed....
>
> Lift up your heads!
>
> Erect on the summit of the world, once again we hurl defiance to the stars.

Here is indulgence of language for its own sake if ever it is to be found.

Between this use of language and the ordinary use of language (to designate, demonstrate, order, beg, insult, persuade and insinuate) there is a third kind of use: the poetic. Of the poet Sartre says:

> As he is already on the outside, he considers words as a *trap to catch a fleeing reality* rather than as indicators which throw him out of himself into the midst of things. In short, all language is for him the mirror of the world.
>
> (Sartre 1967: 6; my italics)

Words reflect the world. When a poet or philosopher comes to reflect on the world in which words are used all manner of connections, disparities, possibilities, incongruities, which have remained dormant in the practical use of language are thrown up. Though the poet or metaphysician may appear to be making assertions about the world, he is, in fact, musing on it, or rather, on its reflection in language. He is not contemplating language as such. He is not doing linguistics or constructing a meta-language. He is, in Sartre's admirable phrase, setting a trap in which to catch reality or at least some facet of it. If he is successful, it should not be surprising if he comes up with oddities of all kinds, paradoxes, and even downright contradictions. Reality was not planned according to the rules and regulations of a local government department.

To say, therefore, that the poet or metaphysician is not primarily concerned with making empirically verifiable statements is merely to state the obvious – though some metaphysicians, and even some poets, might believe the contrary. But to assume that on this account their utterances are meaningless and have no cognitive content is at best arrogant, at worst, absurd. It assumes that if an utterance cannot be fitted into a preferred theory of meaning, it is meaningless. Might not the theory be wrong? It is almost, though not quite, like saying that, if you cannot understand what someone is saying, he is *eo ipso* talking nonsense.

But what of the religious visionary? The poet, after all, is for the most part, talking about human experiences, and the metaphysician is talking about the world or reality in general, even if, as Sartre says, from 'outside', or, as Wittgenstein put it, *sub specie aeternitatis*. But the religious visionary is concerned with the truly transcendental, not just with what stands outside the particularities of the here and now, but what is outside human experience, at least in this life. How does he 'catch reality'?

Though Sartre does not elaborate on the art of catching reality, the technique is well known to students of rhetoric and poetics. It is the trope. In particular simile, metaphor, analogy and symbol. All are based on similarity or resemblance. The simile is based on a direct and obvious comparison, though in what respect or respects the two elements of the comparison resemble each other may be left to the reader or listener to decide. When Burns says: 'O, my Luve's like a red red rose', is he saying that she blushes when she sees him or just that she is beautiful or both and more besides? There is no exact way of telling. Metaphors may be abbreviated similes. 'My rose' says much the same as Burns's line. But it can also be more subtle. It is not just that it drops the comparative 'like', which some scholars think is the distinguishing feature of metaphor – a superficial distinction – but, as the *Concise*

Oxford Dictionary, defining metaphor more astutely, puts it, it is 'the application of a name or descriptive term to an object to which it is not literally applicable'. 'A gentle breeze stroked her face' would be a simple example. Breezes, not being human, cannot be gentle or otherwise, nor can they stroke anything: they are forces of nature that hit an object 'gently', 'harshly', 'violently' – but they do not 'stroke'; only humans do that. These terms 'gently', 'harshly' and 'violently' lead us to the analogical use of language. Though very close to metaphor – all these tropes are very close – analogy is different in this respect, that it is a proper and literal, if extended, use of a word. Examples are 'cause', 'tense', 'communication', 'space', 'intelligent(ce)', 'love'. . . . For example, if we take 'tension', *Chambers Twentieth Century Dictionary* gives: 'stretching: a pulling strain: stretched or strained state . . . electromotive force: a state of barely suppressed emotion, as excitement, suspense, anxiety, or hostility . . . strained relations (between persons): opposition (between conflicting ideas or forces)'.

These are not metaphors. They may be based on resemblances, but they are not based on comparisons. To talk of a 'high tension cable', a 'tension in diplomatic relations', and 'taking the tension on a rope' is not to use the term 'tension' metaphorically. It is not a strange use of the word 'tension'. It is a perfectly normal use. Metaphors shock us; analogues we take in our stride. 'Tension' may come from *tensus*, and ultimately from *tendere*, to stretch, to draw out, to move or strive in a certain direction, but none of its uses are shocking, disturbing or stimulating. This is not to say that the use of 'cause' in 'First Cause' or 'Intelligence' in 'Divine Intelligence' does not pose problems. But, *pace* Kant and others, these problems need be no greater than those that one confronts in trying to interpret and understand a poem. This brings me to symbolism.

If you ask what W.B. Yeats means when he writes in 'The Secret Rose':

> Far-off, most secret, and inviolate Rose
> Enfold me in my hour of hours;

you may be in for an unsatisfactory answer, if not a dusty one. The rose for Yeats was the symbol for so many things – beauty, woman, Ireland, western civilization or civilization in general, love, of course, and much else. Each reader has to interpret it for himself within the perimeters of Yeats's symbolism. This is not simile, certainly. Nor is it analogy or extended meaning. And it is beyond metaphor. We are dealing here with symbolism. Symbolism wanders in and out of poetry. Blake, Yeats, Smart and, of course, Emily Dickinson, and possibly Eliot, were poets who dealt in symbolism. Whether their symbolism is transcendental in the sense of merely transcending the here and now experiences or transcending all sensory experience is not certain. What is certain is that the visionary prophetic utterances in the Song of Solomon, the Psalms, and the Revelation (or Apocalypse) which I have quoted, are certainly attempts to transcend sensory experience, though couched in sensory terms, which are all that are available to us in this life. They are symbolical; but of what?

To attempt to answer that question is futile and fatuous, just as it is futile and fatuous to attempt to translate poetry into prose. The meaning lies in the particular words and images. That is how it has come to the visionary. He has had his spiritual experience in these words and images. As has been said, the seer and prophet is not attempting to find words to express a non-verbal experience. Nor is he necessarily reporting a sensory experience such as a dream or an hallucination. When John says: 'Then I saw a new heaven and a new earth' and so forth, we do not have to assume that he literally saw anything, as one might see New York from the air for the first time or even dream of being on a beach in Hawaii. It is more like, to quote an example Professor John Wisdom once gave, as if Galileo were to express what Newton was later to call the first law of motion in terms of a dream or vision of an endless, frictionless plain on which frictionless spheres moved endlessly at a uniform speed. Of course, that image can be translated into Newton's law, but the point is that the insight would have been arrived at in the vision, and the vision would have been the product of imagination brought to fruition in verbalization.

Unlike Galileo's vision, most prophetic visions remain embedded in the language in which they were generated, as do poetic images. Take the saying: 'Unless a grain of wheat falls into the earth and dies, it remains alone; but if it dies, it bears much fruit' (John xii 24). Taken literally it is a truistic piece of agricultural wisdom, if that. But that is not how it is to be taken. It may, however, be translated into an equally mysterious and paradoxical saying – 'He who loses his life for my sake will find it' (Matthew x 39) – this, however, does not explain its meaning. If anything, it makes it more obscure to the literal-minded. As in poetry, so in prophetic visionary utterances it is not possible to trade one set of words for another. The image is inseparable from the words in which it lies; and so is its meaning. The image of the grain of wheat dying and fructifying is integral to the insight expressed. It is as Wittgenstein says, an image to live by.

Many objections can be brought against this account of prophetic visionary utterance. No doubt it will be offensive to the proverbial pious ears (and eyes). However, some of the objections can be met in anticipation. Perhaps the most serious is that I seem to reduce religious ecstasy and vision, if not to an indulgence of language, to nothing more than contact with language itself and a sort of rummaging about in it. There does not seem to be any of the 'I-Thou' relationship which is supposed to characterize prophetic utterances, no contact with the Almighty. First, I want to say that, whatever may be the case with poetry (and I would deny it of poetry also), I do not wish to suggest that prophetic utterances are merely linguistically and not divinely generated. Nor do I for a moment wish to suggest that there is not or cannot be non-verbal communication with the divine, supernatural and transcendental, just as there can be between human lovers, for instance. What I am concerned with in this paper, however, are prophetic *utterances*. And what I am saying is that whatever contact God, the Absolute, the Transcendental or whatever supranatural power had with the prophet it was by way of language and the images and meanings and insights it generates. So when John tells us that he saw a New Jerusalem where God will dwell with men, where there will be no more death or mourning or crying or pain, that 'the former things have passed away', it is not that he has actually seen anything, except in his imagination, with the help of language. And that language belonged to a long and rich tradition of prophetic writing stretching back through Ezekiel and Isaiah to the Song of Solomon, the Psalms, Job, Ezra and beyond.

It is within this context that we must understand biblical prophetic visionary writing. As symbolic writing it is in language but stretches out beyond it towards something seen through a glass darkly or, as the *New English Bible* puts Paul's words, 'we see only puzzling reflections'(!) (I Cor. xiii 12). And staying with Paul and with I Corinthians, the next chapter neatly sums up what I have been saying. In it he contrasts the language of private ecstasy with prophecy. The distinction he draws is between utterances that cannot be understood by others, that are mysterious, between the utterer and God, not directed to other men; and utterances in the public domain that enlighten, instruct and build up the Church. Paul is charitable enough not to dismiss private ecstatic utterances as meaningless in the worst sense. He has a problem with ecstatic language as he reveals in II Corinthians xii 2–4 where he recounts an ecstatic, but not a prophetic, experience which he had 'whether in the body or out of the body, I do not know, God knows'. Unfortunately, he does not attempt to communicate it to us. I am rather sceptical about this, taking a Wittgensteinian attitude towards private language. But, being charitable in turn, I concede that these non-verbal experiences may occur and can be understood only by those who have had similar experiences. Meanwhile, even by Paul's admission, prophecy, however mysterious, is firmly in the public domain.

It remains to ask whether the language of prophecy is necessarily symbolical. And a further question: is prophecy necessarily confined to language? Can it not be conveyed by music, painting, sculpture or even architecture? To the first question my inclination is to say: yes, it must be symbolical. Whatever the Thomists try to make of analogy – simile and metaphor are not applicable, however interpreted – the only trope that will lead from the sensory to the absolutely transcendental is some form of symbolism. And this symbolism is largely negative. If what the Revelation says is correct, heaven will not be a painful place, but what having God amongst us will be is hard to envisage. As for the other arts. Music certainly conveys spiritual ideas: Kant, Schopenhauer, Pater and others recognized this. But there must be some linguistic backing. The same goes for painting, sculpture and architecture. Whether or not one is prepared to extend 'language' to include all forms of non-verbal communication, ordinary language must have some place, whether as part of vocal music or as the theme and subject matter of painting and sculpture, or in liturgy and worship if it is architecture. However, what the other arts have in common with literature, poetry especially, is that the experience they generate and express is created *in the work* itself. The work is not a vehicle designed to convey an experience already experienced: it is the context in which the experience is experienced, and yet it transcends the immediacy of the experience. The language of ecstasy is not merely an ecstasy of language. It stretches beyond language, the language of the here and now, of the sensory perception, to the New Jerusalem, where there is no night or day, no intruder enters and no friend goes out, yet the gates are never shut, and everyone lives in peace in the light of the Lamb. A pipe-dream, you may say. Perhaps. We shall see. But not, or not intended to be, a mere indulgence of language. That is what makes it the Revelation, the Apocalypse.

BIBLIOGRAPHY

Adams, H. (ed.) (1971) *Critical Theory Since Plato*, New York: Harcourt, Brace, Jovanovich.

Albrektson, B. (1967) *History and the Gods: an Essay on the Idea of Historical Events as Divine Manifestations in the Ancient Near East and in Israel*, Lund: Gleerup.

Alter, R. (1981) *The Art of Biblical Narrative*, London: George Allen & Unwin.

Alter, R. and Kermode F. (eds) (1987) *The Literary Guide to the Bible*, London: Collins.

Aristotle (1908–52) *The Works of Aristotle translated into English*, ed. W.D. Ross, 12 vols, Oxford: Clarendon Press.

Ashton, J. (ed.) (1986) *The Interpretation of John*, Philadelphia & London: Fortress & SPCK.

Auerbach, E. (1953) *Mimesis: The Representation of Reality in Western Literature*, trans. W.R. Trask, Princeton: Princeton University Press.

Augustine (1963) *The Confessions of St Augustine*, trans. R. Warner, New York: Mentor Books.

— (1973–4) 'Epistles' in P. Schaff (ed.) *The Nicene and Post-Nicene Fathers of the Church*, First Series, reprint edition, Grand Rapids: Eerdmans.

Ayer, A.J. (1946) *Language, Truth and Logic*, 2nd edn, London: Gollancz.

Bahti, T. (1981) 'Vico, Auerbach, and Literary History', *Philological Quarterly* 60.

— (1985) 'Auerbach's *Mimesis*: Figural Structure and Historical Narrative', in Jay and Miller.

Barton, J. (1979) 'Natural Law and Poetic Justice in the Old Testament', *Journal of Theological Studies* 30.

— (1980) *Amos' Oracles against the Nations*, Cambridge: Cambridge University Press.

— (1987) 'Begründungsversuche der prophetischen Unheilsankündigung im Alten Testament', *Evangelische Theologie* 47.

Beckett, S. (1963) *Watt*, London: Calder and Boyars.

Benjamin, W. (1977) *The Origins of German Tragic Drama*, trans. J. Osborne, London: New Left Books.

222

Berlin, A. (1982) 'On the Bible as Literature', *Prooftexts* 2.

Bishops' Bible (1568) *The holie Bible*, 1st edn of the version popularly known as the 'Bishops' Bible', London: Richard Iugge.

Blackman, A.M. and Peet, T.E. (1925) 'Papyrus Lansing – a Translation with Notes', *Journal of Egyptian Archaeology* 11.

Bloom, H. (1973) *The Anxiety of Influence*, New York: Oxford University Press.

Booth, W.C. (1961) *The Rhetoric of Fiction*, Chicago and London: University of Chicago Press.

— (1974) *A Rhetoric of Irony*, Chicago and London: University of Chicago Press.

Borges, J.L. (1981) 'Pierre Menard, Author of the *Quixote*', in D.A. Yates and J.E. Irby (eds) *Labyrinths*, Harmondsworth: Penguin Books.

Bornkamm, G. (1969) *Paul*, trans. D.M.G. Stalker, London: Hodder and Stoughton.

— (1986) 'Towards the Interpretation of John's Gospel', in Ashton.

Brown, R.E. (1966) *The Gospel According To John*, 2 vols, Anchor Bible, London: Geoffrey Chapman.

— (1979) *The Community of the Beloved Disciple*, New York & London: Chapman.

Bultmann, R. (1925) 'Die Bedeutung der neuerschlossenen mandäschen und manichäschen Quellen für das Verstädnis des Johannesevangeliums', *Zeitschrift für die neutestamentliche Wissenschaft* 24.

— (1969) 'The Eschatology of the Gospel of John', in his *Faith and Understanding*, vol. 1, ed. R.W. Funk, trans. L.P. Smith, London: SCM.

Burke, K. (1947) *A Grammar of Motives*, Berkeley and Los Angeles: University of California Press.

— (1950) *A Rhetoric of Motives*, New York: Prentice-Hall.

Caird, G.B. (1980) *The Language and Imagery of the Bible*, London: Duckworth.

Caminos, R. (1954) *Late-Egyptian Miscellanies*, London: Oxford University Press.

Chaucer, G. (1957) *The Works of Geoffrey Chaucer*, ed. F.N. Robinson, 2nd edn, London: Oxford University Press.

Clines, D.J.A. (1989) *Job 1-20*, Word Biblical Commentary 17, Waco, Texas: Word Books.

Coleridge, S.T. (1936) *Miscellaneous Criticism*, ed. T.M. Raysor, London: Constable.

— (1972) *Lay Sermons*, ed. R.J. White, London: Routledge and Kegan Paul.

Culler, J. (1983) *On Deconstruction: Theory and Criticism after Structuralism*, London: Routledge and Kegan Paul.

Daly, M. (1985) *Beyond God the Father: Toward a Philosophy of Women's Liberation*, 2nd edn, Boston, Mass.: Beacon Press.

de Beauvoir, S. (1972) *The Second Sex*, trans. H.M. Parshley, Harmondsworth: Penguin Books.

de Jonge, M. (1977) *Jesus: Stranger from Heaven and Son of God*, trans. J.E. Steely, Missoula: Scholars Press.

de Man, P. (1971) *Blindness and Insight*, New York: Oxford University Press.

Detweiler, R. (1980) 'After the New Criticism: contemporary methods of literary interpretation', in R.A. Spencer (ed.) *Orientation by Disorientation*, Pittsburgh: Pickwick Press.

Dixon, P. (1971) *Rhetoric*, London and New York: Methuen.

Dodd, C.H. (1968) *The Interpretation of the Fourth Gospel*, Cambridge: Cambridge University Press.

Dummett, M. (1987a) 'A Remarkable Consensus', *New Blackfriars* 68, 809.

— (1987b) 'Unsafe Premises: a reply to Nicholas Lash', *New Blackfriars* 68, 811.

Eagleton, T. (1983) *Literary Theory: An Introduction*, Minneapolis: University of Minnesota Press.

Eckhart, J. (1924) *Meister Eckhart*, trans. C. de B. Evans, ed. F. Pfeiffer, London: J.M. Watkins.

Edwards, M. (1984) *Towards a Christian Poetics*, London: Macmillan Press.

Eusebius (1976), *Church History*, in *A Select Library of Nicene and Post-Nicene Fathers of the Christian Church: Second Series*, eds P. Schaff and H. Wace, vol. 1, Michigan: Eerdmans.

Ezell, M.J.M. (1987) *The Patriarch's Wife: Literary Evidence and the History of the Family*, Chapel Hill: University of North Carolina Press.

Farrer, A. (1948) *The Glass of Vision*, Westminster: Dacre Press.

Freccero, J. (1975) 'The Fig Tree and the Laurel: Petrarch's Poetics', *Diacritics* 5.

Frei, H.W. (1974) *The Eclipse of Biblical Narrative: A Study in Eighteenth and Nineteenth Century Hermeneutics*, New Haven and London: Yale University Press.

Freud, S. (1957) 'The Psychology of Love, III: The Taboo of Virginity', in J. Strachey (ed.) *The Standard Edition of the Complete Psychological Works of Sigmund Freud*, vol. XI, London: The Hogarth Press.

Friedlaender, W. (1974) *Caravaggio Studies*, Princeton: Princeton University Press.

Frye, N. (1982) *The Great Code: The Bible and Literature*, London, Melbourne and Henley: Routledge and Kegan Paul.

Georgi, D. (1971) 'Forms of Religious Propaganda', in H.J. Schultz (ed.) *Jesus in His Time*, Philadelphia: Fortress Press.

Greer, G. (1981) *The Obstacle Race*, London: Secker and Warburg.

Gregory the Great (1979–85) *Moralia in Job*, ed. M. Adriaen, 3 vols, (Corpus Christianorum. Series Latina, 143, 143A, 143B), Turnhout: Brepols; in English: (1844–50) *Morals on the Book of Job*, ed. C. Marriott, 4 vols, Oxford: J.H. Parker.

Harvey, A.E. (1976) *Jesus on Trial: A Study in the Fourth Gospel*, London: SPCK.

Heaton, E.W. (1977) *The Old Testament Prophets*, revised edn, London: Darton, Longman & Todd.

Heywood, T. (1640) *The Exemplary Lives and Memorable Acts of Nine the Most Worthy Women of the World*, London: R. Royston.

Hoskyns, E.C. (1947) *The Fourth Gospel*, ed. F.N. Davey, London: Faber & Faber.

Hughes, F.W. (1989) *Early Christian Rhetoric and Second Thessalonians*, Sheffield: Sheffield Academic Press.

Hulme, T.E. (1924) *Speculations*, London: Routledge and Kegan Paul.

Hume, D. (1878) *A Treatise of Human Nature*, ed. T.H. Green and T.H. Grose, London: Longman's Green & Co.

— (1932) *The Letters of David Hume*, ed. J.Y.T. Greig, 2 vols., Oxford: Clarendon Press.

Jacobus, M. (1987) *Reading Woman*, London: Methuen.

Jasper, D. (1987) *The New Testament and the Literary Imagination*, London: Macmillan.

Jay, G. and Miller, D. (eds) (1985) *After Strange Texts: The Role of Theory in the Study of Literature*, Alabama: University of Alabama.

Jenkins, D.E. (1987) *God, Miracle and the Church of England*, London: SCM.

Josephus (1930) *Jewish Antiquities: Books I–IV*, trans. H. St. J. Thackeray, London and Cambridge, Mass.: Loeb Classical Library.

Josipovici G. (1988) *The Book of God: A Response to the Bible*, New Haven and London: Yale University Press.

Kant, I. (1951) *Critique of Judgement*, trans. J.H. Bernard, New York: Hafner Press.

Käsemann, E. (1969) 'The Structure and Purpose of the Prologue to John's Gospel', in his *New Testament Questions of Today*, Philadelphia: Fortress Press.

Kennedy, G.A. (1984) *New Testament Interpretation through Rhetorical Criticism*, Chapel Hill and London: University of North Carolina Press.

Kermode, F. (1979) *The Genesis of Secrecy*, Cambridge, Mass.: Harvard University Press.

— (1987) 'John', in Alter and Kermode.

Kinneavy, J.L. (1987) *Greek Rhetorical Origins of Christian Faith*, New York and Oxford: Oxford University Press.

Klemm, D.E. (1987) 'Toward a Rhetoric of Postmodern Theology: Through Barth and Heidegger', *Journal of the American Academy of Religion* 55.

Kugel, J. (1981a) *The Idea of Biblical Poetry*, New Haven: Yale University Press.

— (1981b) 'On the Bible and Literary Criticism', *Prooftexts* 1.

— (1982) 'On the Bible as Literature', *Prooftexts* 2.

Kuhn, T.S. (1962) *The Structure of Scientific Revolutions*, Chicago & London: University of Chicago Press.

Lampe, G.W.H. (1969) 'The Exposition and Exegesis of Scripture to Gregory the Great', in *The Cambridge History of the Bible*, vol. 2, ed. G.W.H. Lampe, Cambridge: Cambridge University Press.

Lausberg, H. (1960) *Handbuch der literarischen Rhetorik*, 2 vols, Munich: M.Hueber.

Lehmann, P. (1975) *The Transfiguration of Politics: Jesus Christ and the Question of Revolution*, London: SCM.

Le Moyne, P. (1652) *The Gallery of Heroick Women*, trans. the Marquess of Winchester, London: Henry Seile.

Liddell, H.G. and Scott, R. (1883) *A Greek-English Lexicon*, Oxford: Clarendon Press.

Lindars, B. (1965) 'Ezekiel and Individual Responsibility', *Vetus Testamentum* 15.

Lodge, D. (1985) *Small World*, Harmondsworth: Penguin Books.

McGann, J.J. (1983) *A Critique of Modern Textual Criticism*, Chicago: University of Chicago Press.

Marks, H. (1987) 'The Twelve Prophets', in Alter and Kermode.

Marsh, J. (1968) *The Gospel of St. John*, Pelican New Testament Commentaries, Harmondsworth: Penguin Books.

Meeks, W.A. (1986) 'The Man from Heaven in Johannine Sectarianism', in Ashton.

Mill, J.S. (1843) *A System of Logic: Ratiocinative and Inductive*, 8th edn, new impr. 1959, London: Longmans.

Miller, J.H. (1981) 'The Two Allegories', in M. Bloomfield (ed.) *Allegory, Myth and Symbol*, Harvard English Studies 9, Cambridge, Mass.: Harvard University Press.

Millett, K. (1977) *Sexual Politics*, London: Virago.

Mitchell, J. (1975) *Psychoanalysis and Feminism*, Harmondsworth: Penguin Books.

Muilenburg, J. (1969) 'Form Criticism and Beyond', *Journal of Literature* 88.

Nichols, J. (ed.) (1823) *The Progresses and Public Processions of Queen Elizabeth*, 3 vols, London: J. Nichols and Son.

Nietzsche, F.W. (1966) *Beyond Good and Evil*, trans. W. Kaufmann, New York: Random House.

—— (1974) *The Gay Science*, trans. W. Kaufmann, New York: Vintage Books.

Nuttall, A.D. (1980) *Overheard by God: Fiction and Prayer in Herbert, Milton, Dante and St John*, London & New York: Methuen.

Nygren, A. (1949) *Commentary on Romans*, trans. C.C. Rasmussen, Philadelphia: Muhlenberg Press.

Ogden, S.M. (1982) *The Point of Christology*, London: SCM.

Pascal, B. (1966) *Pensées*, trans. A. J. Krailsheimer, Harmondsworth: Penguin Books.

Pease D. (1987) 'Critical Communities', in J.A. Buttigeig (ed.) *Criticism without Boundaries: Directions and Crosscurrents in Postmodern Critical Theory*, Notre Dame: University of Notre Dame Press.

Plato (1963) *The Collected Dialogues of Plato, Including the Letters*, eds E. Hamilton and H. Cairns, New York: Bollingen Foundation.

Pointon M. (1981) 'Artemisia Gentileschi's "The Murder of Holofernes"', *American Imago* 38.

Pope, M. (1973) *Job*, The Anchor Bible 13, 3rd edn, New York: Doubleday.

Prebble, J. (1961) *Culloden*, London: Secker and Warburg.

Prickett, S. (1986) *Words and The Word: Language, Poetics and Biblical*

Interpretation, Cambridge: Cambridge University Press.

Quinton, A. (1985) *The Divergence of the Twain: Poet's Philosophy and Philosopher's Philosophy*, Coventry: University of Warwick.

Ricoeur P. (1969) *The Symbolism of Evil*, trans. E. Buchanan, Boston: Beacon Press.

— (1970) *Freud and Philosophy: An Essay on Interpretation*, trans. D. Savage, New Haven and London: Yale University Press.

— (1979) 'Epilogue: The Sacred Text and the Community', in W.D. O'Flaherty (ed.) *The Critical Study of Sacred Texts*, Berkeley Religious Studies Series 2, Berkeley: Graduate Theological Union.

— (1981) 'The narrative function', in his *Hermeneutics and the Human Sciences*, trans. J.B. Thompson, Cambridge: Cambridge University Press.

— (1985) *Temps et récit*, vol. III, Paris: Editions du Seuil.

Robinson, J.A.T. (1985) *The Priority of John*, ed. J.F. Coakley, London: SCM.

Rogers, K.M. (1966) *The Troublesome Helpmate*, Seattle and London: University of Washington Press.

Ruskin, J. (1906) 'Mornings in Florence', in *Works*, vol. 23, E.T. Cook and A. Wedderburn (eds), London: George Allen.

Ruysbroeck, J. (1916) *The Adornment of the Spiritual Marriage. The Sparkling Stone. The Book of Supreme Truth*, trans. C.A. Wynschenk, ed. E. Underhill, London: J.M. Dent.

Said, E.W. (1985) *Beginnings: Intention and Method*, New York: Columbia University Press.

Sartre J.-P. (1938) *La Nausée*, Paris: Gallimard.

— (1967) *What is Literature?*, trans. B. Frechtman, London: Methuen.

— (1976) *Critique of Dialectical Reason*, ed. J. Rée, trans. A. Sheridan-Smith, London: NLB.

Scharlemann, R.P. (1981) *The Being of God: Theology and the Experience of Truth*, New York: Seabury Press.

Shirley, J. (1686) *The Illustrious History of Women*, London: J. Harris.

Sowernam, E. (1617) *Esther hath hang'd Haman: Or, An Answere to a lewd Pamphlet, entituled, The Arraignment of Women*; repr. in K.U. Henderson and B.F. McManus (eds) (1985) *Half Humankind: Contexts and Texts of the Controversy about Women in England, 1540–1640*, Urbana: University of Illinois Press.

Spear, R.E. (1975) *Caravaggio and His Followers*, rev. edn, New York: Harper and Row.

Steiner, G. (1988) 'The Good Books', *The New Yorker*, January 11, 1988.

Sternberg, M. (1985) *The Poetics of Biblical Narrative: Ideological Literature and the Drama of Reading*, Bloomington: Indiana University Press.

Stocker, M. (1986) *Apocalyptic Marvell: The Second Coming in Seventeenth-Century Poetry*, Brighton: Harvester.

— (1987) 'Remodelling Virgil: Marvell's New Astraea', *Studies in Philology* 84.

Strahan, J. (1913) *The Book of Job Interpreted*, Edinburgh: T. and T. Clark.

Strong, R. (1977) *The Cult of Elizabeth: Elizabethan Portraiture and Pageantry*,

London: Thames and Hudson.

Sutherland, S.R. (1984) *God, Jesus and Belief: The Legacy of Theism*, Oxford: Basil Blackwell.

Swetnam, J. (1615) *The Arraignment of Lewde. . . women*, London: T. Archer.

Temple, W. (1945) *Readings in St. John's Gospel: First and Second Series*, London: Macmillan.

Tennenhouse, L. (1986) *Power on Display: The Politics of Shakespeare's Genres*, New York: Methuen.

Thucydides (1928) *History of the Peloponnesian War: Books I and II*, trans. C.F. Smith, London and Cambridge, Mass.: Loeb Classical Library.

Tillich, P. (1953–64) *Systematic Theology*, 3 vols, Welwyn: James Nisbet.

van Buren, P.M. (1963) *The Secular Meaning of the Gospel: Based on an Analysis of its Language*, London: SCM.

Via, Jr. D.O. (1985) *The Ethics of Mark's Gospel – In the Middle of Time*, Philadelphia: Fortress Press.

Warner, F.le P. (1983) *Moving Reflections*, Gerrards Cross: Colin Smythe, Oxford Theatre Texts.

Warner, M. (1987) *Monuments and Maidens: The Allegory of the Female Form*, London: Pan Books.

Warner, M.M. (1984) 'Philosophical Autobiography: St Augustine and John Stuart Mill', in A. Phillips Griffiths (ed.) *Philosophy and Literature*, Royal Institute of Philosophy Lecture Series 16, Cambridge: Cambridge University Press.

— (1989) *Philosophical Finesse: Studies in the Art of Rational Persuasion*, Oxford: Clarendon Press.

Watson, R.A. (1892) *The Book of Job*, Expositor's Bible, London: Hodder and Stoughton.

Weiskel, T. (1976) *The Romantic Sublime*, Baltimore: Johns Hopkins University Press.

Westcott, B.F. (1908) *The Gospel According to John*, 2 vols, London: John Murray.

Whately, R. (1832) *Elements of Rhetoric*, 4th edn, Oxford: J. Murray.

White, H. (1978) *Tropics of Discourse: Essays in Cultural Criticism*, Baltimore and London: Johns Hopkins University Press.

Wilder, A. (1971) *Early Christian Rhetoric*, 2nd edn, Harvard: Harvard University Press.

Wittgenstein, L. (1958) *Philosophical Investigations*, trans. G.E.M. Anscombe, Oxford: Basil Blackwell.

— (1965) 'A Lecture on Ethics', *The Philosophical Review* 74.

— (1966) *Lectures and Conversations on Aesthetics, Psychology and Religious Belief*, ed. D.C. Barrett, Oxford: Blackwell.

Woodbridge, L. (1984) *Women and the English Renaissance: Literature and the Nature of Womankind, 1540–1620*, Brighton: Harvester.

Wuellner, W. (1976) 'Paul's Rhetoric of Argumentation in Romans', *The Catholic Biblical Quarterly* 38.

Yates, F.A. (1977) *Astraea: The Imperial Theme in the Sixteenth Century*, Harmondsworth: Penguin Books.

Index of biblical references

General Index